CLASSICAL
HEBREW COMPOSITION

CLASSICAL
HEBREW COMPOSITION

BY

J. WEINGREEN, M.A., Ph.D.

PROFESSOR OF HEBREW AT
TRINITY COLLEGE, DUBLIN

OXFORD
AT THE CLARENDON PRESS
1957

Oxford University Press, Amen House, London E.C.4

GLASGOW   NEW YORK   TORONTO   MELBOURNE   WELLINGTON
BOMBAY   CALCUTTA   MADRAS   KARACHI
CAPE TOWN   IBADAN   NAIROBI   ACCRA   SINGAPORE

PRINTED IN GREAT BRITAIN

PREFACE

A STUDENT's knowledge of a classical language may be assessed in terms of his competence in writing compositions in the correct idiom of that language. Teachers of classical Hebrew have long felt the need for a textbook designed for the training of students in writing Hebrew compositions in the style of the Old Testament. This book is offered in the hope that it will fill the vacuum. It is assumed that the student has already covered the general groundwork of Hebrew grammar, that he has worked through the exercises accompanying the rules of grammar, and that he has also studied some Old Testament Hebrew texts.

Experience in teaching Hebrew over a long period has convinced me that the system of providing the student with English texts for translation into Hebrew, without any accompanying aids, imposes a strain upon him and often leads him to the frustrating experience of producing faulty Hebrew renderings. Corrections made subsequently may not be effective as permanent guides since they remain unorganized and, often, difficult to locate when required. On the other hand, I have found that, when the student is provided with aids in advance, he produces good Hebrew renderings of the English text and, at the same time, enjoys the work of translation.

With a view to assisting both teacher and student the following materials have been provided:

(1) Fifty pieces of prose and five of verse, composed in the style of the Authorized English Version of the Old Testament, are presented. To sustain the student's interest in the texts, the themes selected deal with Old Testament personalities and events in chronological order and are written in apocryphal fashion.

(2) Each text is accompanied by copious notes, in which the relevant rules of Hebrew syntax are explained rationally while, at the same time, the student's memory is constantly

refreshed on points of grammar acquired earlier. For those who have studied my *Practical Grammar for Classical Hebrew* (The Clarendon Press, Oxford), there are special references to that book under the symbol WHG.[1]

(3) An English–Hebrew vocabulary is appended. This vocabulary is designed not only to supply the words required for the translation of the texts, but also further to assist the student; the main parts of difficult verbs and nouns are given and frequent reference made to the notes which accompany the texts.

(4) An index to the notes is supplied. This will enable the student to revise the rules of syntax and, since he can refer to several manifestations of the rules engaging his attention, will help him to understand the modes of Hebrew thinking more fully.

In the texts offered in this book idiomatic usages recur with deliberate frequency and, at every recurrence, reference is made to the original note. In this way the student gradually acquires a feeling for the correct, idiomatic forms of expression and thus develops an appreciation for the language. Further-more, the presence of references back to the original note permits selection of texts for translation, without the loss of notes on earlier texts which may have been omitted.

The method employed in this book is a reversal of the convention of stating the rules of Hebrew syntax and then producing examples to illustrate them. Samples of English usage emerge from the continuous texts provided and these are modified in terms of Hebrew thinking in a manner which endows the process of translation with understanding and interest. It is not claimed that all the minutiae of Hebrew syntax have been covered in the notes accompanying the texts. As in my *Hebrew Grammar*, the aim has been practical and the scope restricted to workable limits.

I have to thank the Board of Trinity College, Dublin, for their ready permission to make use of examination papers

---

[1] WHG = Weingreen, *Hebrew Grammar*.

set by me in former years and published by the college in the annual collections of examination papers. I wish also to express my gratitude to Professor H. H. Rowley of Manchester University and to Professor D. Winton Thomas of Cambridge University for their kindness in examining the English–Hebrew vocabulary and for their very helpful suggestions. The readers of the Clarendon Press have earned my gratitude for their painstaking care in proof-reading and in ensuring consistency in the notes. I dedicate this book to my wife, whose constant encouragement and practical help in this work bear testimony to her love for and appreciation of the grandeur of the Old Testament.   J.W.

Trinity College, Dublin
12 *October* 1956

CONTENTS

CONTENTS

I

THERE was[1] a famine in the land of Canaan, for the people were sinful unto[2] the Lord. And the Lord spoke unto[2] Abraham and he said unto[2] him: 'Behold, there is a famine in the land. Take,[3] therefore,[4] thy wife and thy brother's son and all which thou possessest[5] and go down[6] to the land[7] of Egypt, for there is[8] bread in Egypt.' And Abraham did[9] as[10] the Lord commanded him[11] and he took[3] his wife and his brother's son and his flocks[12] and his herds[12] and he went down[6] with[13] them to Egypt[14] and he dwelt[15] there. And the Lord spoke unto Abraham in the land of Egypt, saying:[16] 'Behold, thy children shall be slaves in this land and they will serve the Egyptians[17] and they will build great[18] cities for them.[19] And it shall come to pass,[20] when they cry[21] unto[22] me, by reason of[23] their service, that[24] I shall hear their cry and I shall send My plagues upon the Egyptians[17] and I shall bring thy children forth[25] from this land and I shall bring them into[26] the land of Canaan, which I have sworn[27] unto[2] thee to give[28] unto[2] them. And they will fight[29] the inhabitants of Canaan and I shall give them[30] victory[31] over them[32] and I shall deliver[33] their cities into their hands[34] and they shall dwell in them. And it shall come to pass,[20] if they serve[35] Me in truth and keep[35] My commandments[36] which I shall command them[37] and do[35] that which is[38] pleasing[39] in My sight,[40] that[24] I shall send My blessings upon them and upon the fruit of their land and they shall know that I am the Lord, their God, Who[41] brought them forth from the land of Egypt and Who[42] brought them into the land of Canaan and Who[43] did battle[44] for them against their enemies. But,[45] if they hearken[35] not to My voice,[46] according to all[47] which I shall command them, and they go[35] in the way of the nations amongst[48] whom they shall dwell and serve[35] their gods, then[49] I shall send prophets unto[50] them to bring them back[51] unto[2] Me, to serve Me.[52] Behold, I have made[53] a covenant with[54] thee to give the land of Canaan to[2] thy seed,[55] as[56]

B

an everlasting[57] possession. Not with[13] thee alone[58] have I made[53] this covenant, but also with[13] the generations who[59] will come after[60] thee. Fear not,[61] O[62] My servant, for I shall not forget thy children when they are in[63] distress, but[64] I shall remember this covenant which I have made[53] with thee, and they shall be My people[65] and I shall be their[66] God.'

NOTES ON I

[1] Begin with Waw consecutive (and shortened imperfect)—'*and* there was' or '*now*, there was', WHG 92 (*e*) and (*f*).

[2] When the preposition 'to', 'unto' occurs in the English, if it denotes a dative or indirect object, as 'he gave unto me', 'he told (to) me', 'he was sinful unto the Lord', the inseparable preposition ל is used. When, however, it follows a verb of motion or speech, as 'he came unto me', 'he spoke (said) unto me', אֶל is used.

[3] The verb לָקַח is a class on its own, the imperfect being יִקַּח, the imperative קַח and the infinitive construct קַחַת, WHG 149.

[4] 'therefore' has the effect of emphasis, for which נָא serves. Other emphatic words, in the English, are 'now', 'then', which, in their contexts, do not refer to points of time, but are, simply, emphatic words.

[5] Either contract to 'and all which is thine (literally to thee)', וְאֶת־כָּל־אֲשֶׁר לָךְ (pausal), or expand to 'and all the possession(s) which thou possessest', וְאֶת־כָּל־הָרְכוּשׁ אֲשֶׁר רָכַשְׁתָּ. Two further points are to be noted:

(*a*) The word כֹּל, which we translate as 'all', is a noun with the meaning 'whole', 'totality'. Therefore, the idea 'all which . . .' is, in Hebrew thinking, 'the whole-of (that) which . . .', i.e. it is a direct object and must be preceded by אֶת־.

(*b*) In the second alternative expression, the perfect רָכַשְׁתָּ is used, since the perfect denotes that an act or state-of-being is completed, WHG 56. One can only speak of possessing anything, when the state of possessing is completed.

[6] It is important to realize that, unlike English, Hebrew has not the basic idea 'went' which is modified by the prepositions 'down', 'up', 'in', 'out (*or* forth)', 'around', &c. In Hebrew one must think of such verbs as 'went-down', i.e. 'descended', יָרַד; 'went-up', i.e. 'ascended', עָלָה; 'went-in', i.e. 'entered', בָּא; 'went-out', i.e. 'departed', יָצָא; 'went-around', סַב.

[7] A few words take the so-called old accusative case ending (to denote direction or motion-towards, WHG 66) when in the construct arrangement. One is אֶרֶץ, as אַרְצָה מִצְרַיִם, 'to the land of Egypt', another being בַּיִת, as בֵּיתָה פַרְעֹה, 'to the house of Pharaoh'.

[8] Though יֵשׁ might be used to express 'there is', it is not really necessary— 'for bread (is) in Egypt'.

[9] Note this doubly weak verb עָשָׂה, WHG 225 (*b*).

[10] A preposition cannot govern a verb. It is, therefore, associated with a nominal idea represented by the relative אֲשֶׁר, with the meaning 'as (the thing) which', כַּאֲשֶׁר.

[11] צִוָּה אֹתוֹ יהוה—the object (direct or indirect with ל) comes between the verb and the subject, probably because of the extension of the idea that the main portion of the phrase is first expressed and the subject limiting its application follows, WHG 57 (d). Similarly, 'the Lord gave (to) him' is נָתַן לוֹ יהוה.

[12] 'flocks' and 'herds' are represented by the singulars as collectives (e.g. the English word 'sheep'), namely, צֹאן and בָּקָר.

[13] Parallel with note 2 above, one must consider whether the preposition 'with' denotes the idea of instrument (i.e. 'by means of'), in which case the inseparable preposition בְ is used, or whether it is in the sense of 'together with', in which case עִם or אֵת is to be used. 'He smote the man with a sword' requires בְ: 'he went with the man' requires עִם or אֵת.

[14] Old accusative case ending, WHG 66, 67.

[15] WHG 188, 189.

[16] In this context, the sense of 'saying' is 'as follows' and precedes the actual words spoken. The infinitive construct with the prefixed inseparable preposition ל (and not the participle)—לֵאמֹר—is used, as if meaning '(that is) to say', WHG 162 note.

[17] Though one would expect הַמִּצְרִים, the land—מִצְרַיִם—often represents its people, when the reference is to the people as a whole. When the context implies a number or group of nationals, the generic form (the masculine singular of which ends in ִי.) is used in the plural.

[18] Though the irregular plural of עִיר, namely עָרִים, has the termination of a masculine plural, the noun is, nevertheless, feminine and the adjective qualifying it must, necessarily, be feminine plural.

[19] The order of words in the Hebrew is 'will build for them great cities'.

[20] Simply 'and it shall be', וְהָיָה, perfect with Waw consecutive.

[21] This must be rephrased, in terms of Hebrew thinking, to 'in their crying'— i.e. infinitive construct (which is a verbal noun) and the suffix. The difference between (a) the verbal noun (infinitive construct), and (b) the verbal adjective (participle) may be seen in the phrases (a) 'seeing is believing', and (b) 'I am seeing'. For the form of Qal infinitive construct with suffix, see WHG 131, 132.

[22] Since the idea of crying implies speech, the preposition which follows is אֶל, as in note 2 above. Note that if the verb קָרָא is used, then קָרָא אֶל means 'prayed' 'addressed', while קָרָא לְ means either 'summoned' or 'named', according to the context.

[23] The Hebrew is, simply, 'out of', מִן.

[24] The English idiom requires the sequence 'and it shall come to pass . . . that I shall hear', whereas in Hebrew it is 'and it shall come to pass . . . and I shall hear'.

[25] The Hiphil of יָצָא, 'went forth', namely הוֹצִיא, 'caused to go forth', produces the derived idea 'brought forth', WHG 212.

[26] The Hiphil of בָּא (root בוא)—'went in', 'came in', namely הֵבִיא, 'caused to go in', produces the derived idea 'brought in', WHG 212.

[27] The Niphal of שׁבע, namely נִשְׁבַּע, reminds us of the English 'was sworn in', i.e. took an oath.

4   NOTES ON I

²⁸ See WHG 148 for infinitive construct Qal.

²⁹ Niphal of לחם, i.e. נִלְחַם, 'fought' (WHG 103 footnote b), and is usually followed by the inseparable preposition בְּ.

³⁰ Indirect object and has the inseparable preposition לְ; see note 2 above— it obviously means 'to them'.

³¹ The noun is יְשׁוּעָה, usually rendered 'deliverance', 'salvation' but means 'victory' when referring to a battle.

³² עַל takes suffixes of the plural noun, WHG 87.

³³ The context shows that the sense is 'hand over', i.e. 'give'.

³⁴ The singular 'hand' is used and has the sense of 'power'.

³⁵ Imperfect, since the reference is to future time.

³⁶ The plural of מִצְוָה is usually written defectively as מִצְוֹת (instead of the expected מִצְווֹת), the last syllable having the letter Waw with the vowel-sign Holem over it.

³⁷ Direct object.

³⁸ 'that which' may be expanded to the idea 'the (thing) which' and, being a direct object, is preceded by אֵת, in the formula אֵת אֲשֶׁר (the relative representing the noun 'thing' understood). However, in association with the adjective which follows, namely (next note)

³⁹ 'pleasing' which, in Hebrew, is 'good', the whole phrase is, simply, אֵת הַטּוֹב 'the good (thing)'.

⁴⁰ 'sight' is the English paraphrase for 'eyes'. Similarly 'hearing' represents the Hebrew 'ears'.

⁴¹ If the perfect (Hiphil of יָצָא) is used with the relative then it must be in the 1st person singular אֲשֶׁר הוֹצֵאתִי, 'who (i.e.) I brought forth'. As an alternative, one may rephrase 'the (one) bringing forth', הַמּוֹצִיא—i.e. with the participle and article. The participle, as a verbal adjective, is descriptive of (or qualifies) the noun 'the Lord'. See WHG 66 for the note that the participle with the article may represent the English verb in the past tense and the relative.

⁴² As in the preceding note, the Hebrew will be either אֲשֶׁר הֵבֵאתִי, ('who (i.e.) I brought in' or הַמֵּבִיא, 'the (one) bringing in', using the Hiphil of בָּא (root בוא) note 26 above.

⁴³ As in preceding two notes, either 'who (i.e.) I did battle', אֲשֶׁר נִלְחַמְתִּי, or 'the (one) doing battle', הַנִּלְחָם.

⁴⁴ Meaning 'fought', see note 29 above.

⁴⁵ The Waw conjunctive (and consecutive) does not only mean 'and', but whatever linking word is required by the context in English. The introductory part may be expanded to 'but (וְ) it shall come to pass, if . . .'.

⁴⁶ Either 'to My voice' or 'in My voice', meaning 'obey Me'.

⁴⁷ Since כְּ means 'as', 'according to', use simply 'as all', כְּכֹל.

⁴⁸ There is no compound relative construction in Hebrew. We must restore the more primitive thinking of the Hebrew which, in this instance, is 'the nations who they shall dwell amongst them', WHG 135.

⁴⁹ Following note 45 above, it will be the perfect with Waw consecutive.

⁵⁰ Since motion is involved, אֶל will be used, as in note 2 above. The order of words is 'then (וְ) I shall send unto them prophets'.

⁵¹ The Hiphil of שָׁב (root שוב) 'came back', 'returned', namely הֵשִׁיב 'caused

to come back' produces the derived idea 'brought back', WHG 200 for the form of Hiphil.

⁵² Though the personal pronoun (as object) may be kept separate from the verb, yet the effect is better if the infinitive construct with suffix is used, WHG 131. However, if one is not sure of the correct modifications in pointing, it is safer to keep the infinitive construct without suffix and use the personal pronoun (as object.)

⁵³ In Hebrew usage one *cuts* (not makes) a covenant, reminding us of the sacrificial ceremony involved. Note also that the Qal perfect 1st singular of the verb כָּרַת is כָּרַתִּי (for כָּרַתְתִּי, the first ת having assimilated into the next).

⁵⁴ The order is 'I have made (literally cut) with thee a covenant'.

⁵⁵ A segholate noun, WHG 82, 83 note (a), originally זַרְעְ, with suffix זַרְעִי, &c.

⁵⁶ The sense is not 'like', but 'for', i.e. לְ.

⁵⁷ Hebrew is very deficient in adjectives, but the adjectival effect is often achieved by the construct arrangement of two nouns, as here, 'a possession of eternity'. The noun (said to be in the genitive) following the one in the construct limits the application of the construct noun or gives it a description, in the same way as an adjective. Similarly, 'golden vessels' is expressed as 'vessels of gold', 'a holy mountain' is, in Hebrew thought, 'a mountain of holiness'.

⁵⁸ לְבַד, meaning 'except', takes suffixes; 'with thee alone' is, in Hebrew thinking, 'with thee, thou alone'.

⁵⁹ Either literally or 'the (ones) coming'—i.e. the participle plural with the article; see notes 41–43—הַבָּאִים.

⁶⁰ This plural noun, representing a preposition, takes suffixes of the plural noun, WHG 87, 88.

⁶¹ (a) The imperative is never used with the negative: one must restore the phrasing 'thou shalt not . . .'. If the negative command or prohibition is meant to be permanent, the negative is לֹא; for immediate application it is אַל, WHG 77. (b) The verb יָרֵא 'was afraid, feared' is a stative (WHG 95–97) and doubly weak, being both a Pe Yod and a Lamed 'Alep. Since the normal stative (e.g. כָּבֵד) has Pataḥ in the second syllable of the imperfect (יִכְבַּד), the imperfect Qal of our verb is first (theoretically) יִיְרָא, but the vowelless יְ quiesces into the preceding Ḥireq vowel, resulting in יִירָא and, since the terminal letter א is silent, the second syllable ends in a vowel (sound) and is open, requiring a long vowel and giving rise to יִירָא, WHG 211 (b).

⁶² The vocative is expressed by defining the noun, either with the article or suffix.

⁶³ The idiomatic expression is בַּצֵּר לָהֶם (literally 'in (it) being straitened (infinitive construct) for them'); the root being צרר.

⁶⁴ Waw consecutive with perfect, see note 45 above.

⁶⁵ Rephrase: 'they shall be unto me as (literally for) a people'.

⁶⁶ Rephrase: 'I (personal pronoun before the verb for emphasis) shall be unto them as (literally for) a God.'

II

THE Lord appeared[1] unto[2] Abraham in a dream of the night
and He spoke unto him, saying:[3] 'Thou hast[4] been a faithful
servant unto[2] Me, for thou hast walked before[5] Me in righteousness and truth all the days of thy life[6] and thou hast done
that which is[7] good in My sight.[8] Go thou[9] up, therefore,[10]
upon the mountain opposite which[11] are thy tents[12] and lift
up[13] thine eyes and see the land of Canaan, for unto[2] thee have
I given[14] it and unto thy seed[15] for ever.' And Abraham said:[16]
'I pray Thee,[17] O Lord, Thou[4] knowest[18] that I have not[19] a
son and my wife is exceedingly[20] old and one of my household[21]
will inherit[22] me.' And the Lord said unto him:[23] 'Wherefore
speakest[24] thou thus?[25] Thy wife, Sarah,[26] will bear thee[27] a
son and he will walk in thy ways and I shall[28] bless him.' And
it came to pass,[29] in the morning, that[30] Abraham told[31] Sarah
all[32] which the Lord had spoken unto him.[33] And Sarah said:[16]
'Blessed[34] be the Lord, Who hath not forsaken His handmaid
for, behold, I am old[35] and I said[36] in my heart: "I shall not[19]
have a son", but I trust[37] in the Lord.' And Abraham built an
altar in that place and he offered[38] up sacrifices to the Lord and
he called in the name of the Lord. And it came to pass,[29] after
many days, that[30] Sarah bore a son unto[2] Abraham, her husband, according to[39] the word of the Lord, and she called his
name Isaac, for she said: 'I laughed when they said[40] unto[2]
me: "Thou[41] wilt bear a son."' And the lad grew[42] up and he
walked[43] in the ways of his father and he did[44] only that which
was[45] good in his eyes. And Abraham rejoiced greatly,[46] for
he knew that the Lord was[47] with[48] the lad. And he prayed unto
the Lord and he said:[49] 'O Lord, Thou hast indeed[50] remembered Thy servant[51] and hast done kindness to[52] me and hast
given[53] me a son who will inherit[22] me. Bless, I pray Thee,
this lad, that he may be[54] a faithful servant before[5] Thee all
the days of his life.'[6] And the Lord said unto him:[23] 'Behold,
thy son[55] shall become a great nation[56] and I shall multiply[57]

them as the stars of the heavens and as the dust of the ground, and they shall inherit the land which I have sworn[58] to thee to give[59] unto thy seed.'[60] And Abraham bowed[61] himself before[5] the Lord.

NOTES ON II

[1] The Niphal of רָאָה 'saw', namely נִרְאָה meaning 'was seen', has the derived sense of 'appeared'. Begin with imperfect and Waw consecutive (cf. I, 1) and see WHG 227 (d) for the form.   [2] See note in I, 2, for ל or אֶל.   [3] I, 16.

[4] Either introduce the clause with the personal pronoun which would emphasize 'thou' or, alternatively, reverse the order to 'a faithful servant hast thou been', which would emphasize the fact of his having been a faithful servant.

[5] The English preposition 'before' is expressed by the formula 'to the face of', לִפְנֵי, so that 'before me', 'before thee', &c., must be thought of as 'to my face', 'to thy face', &c., לְפָנַי, לְפָנֶיךָ since פָּנִים is a plural noun.

[6] When the context indicates that the word 'life' means duration of earthly existence, as here, the Hebrew word is (the plural) חַיִּים. When, however, it refers to the vital element in earthly creatures, the word to be used is נֶפֶשׁ (which is usually translated 'soul').   [7] I, 39.   [8] I, 40.

[9] Since the imperative singular necessarily refers to the 2nd person singular, 'thou' is implied in the Hebrew form. Similarly the plural implies 'ye'.

[10] I, 4.

[11] (a) Following upon I, 48, the order of Hebrew thinking is 'the mountain which thy tents are opposite it'. (b) Furthermore, the Hebrew idiom is 'from opposite to . . .'.

[12] אֹהֶל is a segholate noun, originally אָהֶל, WHG 82, 83.

[13] For the doubly weak verb נָשָׂא, see WHG 185 (c).

[14] נָתַתִּי (for נָתַנְתִּי), WHG 148.   [15] I, 55.

[16] For this form—imperfect with Waw consecutive, see WHG 162 (a) and (b).

[17] When introducing a request with 'I pray thee' and a note of urgency is implied, the longer form אָנָּה is used.

[18] (a) Since one cannot speak of 'knowing' unless that state is a completed one, the perfect often corresponds to the English present tense of this verb: יָדַעְתָּ suggests that 'thy knowing is complete' i.e. 'thou knowest'. (b) Similarly, in the cases of the verbs זָכַר, 'remembered', אָהֵב, 'loved', שָׂנֵא, 'hated'.

[19] For the modes of expressing possession in point of time, see WHG 72.

[20] The adverb follows the adjective (and verb) it modifies.

[21] The noun בַּיִת ('house') has an extended meaning of 'household'. 'One', in this context, is not used numerically but, rather, in the sense of a 'member' of the household; in Hebrew it is בֶּן־בַּיִת (literally 'a son of the house(hold)').

[22] The verb יָרַשׁ, curiously, partakes of the characteristics of both the Pe Yod and Pe Waw. The imperfect Qal is יִירַשׁ (as with Pe Yod), but the infinitive construct is רֶשֶׁת (as with Pe Waw). In this context, the active participle Qal יֹרֵשׁ may be used in its adjectival or qualifying sense, i.e. '(one) inheriting me'.

²³ The order of words will be: 'and said unto him (אֵל) the Lord'.

²⁴ The imperfect is often used to implied continued action. Here it would mean 'why dost thou keep on speaking?'.

²⁵ When a sentence is introduced by the adverb 'thus', the Hebrew is כֹּה, but when it occurs at the end of a sentence, it is better to use כָּזֹאת (literally 'like this') instead. Note that the feminine singular (like the Latin neuter) implies 'thing'.

²⁶ Since, in Hebrew, the main idea is first expressed and is limited in its application or is qualified by the following word, (WHG 57 (d)), the order of words will be: 'Sarah, thy wife'.

²⁷ Indirect object, meaning 'to thee'. Use prefixed לְ, I, 2.

²⁸ One may use the normal perfect with Waw consecutive, but, since there is a change of subject and the emphasis is on 'I', the personal pronoun and imperfect may be used. If you are not sure of the modifications involved with the verbal suffix, the personal pronoun (as object) may be kept separate.

²⁹ 'and it was'—וַיְהִי. WHG 92 (e).   ³⁰ Cf. I, 24.

³¹ Indirect object, meaning 'to Sarah'. Use prefixed לְ, I, 2.

³² I, 5 (a).   ³³ Note 23 above.

³⁴ Either the passive participle Qal—בָּרוּךְ—or, when preceded by the jussive יְהִי 'may (let) it be', often the Pual participle מְבֹרָךְ, WHG 169.

³⁵ The verb זָקֵן 'was old' is a stative. The perfect (here preceded by the personal pronoun to emphasize the person) expresses a completed state (meaning, possibly, 'I have become old')—אֲנִי זָקַנְתִּי. Note: אֲנִי זְקֵנָה with the feminine singular adjective would mean 'I (am) an old (woman)'.

³⁶ The imperfect Qal of אָמַר is יֹאמַר in the 3rd masculine singular, but the 1st singular is (not אָאמַר, but contracted in spelling to) אֹמַר, WHG 162.

³⁷ (a) As in note 18 above, one cannot speak of trusting, till that state is a completed one, so that the perfect may be used. On the other hand, if the context conveys the idea of continued trust—'I keep on trusting'—then the imperfect is to be used. (b) In this phrase, if the order is reversed, namely, 'in the Lord I trust', the emphasis is upon the object of trust.

³⁸ The cognate verb and noun is normally used: זָבַח זֶבַח, 'he sacrificed a sacrifice'; הֶעֱלָה עֹלָה, 'he brought up (Hiphil) a burnt offering (literally something brought up)'; or הִקְרִיב קָרְבָּן, 'he brought near a sacrifice (literally something brought near)'.

³⁹ Simply 'as', cf. I, 47.

⁴⁰ The Hebrew form of thinking must be restored, namely: 'In their saying'—i.e. the infinitive construct Qal with suffix, I, 21.

⁴¹ The personal pronoun before the verb emphasizes the person.

⁴² The verb גָּדַל 'was big, great', is a stative by nature. The imperfect Qal is, therefore, יִגְדַּל, WHG 95–97.

⁴³ Note this defective verb: perfect הָלַךְ, imperfect יֵלֵךְ, &c. WHG 237.

⁴⁴ Note this doubly weak verb, WHG 225 (b).

⁴⁵ I, 39.   ⁴⁶ עַד־מְאֹד (literally 'till exceedingly').

⁴⁷ 'was' does not mean 'had been', though the English idiom requires it. In Hebrew the thought is 'he knew that the Lord is with him'.   ⁴⁸ I, 13.

⁴⁹ The pausal form וַיֹּאמַר, followed by the words spoken, WHG 162 (a).

[50] The infinitive absolute before the finite verb for emphasis, WHG 79.

[51] עֲבָד, originally עָבְדְּ, is a segholate noun, WHG 82.

[52] In Hebrew one does kindness *with* (not *to*). Other English renderings are: 'dealt kindly with', 'showed kindness to'.

[53] Indirect object, meaning '*to* me', with לְ, I, 2.

[54] The effect required is obtained by the jussive (יְהִי, 'let him', or 'may he be, become') and the Waw conjunctive.

[55] By placing the subject before the verb, the former is emphasized.

[56] In Hebrew '*as* (i.e. לְ, I, 56) a great nation'.

[57] Hiphil of רָבָה ('was many'), i.e. 'caused to be many'.   [58] I, 27.

[59] WHG 148.   [60] I, 55.

[61] The verb שׁחה ('was low') is one of the so-called Lamed He verbs which was originally a Lamed Waw (שׁחו). In the Hithpalel (required here as a reflexive), the perfect is הִשְׁתַּחֲוָה, the imperfect יִשְׁתַּחֲוֶה and the shortened imperfect (for the Waw consecutive) is יִשְׁתַּחוּ; the terminal Waw quiesces. Note the metathesis of the first radical sibilant letter with the תְ of the prefix הִתְ, WHG 120 note.

III

IT came to pass,[1] when Eliezer heard[2] that Rebecca was[3] of the family of Abraham, that[4] he rejoiced greatly[5] and he came with[6] her to the house of[7] her brother, Laban.[8] And Eliezer spoke unto Laban and he said unto him: 'I am the servant of Abraham,[9] who dwelleth[10] in the land of Canaan. And the Lord blessed[11] my master exceedingly[12] and he gave him[13] flocks[14] and herds, gold and[15] silver and many servants. And he has a son,[16] whose name[17] is Isaac, who will[18] inherit him after his death. And Abraham called me before him[19] and he said unto me: "Behold, now,[20] I am old[21] and I know not[22] the day of my death. Swear,[23] now[20] unto me, that thou wilt not take[24] a wife for my son from the daughters of the Canaanites,[25] amongst whom[26] I dwell. Arise and go forth to the land of my birth,[27] to the house of my kinsman,[28] and take [29] a wife for my son from there, that I may see[30] the wellbeing[31] of my son before[32] I die." And I hearkened to the voice[33] of my master and I arose and I went forth from the land of Canaan and I journeyed unto this place. And, now,[34] tell me,[35] I pray thee, wilt thou let the girl go[36] with[6] me to be a wife[37] unto Isaac

or[38] not, that I may know[39] whether[40] I may return to the house
of my master with[6] her or whether[38] I should seek a wife for
his son from another place.' And it came to pass, when Laban
heard[2] the words of Eliezer, that[4] he said unto him: 'The Lord[41]
hath done this thing.[42] Let us call[43] the girl and ask her. And
if she will say: "I will go[44] with this man to the house of
Abraham, to be a wife[37] unto Isaac", then[45] thou mayest take
her with thee.' And they did as Laban said and they called[46]
Rebecca and they asked her, saying:[47] 'Wilt thou go with this
man to be a wife[37] unto Isaac, the son of Abraham?' And she
answered[48] and said:[49] 'I will go.'[44] Then[45] Eliezer lifted up his
voice and he cried in a loud[50] voice: 'Blessed[51] be the Lord,
God of my master, Who hath brought[52] me hither.'[53] And it
came to pass, on the morrow, that[4] Eliezer said unto Laban:
'Let me go,[54] I pray thee, that I may return[55] to the house of
my master with[6] the girl.' And Laban said: 'Go[56] in peace,[57]
and may the Lord bless[58] our sister in the house of Isaac.' And
Eliezer arose[59] and he placed[60] Rebecca upon the camel and
they went forth, to go[61] to the land[62] of Canaan.

NOTES ON III

[1] II, 29.

[2] Though the direct translation כַּאֲשֶׁר שָׁמַע אֱלִיעֶזֶר is good Hebrew, the more
idiomatic form of expression is 'as Eliezer's hearing' ('as the hearing-of Eliezer'),
i.e. the infinitive construct with prefixed inseparable preposition כְּ, that is
כִּשְׁמֹעַ אֱלִיעֶזֶר.

[3] He heard that Rebecca *is* . . .. If one were to translate 'was' with the verb in
Hebrew, it would mean 'had been', II, 47.   [4] I, 24.

[5] II, 46.   [6] I, 13.

[7, 8] Firstly, the order of the words must be 'to the house of Laban, her brother',
II, 26. Secondly 'house-of', though in the construct state, nevertheless takes the
old accusative ending, I, 7.

[9] Since the main part of this sentence is the fact that he is Abraham's servant,
the order of the words should be reversed to 'the servant of Abraham am I', giving
prominence to his status.

[10] The direct translation, with the relative, is not idiomatic Hebrew. One must
rephrase 'the (one) dwelling', הַיֹּשֵׁב, i.e. the participle with the article. Since
the participle is, in effect, a verbal adjective, it qualifies or describes the noun
preceding it, 'Abraham', WHG 66.

[11] Since there is a change of theme, it is better to translate וַיהוה בֵּרַךְ, i.e.

'and the Lord, He blessed', rather than the more usual וַיְבָרֶךְ יהוה with the imperfect and Waw consecutive.

[12] II, 20, 46.   [13] Indirect object—'to him'—לוֹ.

[14] I, 12.

[15] The conjunction, when immediately before the tone-syllable and connecting a pair of words, is וָ, WHG 41, 7.

[16] 'to him (is) a son'.   [17] Modify to 'and his name'.

[18] Similarly, modify to 'and he will inherit . . .', II, 22.

[19] 'to his face', II, 5.   [20] I, 4.   [21] II, 35.

[22] II, 18—use the perfect.

[23] Use the emphatic imperative (WHG 88 (b)) to give the effect of urgency. Note the Niphal is used, I, 27.

[24] The formulation of a negative oath in Hebrew is, roughly: '(may God punish me) if I do', the words in brackets being understood. When transferred to English thought, it means 'I swear that I shall not do'. Conversely, a positive oath is made in the formula '(may God punish me) if I do not', i.e. 'I swear that I shall'. In our context, the Hebrew words are: 'Swear to me, if thou wilt take . . .'. For the verb לָקַח, see I, 3.   [25] 'Canaan', I, 17.

[26] 'who I dwell amongst them (or him)', I, 48.

[27] (a) The noun מוֹלֶדֶת is one of many nouns of *location* formed by a preformative מ before the root. This word means 'a place of birth'. Similarly, מִזְבֵּחַ, 'a place of sacrificing', i.e. 'an altar'; מִשְׁכָּן, 'a place of dwelling', i.e. 'a dwelling place' (sometimes 'tabernacle'); and מָבוֹא, 'a place of going in', i.e. 'entrance'.

(b) This noun is a segholate, originally מוֹלַדְתְּ and, with suffix, is מוֹלַדְתִּי &c. (on the analogy of מֶלֶךְ originally מַלְךְ, WHG 82).   [28] 'brother'.

[29] Instead of using the imperative, the perfect with Waw consecutive is more idiomatic, following the preceding imperative, i.e. 'go forth . . . and thou shalt take'.

[30] Expand to 'in order that I shall see'. Note how the finer shades of meaning are not indicated in Hebrew by special modifications in speech, but are understood from, or implicit in, the context.

[31] The noun שָׁלוֹם means 'peace', 'well-being'.

[32] בְּטֶרֶם אָמוּת, 'before I shall die'.   [33] I, 46.

[34] There is a break in subject-matter and a new idea introduced by וְעַתָּה.

[35] Indirect object, 'to me'.

[36] שָׁלַח in Qal means 'sent'. The intensive Piel produces the derived idea 'sent away', 'dismissed', 'let go'. The Piel is, therefore, appropriate here, with the He interrogative.   [37] 'to be as (in Hebrew 'for') a wife'.

[38] In an interrogative sentence, the alternative 'or' is אִם.

[39] Expand to 'in order that I shall know', cf. note 30 above.

[40] 'whether . . . or' is הֲ . . . אִם, since a question is implied.

[41] The emphasis is on 'the Lord'; therefore it precedes the verb.

[42] Either direct translation or זֹאת, II, 25.

[43] The Lamed 'Alep verb, having a weak terminal radical, has no extension of the 1st imperfect for the cohortative. The modification in meaning is implicit

in the context. The cohortative, however, is to be used with the following verb, since the sense is 'and let us ask'. Since 'let us call' means 'let us summon', the verb קְרָא will be followed by לְ, I, 22.

[44] The cohortative makes the statement stronger.

[45] The Waw consecutive with the perfect—'and thou shalt take'—is modified by the context, implicitly in Hebrew and explicitly in English, to 'then thou mayest take', I, 45.

[46] 'summoned' is קְרָא לְ, I, 22.   [47] I, 16.

[48] For this doubly weak verb, see WHG 225–6.   [49] II, 49.

[50] Simply, 'a great voice'—קוֹל גָּדוֹל.   [51] II, 34.

[52] Hiphil of בָּא (root בוא), WHG 212 (d).   [53] הֵנָּה.

[54] Note 36 above.

[55] The cohortative with Waw conjunctive, giving the effect of 'and let me return', וְאָשׁוּבָה.   [56] II, 43.

[57] בְּשָׁלוֹם or לְשָׁלוֹם.

[58] Imperfect as jussive, with Waw conjunctive.   [59] WHG 197.

[60] WHG 197.   [61] II, 43, לָלֶכֶת.   [62] I, 7.

IV

IT came to pass,[1] after these things, that[2] Isaac called his son Jacob[3] and he said unto him: 'Thou knowest[4] that we are strangers in this land and its inhabitants worship[5] strange[6] gods, the work of the hands of man. Take not[7] a wife from the daughters of the Canaanites,[8] in whose[9] land we dwell, but go[10] to the house of thy mother's brother and take[10] unto thyself[11] a wife from his household.'[12] And Jacob hearkened to the voice[13] of his father and he went forth to go[14] to Aram, to the house[15] of Laban. And it came to pass,[1] in that night, that[2] Jacob slept[16] upon the ground and he dreamed a dream and he heard a voice calling[17] unto[18] him, saying:[19] 'I am the God of Abraham and of thy father Isaac.[20] Behold, the land upon which[21] thou sleepest shall I give unto thee[22] and unto thy seed[23] after thee,[24] as an everlasting possession,[25] for thou walkest[26] in My ways and doest[27] that which is pleasing[28] in My sight.[29] And I shall[30] be with thee[31] in the way that thou[32] walkest and I shall keep thee from all harm.'[33] And it came to pass, in the morning, that[2] Jacob awoke[34] from his sleep and he remembered the dream which he had dreamed and he said unto himself:[35] 'Lo![36] This place is holy and I knew not and I slept[16] there.' And he prayed unto[37] the Lord and he said:[38] 'O Lord, God of my father, Isaac, Thou hast done[39] kindness to[40] Thy servant this day. And it shall come to pass, when I return in[41] peace to my father's house, that[2] I shall pass by this place and I shall make sacrifice unto[42] thee.' And Jacob journeyed to the land[43] of Aram and, on the third[44] day, he came to the house of his mother's brother, Laban.[45] And Jacob said unto Laban: 'I am the son of thy sister, Rebecca;[45] my father hath sent me hither to dwell with thee.[31] And now,[46] if it pleaseth thee,[47] let me abide[48] here with thee.'[31] And Laban said unto him:[49] 'Behold, thou art my kinsman;[50] abide with[31] me.' And Jacob dwelt in the house of Laban and he kept Laban's sheep[51] and he was as one of the household.[52] And the Lord blessed Laban, on account of Jacob and his sheep increased, beyond reckoning.[53]

NOTES ON IV

[1] II, 29.   [2] I, 24.   [3] I, 22, and II, 26.

[4] Precede with the personal pronoun to emphasize the person; see also II, 18.

[5] 'serve'.   [6] 'other gods'.   [7] I, 61 (a).

[8] I, 17.   [9] 'who, I dwell in his land', cf. I, 48.

[10] I, 45, and III, 29, 'and thou shalt go', 'and thou shalt take'.

[11] 'to thee'.   [12] II, 21.   [13] Cf. I, 46.

[14] II, 43; III, 61.   [15] I, 7.

[16] The verb שָׁכַב is a stative by nature, since it describes a state-of-being; the imperfect is, therefore, יִשְׁכַּב, WHG 97.

[17] Active participle Qal.

[18] With preposition אֶל, since it involves speaking, I, 2.   [19] I, 16.

[20] (a) There must be nothing between a noun in the construct state and the following noun upon which it depends. The English construction 'and of thy father . . .' is impossible in Hebrew and one must expand to 'and the God of thy father'.

(b) Note that the order of thought is 'of Isaac, thy father', II, 26.

[21] 'the land which thou liest upon it (feminine)', cf. I, 48.   [22] I, 2.

[23] I, 55.   [24] I, 60.   [25] I, 56, 57.

[26] Though the active participle Qal gives the direct translation, the sense would seem, rather, to be 'thou hast walked'—perfect.

[27] If the preceding verb is put in the perfect, then this must be the (shortened) imperfect with Waw consecutive.

[28] I, 39.   [29] I, 40.   [30] Note 4 above.

[31] I, 13.   [32] 'the way which thou walkest in it', cf. I, 48.

[33] 'evil'.

[34] The verb יָקַץ, 'was awake' is both a stative and a Pe Yoḏ. In the imperfect Qal the first radical Yoḏ quiesces into the preceding homogeneous vowel and the second syllable has Pataḥ, i.e. יִיקַץ.

[35] The Hebrew idiom is 'said in his heart'.

[36] A stronger word than הִנֵּה seems necessary; אָכֵן or אָמְנָם, 'indeed', 'surely' would suit. If it is felt that the idea of holiness should be stressed, the order should be 'holy is this place'.

[37] Use the preposition אֶל, since praying involves speaking, I, 2.

[38] II, 49.   [39] See note 4 above.   [40] II, 52.

[41] Rephrase 'in my returning', infinitive construct with suffix, cf. I, 21.

[42] II, 38.   [43] I, 7.

[44] Note that the ordinal numbers—WHG 244-5—are adjectives, following the noun they qualify and agreeing with them in gender. From 'second' to 'tenth' the masculine ending is ִי. and the feminine ִית..

[45] II, 26.   [46] III, 34.

[47] Either 'if it is good in thine eyes' or 'if I have found favour in thine eyes'.

[48] Cohortative.   [49] 'and said to him Laban', I, 11.

[50] II, 28.

[51] Either the construct 'sheep of Laban' or 'the sheep (absolute) which (belonged) to Laban'.

[52] 'as one of (construct) the sons of his house', cf. II, 21.

[53] In Hebrew this expression is 'till there is not (any) reckoning' (or 'number'), עַד אֵין מִסְפָּר.

V

IT came to pass,[1] when Jacob heard[2] that Esau was[3] seeking his life,[4] that[5] he arose and he went forth from his father's house, to go[6] to the house of Laban,[7] his mother's brother, as his[8] father commanded him,[9] for he feared[10] lest Esau would slay him. And he came to the house of Laban[7] and he dwelt there with him[11] and he kept his sheep. Now[12] Laban had two[13] daughters; the name of the elder[14] was[15] Leah and the name of the younger[16] was[15] Rachel. And Jacob loved[17] Rachel, for she was exceedingly[18] beautiful. And Jacob said unto Laban: 'I have been a faithful[19] servant unto thee[20] all these days and I have kept thy sheep. Give me,[21] I pray thee, thy younger[16] daughter, Rachel,[22] as[23] a wife, for I love[24] her, and I shall serve thee seven[25] years for her.' And Jacob's words pleased[26] Laban exceedingly and he said unto him:'It is better[27] that I should give her to thee than that I should give her to a man whom[28] I know not. Abide[29] here with me[11] another seven[30] years and serve me, as[8] thou hast said. And it shall come to pass, when the seven years are full,[31] that[5] I shall give her to thee as a[23] wife.' And Jacob served Laban seven years, and it came to pass, when the seven years were full,[31] that[5] Jacob said unto Laban: 'Give me,[21] I pray thee, my wife, for the seven years are full.'[32] And Laban gathered[33] together the inhabitants of his city and he made a great feast,[34] but[35] he sent Leah unto Jacob instead of Rachel. And Jacob was exceedingly wroth[36] and he said unto Laban: 'What is this[37] that thou hast done unto me? Did I not serve thee these seven years for thy younger[16] daughter, Rachel?[22] Why didst thou not do as[8] thou didst say?' And Laban said unto[38] him: 'If thou wilt serve me another seven[30] years, then[35] I shall give thee also Rachel as[23] a wife.' And Jacob did as[8] Laban said and he served him another[30] seven years, and he took also Rachel unto himself[39] as a[23] wife. And Jacob said unto himself:[40] 'I shall avenge myself[41] against Laban, for he hath requited[42] me evil[43] for good.'[44] And Jacob kept the matter in his heart.

NOTES ON V

[1] II, 29.   [2] III, 2.

[3] The Hebrew thought is 'Jacob heard that Esau *is* seeking . . .', cf. II, 47.

[4] נֶפֶשׁ; a segholate noun, originally נַפְשׁ, and, with suffix, נַפְשִׁי, II, 6.

[5] I, 24.   [6] III, 61.   [7] I, 7.   [8] I, 10.

[9] I, 11.   [10] I, 61 (*b*).   [11] I, 13.

[12] 'and to Laban (were) two daughters', see I, 45.

[13] Literally in Hebrew, 'a pair-of', since the numerals, from 2 to 10, are really nouns, WHG 243 (*b*)—שְׁתֵּי.

[14] 'the big (one)'.

[15] 'was' is unexpressed in Hebrew, II, 47—the sense is the 'name (being) . . .'.

[16] 'the small (one)'.

[17] The verb אָהֵב is a stative, since it denotes a state-of-being; the imperfect, therefore, is יֶאֱהַב; it being also a Pe Alep, WHG 97 note and 155 on stative Pe guttural verbs.

[18] II, 20.   [19] Cf. II, 4.   [20] I, 2.

[21] '*to* me'.

²² The order of words is 'Rachel, thy younger daughter', II, 26.

²³ I, 56.   ²⁴ Use the perfect, see II, 18.

²⁵ Though the plural of שָׁנָה is שָׁנִים, it is a feminine noun and, therefore, requires the feminine numeral.

²⁶ (a) Rephrase: 'And Jacob's words were good in the eyes of Laban.' (b) Do not translate with the verb הָיָה and the adjective, as טוֹבִים . . . וַיִּהְיוּ. Use the verb יטב. This is a defective verb: the perfect is טוֹב (see WHG 206) and the imperfect יִיטַב (WHG 188), the latter type being a Pe Yoḏ; see also WHG 238 B.

²⁷ (a) 'better' is expressed by the adjective טוֹב followed by מִן of comparison, WHG 136. (b) The entire sentence must be rephrased, as follows: 'Better is my giving her to thee than my giving her to . . .', i.e. the infinitive construct Qal and suffix, WHG 148.

²⁸ 'to a man who I know not him', using the perfect, II, 18; see also I, 48.

²⁹ יָשַׁב, 'abode', 'stayed', as well as 'sat', 'dwelt'.

³⁰ 'yet other seven years'—the order of words being 'yet seven years (note 25) other (ones—feminine plural).

³¹ (a) The verb מָלֵא, meaning 'was full with' and taking a direct object, is a stative. (b) The Hebrew thinking is 'in (or 'as') the being-full of the seven years' —infinitive construct—בִּמְלֹאת or כִּמְלֹאת. The reference is to future time, if the context speaks of the future; when the context refers to the past, then the infinitive construct, likewise, indicates the past.

³² The verb מָלֵא is to be used in the perfect, since one can only speak of anything being full when that condition is a complete one.

³³ In English it is the context which determines whether the phrase 'gathered together' is transitive or intransitive. In Hebrew, however, the verbal forms make this distinction clear. The Qal אָסַף, the Piel קִבֵּץ and the Hiphil הִקְהִיל ('caused to assemble') all mean 'brought together', 'gathered'. The Niphal of these verbs means 'were gathered together', 'gathered themselves together' (the Hithpael is also used with the first two roots).

³⁴ A 'feast' (with small 'f') is מִשְׁתֶּה from the root שָׁתָה, 'drank', whereas 'Feast' (with capital 'F' and having a religious significance) is חַג from the root חָגַג, 'celebrated', 'kept the Feast'.   ³⁵ Conjunction, I, 45.

³⁶ Apart from the verb קָצַף, the idiom is either וַיִּחַר אַפּוֹ, 'and his anger was hot' or וַיִּחַר לוֹ, 'and it was hot to him'—from the root חָרָה, 'was hot'.

³⁷ The feminine singular demonstrative adjective; see end of II, 25.

³⁸ I, 11.

³⁹ לוֹ 'to him'.   ⁴⁰ 'said in his heart'.

⁴¹ Niphal of נקם with עַל or מִן, use the cohortative for emphasis.

⁴² גָּמַל or the Piel שִׁלֵּם.

⁴³ feminine singular—'(an) evil (thing)'; see end of II, 25.

⁴⁴ feminine singular—'(a) good (thing)'; see end of II, 25. N.B. say, 'instead of good.'

VI

WHEN[1] Laban came back from the field to his house, he[2] heard that Jacob had fled and that he had taken with[3] him his wives and his sons and his servants and his flocks.[4] And Laban was exceedingly wroth[5] and he called unto[6] his sons and he said unto them: 'Behold, Jacob hath gone forth from my house, while we were[7] in the field, and he hath taken with him all which is mine.[8] Let us pursue him,[9] for he is on the way, going[10] to the land of[11] Canaan, to his father's house.' And they arose and they pursued[9] Jacob all that day and all that night[12] and, on the second day, they saw the tents[13] of Jacob before them.[14] And Laban and his sons slept on the mountain that[15] night, for they said: 'When it is morning[16] we shall fall upon him and slay him and bring back[17] that which is ours.'[8] And the Lord spoke unto Laban in a dream and he said unto[18] him: 'I am the God of Jacob. If thou comest nigh unto him, thou shalt surely die.'[19] And Laban was exceedingly afraid,[20] for he knew that the Lord was[21] with[3] Jacob. And it came to pass, in the morning, that Laban lifted his voice and he called unto[22] Jacob and he said:[23] 'Why didst thou depart from me[24] and didst not tell me?[25] Didst thou think[26] there was evil in my heart against thee? And now, let us make[27] a covenant, I and thou, that there may be[28] peace between me and thee[29] and between thy sons and my sons,[29] for we are kinsmen.'[30] And Jacob answered[31] and said:[32] 'I fled from thy house whilst thou wast[33] in the field, for I was afraid that[34] thou wouldst not allow me[35] to go away from thee,[24] for thou knowest[36] that the Lord hath blessed thee for my sake. But now I know[36] that thou art not[37] mine enemy and dost not hate[38] me. I shall make[27] a covenant with thee, as[39] thou hast said.' And they made a covenant there on[40] that day and they swore[41] to one another[42] and they separated[43] from one another.[44] And Laban arose, he and his sons with him, and he departed, to go to his city. And Jacob journeyed to the land of[45] Canaan and he came to the land of Canaan, he and all his household[46] and all which he possessed.[47]

NOTES ON VI

[1] To imitate the biblical style, we should begin with 'and it came to pass, when Laban . . .'. The subservient clause should be rephrased, in the Hebrew pattern, to 'in Laban's returning' ('in the returning-of Laban')—infinitive construct with prepositional prefix, cf. I, 21.

[2] If we begin the sentence with וַיְהִי, we must continue with 'that he heard'—in Hebrew thought 'and he heard'.

[3] I, 13.   [4] I, 12.   [5] V, 36, and II, 20, 46.

[6] This means 'summoned', קָרָא לְ, I, 22.

[7] In Hebrew thinking, 'in our being'—infinitive construct with suffix.

[8] 'to me' (WHG 72), 'to us', &c., as expressing possession.

[9] When 'to pursue' means to chase or run after, then רָדַף is followed by אַחֲרֵי; if it is used in the sense of 'persecute', then it takes the direct object.

[10] 'to go'.   [11] I, 7.

[12] Note that the noun לַיְלָה, though ending in הָ, is masculine, since it is not an accented terminal syllable and is merely an extension of the form לֵיל, found in poetry.

[13] II, 12. This segholate in the construct plural is אָהֳלֵי with a composite shewa (Ḥaṭēp Qāmeṣ) under the guttural, instead of the simple vocal shewa (under a normal letter as קָדְשֵׁי).

[14] II, 5.   [15] 'in that night'.

[16] In Hebrew 'in the being-of-the morning'—infinitive construct.

[17] I, 51.   [18] I, 2.

[19] The infinitive absolute before the finite verb expresses emphasis, WHG 79 and 206–7.

[20] I, 61 (b), and II, 20, 46.

[21] 'was', in this instance, does not mean 'had been', but is required by the English. The Hebrew thinking is that 'he knew that the Lord is with Jacob', II, 47.

[22] The sense here is not 'summoned' (as in note 6 above) but of speaking in a loud voice—addressing. The preposition, then, is אֶל, I, 2.

[23] II, 49.

[24] Hebrew thinking is more exact than the English in phrases expressing movement away from a person or thing: he 'departed from with' a person. Similarly, 'he went down from upon the throne', 'he destroyed them from upon the face of the earth'.

[25] 'to me'.   [26] 'say'.   [27] I, 53; use cohortative.

[28] Expand to 'in order that there shall be . . .'.

[29] 'between me and between thee, between thy sons and between . . .'.

[30] 'brothers'. Note the plural of אָח is אַחִים, WHG 289.

[31] For this doubly weak verb, see WHG 225 (b), 226.

[32] II, 49.   [33] 'in thy being', as in note 7 above.

[34] WHG 179. The verb 'was afraid' is often followed by פֶּן, 'lest'.

³⁵ נָתַן has an extended meaning of 'allow', 'permit'.

³⁶ Perfect, II, 18.   ³⁷ אֵין takes suffixes, אֵינֶנִּי, 'I am not', אֵינְךָ, 'thou art not', &c.

³⁸ Perfect, II, 18. It follows the pattern of יָרֵא in inflection, WHG 179.

³⁹ I, 10.   ⁴⁰ *in* that day'.   ⁴¹ I, 27.

⁴² 'One to the other'. Note: there are three ways of expressing the relationship 'one another': זֶה . . . זֶה, 'this (one) . . . this (one)'; אִישׁ . . . אָחִיו, 'a man . . . his brother'; אִישׁ . . . רֵעֵהוּ, 'a man . . . his neighbour'.

For feminine nouns the feminines of the above are, naturally, used. The first formula suggests a primitive society (and thinking), the second implies a tribal society and the third a more socially developed system.

⁴³ Niphal of פרד. The Niphal is a passive reflexive or middle—'were separated, separated themselves'.

⁴⁴ 'one from *with* the other', notes 24 and 42 above.   ⁴⁵ I, 7.

⁴⁶ II, 21.   ⁴⁷ I, 5, and 5 (*b*).

VII

JOSEPH dreamed[1] a dream and he related[2] it to his brothers[3] and he said unto them: 'Hear ye, now,[4] my dream which I dreamed. Behold, in my dream, the sun and the moon and the stars of the heavens were bowing[5] down before me[6] to the ground.'[7] And, when Joseph's brothers heard[8] the words of their younger[9] brother, they hated[10] him and could not speak peaceably[11] with[12] him. And they said to one another:[13] 'Doth our brother think[14] that he will rule over[15] us?' And it came to pass, when Jacob heard[8] the words of his sons which they had spoken about[16] Joseph, that he feared[17] greatly,[18] and he called Joseph[19] and he said unto him: 'Wherefore didst thou relate thy dream to thy brethren?[3] Surely[20] thou knowest[21] that they hate[22] thee and they seek thy harm.[23] Abide,[24] therefore,[4] with[12] me and go not forth[25] into the field with[12] them, lest they do thee evil.'[26] But[27] Joseph hearkened not to the voice of his father[28] and he went forth into the field to see his brethren[3] and to inquire after[29] their welfare, for he said unto himself:[30] 'My brethren will not do me any harm,[23] for they know[21] that my father loveth[21] me and they fear[31] his fierce anger.'[32] And it came to pass, when the sons of Jacob saw[33] Joseph, that they said to one another:[13] 'Behold, the dreamer cometh. Let us seize him[34] and sell[35] him as[36] a slave to Egypt, and we shall see whether[37] his dream is true[38] or not.' And, as Joseph drew near[39] unto them and asked after[29] their welfare, they seized him[34] and brought him to the house of a merchant, an Egyptian, and they sold him to the merchant as[36] a slave. And they returned unto their father[28] and they said unto him: 'Behold, thy son, Joseph, is dead. An evil beast hath devoured him.' And, when Jacob heard[8] these words, he sat down upon the ground and he put dust[40] upon his head and he cried in a loud[41] voice: 'Woe to me, for my son Joseph is dead. Would that[42] I had died instead of thee, my son.' But[27] the sons of Jacob said not a word, when they saw[43] their father sitting upon the ground and mourning[44] for his son. And the Lord was with[12] Joseph in the house of his master[45] and He blessed him there. And Joseph became chief[46] over all the slaves in the house and, in whatever[47] he did, he prospered.[48]

NOTES ON VII

[1] Begin, as usual, with Waw consecutive (and imperfect).

[2] The verb 'related', in a descriptive sense, is the Piel of סֵפֶר. When the sense is 'informed', the Hiphil of נגד—הִגִּיד, usually translated 'told', is used.

The object 'it', in this sentence, is not represented in the Hebrew, but is supplied by the English.

[3] Note the forms of אָח in the plural with suffixes, WHG 289.   [4] I, 4.

[5] He saw 'the sun . . . bowing down'; 'were' is required by the English. For the verb שחה (שְׁחוּ), see II, 61.

[6] II, 5.   [7] The old accusative case ending—אַרְצָה.

[8] The Hebrew thinking requires (the fuller) 'and it came to pass', followed by the rephrasing 'as the hearing of'—infinitive construct.   [9] V, 16.

[10] If you begin the sentence with 'and it came to pass', you must continue with 'and they hated . . .'.

[11] 'in peace'.   [12] I, 13.   [13] VI, 42.

[14] 'think' in Hebrew is 'say', הַאֹמֵר אָחִינוּ. Note the pointing of the interrogative הַ before a guttural, WHG 80, and the forms of אָח in the singular with suffix, WHG 288.

[15] מָשַׁל is usually followed by בּ (and not by עַל).

[16] עַל has an extended meaning of 'concerning', 'about'.

[17] I, 61 (b).   [18] II, 46.   [19] It means 'summoned', קָרָא ל I, 22.

[20] 'Surely', anticipating a positive response, is expressed by the negative interrogative הֲלֹא. 'Dost thou not know?' implies 'Surely thou knowest'.

[21] II, 18.   [22] Perfect. II, 18.

[23] 'evil'—feminine singular adjective, V, 43.

[24] V, 29.   [25] I, 61 (a).

[26] The direct translation would be יַעֲשׂוּ עִמְּךָ רָעָה, 'they will do evil with thee'. An alternative is the Hiphil of the double 'Ayin verb רַע (root רעע), meaning 'caused to be evil, did evil'. The Hiphil perfect is הֵרַע and the imperfect יָרַע, the terminal guttural inducing the furtive Paṭaḥ (see the normal double 'Ayin verb, WHG 233). This verb is usually followed by the inseparable preposition ל.

[27] I, 45.   [28] For the forms of אָב in the singular with suffixes, see WHG 288.

[29] 'inquired after' is שָׁאַל ל.   [30] V, 40.

[31] The stative verb יָרֵא, 'was afraid, feared', when followed by מִפְּנֵי (literally 'from the face of') implies physical fear and, with the direct object, implies fear of reverence. 'He feared the king' is יָרֵא מִפְּנֵי־הַמֶּלֶךְ, but 'He feared the Lord' is יָרֵא אֶת־יהוה.

[32] In Hebrew 'the fierceness of his anger', חֲרוֹן אַפּוֹ.

[33] 'as the seeing-of the sons of Jacob'—infinitive construct.

[34] Note the Pe 'Alep verb, WHG 162. Use the cohortative.

[35] It means 'and let us sell', i.e. the cohortative.   [36] I, 56.

[37] III, 40.   [38] 'truth'.   [39] 'as the drawing near of Joseph . . .'.

[40] Use either the verb זָרַק, 'sprinkled' or the Hiphil of עָלָה 'caused to come up', i.e. 'brought up'.   [41] III, 50.

[42] (a) מִי־יִתֵּן ('who will give', i.e. 'grant') expresses 'would that'. The complete thought is 'who will grant my dying'—infinitive construct. (b) תַּחַת takes suffixes of the plural noun, WHG 87, 88.

[43] 'as (or in) their seeing'—infinitive construct with suffix.

[44] Hithpael of אָבַל followed by ל or עַל.

[45] The plural אֲדוֹנִים is generally used, except with the 1st singular prefix.

[46] In Hebrew 'was for a head', i.e. 'as a head'.

[47] וּבְכֹל, see I, 5 (a).   [48] Hiphil of צלח.

VIII

JACOB heard[1] that there was[2] bread in the land of Egypt, and he called unto[3] his sons and he said unto them: 'Behold, now,[4] I have heard that there is bread in Egypt. Go ye down[5] thither[6] and bring[7] food for us from there, that[8] we may live and not[9] die.' And the sons of Jacob did as[10] their father commanded them[11] and they went down to Egypt,[12] but[13] they knew not that Joseph was the ruler over[14] all the land of

Egypt. And Joseph saw[15] them among those who had come[16] to Egypt,[12] and he drew near unto[17] them and he asked them, saying:[18] 'Who are ye? Whence have ye come? And why have ye come down to Egypt?'[12] And Judah answered and said:[19] 'My lord, we are the sons of one man in the land of Canaan, and we have come down hither, for we heard that there is bread in the land of Egypt, for there is a famine in the land of Canaan, as[10] my lord knoweth.' And Joseph said unto them: 'Ye are spies; to see the land of Egypt have ye come down hither.' And Judah said: 'Nay,[20] my lord, thy servants are not spies, for we are truthful men.'[21] And Joseph said: 'Give me[22] a sign that thou speakest the truth.' And Judah said: 'We have a young[23] brother, who is[24] with[25] our father in the land of Canaan. He did not come down with us, for our father is very old.' And Joseph said: 'When ye come again[26] to Egypt,[12] let your young brother come down[27] with[25] you, that I may know[28] that ye are righteous men.'[29] Then[30] the sons of Jacob said to one another:[31] 'This evil[32] hath come upon us, for we sinned against[33] our brother, Joseph,[34] when we sold him[35] as[36] a slave and we hearkened not when he cried[37] unto us.' And they knew not that Joseph understood their words, for he had with him[38] an Egyptian who knew the language[39] of Canaan and who was as[36] a mouth to him.[40] And Joseph said unto them: 'Swear[41] unto me that ye will bring down[42] your young brother with you, that I may know[28] whether ye have spoken the truth or not.' And they swore[41] unto him, as[10] he commanded them. And Joseph said: 'Let one of you abide[42] here in Egypt, till ye return[43] with[25] your young brother.' And Simeon did not go up to the land of Canaan with[25] his brothers, but[30] remained[44] in Egypt.

NOTES ON VIII

[1] Begin, as usual, with Waw consecutive (and imperfect).

[2] He heard that 'there *is* bread . . .'.   [3] 'summoned', קְרָא ל, I, 22.

[4] I, 4.   [5] The plural imperative obviously implies 'ye' in Hebrew, II, 9.

[6] שָׁמָּה, with old accusative case ending.

[7] I, 26, for the verb. The order of words is 'bring for us food'.

[8] 'in order that we shall live'.   [9] 'and we shall not die'.

¹⁰ I, 10.

¹¹ The order of words is 'as commanded them their father'.

¹² Old accusative case ending.   ¹³ I, 45.   ¹⁴ VII, 15.

¹⁵ For the shortened imperfect Qal with Waw consecutive of רָאָה, see WHG 227 (d).

¹⁶ Rephrase to 'among the (ones) coming'—active participle plural Qal.

¹⁷ I, 2.   ¹⁸ I, 16.   ¹⁹ II, 49.   ²⁰ The negative לֹא.

²¹ Following I, 57, the Hebrew phrase will be 'men of truth'.

²² Indirect object, 'to me'.

²³ 'small', cf. V, 16—'to us (is) a small brother'.

²⁴ Alter to 'and he is . . .'.   ²⁵ I, 13.

²⁶ 'In your coming (infinitive construct) again (עוֹד)'.

²⁷ The 3rd masculine singular imperfect serves as a jussive, as there is no shortened form in this verb.

²⁸ Either 'in order that I shall know' or, simply, the perfect with Waw consecutive and this modification is understood from the context.

²⁹ Either 'men, righteous (ones)' or 'men of righteousness', I, 57.

³⁰ I, 45.   ³¹ VI, 42.   ³² V, 43.

³³ 'sinned to'.   ³⁴ Cf. II, 26, for order of words.

³⁵ 'in our selling'—infinitive construct with suffix.   ³⁶ I, 56.

³⁷ 'in his crying'—infinitive construct with suffix.

³⁸ 'for with him (was) . . .'.   ³⁹ שָׂפָה, 'lip' is used for a language.

⁴⁰ The order is 'was to him for a mouth'.

⁴¹ I, 27.   ⁴² V, 29 and 27 above.

⁴³ 'till your returning'—infinitive construct.

⁴⁴ Either יֵשׁ or Niphal of שָׁאַר.

IX

It came to pass,¹ after these things, that Joseph sent his brothers away² from him³ and they went up from the land of Egypt and they came to the land of⁴ Canaan, unto their father Jacob.⁵ And they told him,⁶ saying: 'Behold, thy son Joseph⁵ liveth and he is ruler over⁷ all the land of Egypt.' And Judah said unto his father: 'Thus said thy son, Joseph:⁵ "Come down⁸ unto me,⁹ to Egypt,⁴ thou and all thy household¹⁰ with¹¹ thee, and dwell with¹¹ me, for the famine is grievous¹² in the land of Canaan, and in Egypt there is bread."' And Jacob fell down upon his face to the ground⁴ and he said:¹³ 'Blessed¹⁴ art thou, O Lord, God of my father Isaac, who didst not forsake Thy servant,¹⁵ for my son, Joseph,⁵ liveth. I will

go down[16] to Egypt,[4] that I may see him[17] before I die.'[18] And
the sons of Jacob did as[19] Joseph commanded them, and they
took[20] their father and their wives and their sons and their
daughters and their flocks[21] and their herds[21] and all which
they possessed[22] and they went forth, to go down to the land
of[4] Egypt. And it came to pass, before they came[23] to the
border of Egypt, and they were still[24] on the way, that they
sent a messenger unto Joseph, saying: 'Behold, thy father and
thy brethren and all their household are coming down to thee[9]
to Egypt,[4] as[19] thou hast said, and behold, they are[25] on the
way.' And Joseph went[26] to Pharaoh's palace and he appeared[27]
before the king and he said unto him: 'Behold, my father and
my brethren and all their household[10] are coming down to me[9]
to Egypt.[4] Let them dwell,[28] I pray thee, in the land of Goshen,
for they are herdsmen.'[29] And Pharaoh said unto him:[30] 'Is
not the whole land in thy hands?[31] Do as is right[32] in thine
eyes.' And Joseph arose and he went forth to meet[33] his father,
to do him honour.[34] And Jacob lifted up his eyes and he saw,
and behold, a man was[35] riding towards[33] him and he knew
that he was[36] Joseph. And Joseph drew near unto his father
and he kissed him[37] and he wept[38] and his father also wept
with[11] him. And Joseph said unto his brethren: 'The Lord[39]
hath sent me hither, that I may feed you[40] and all your household[10] all the days of the famine. Dwell in the land of Goshen,
for there is pasture for the sheep which ye have.'[41] And,
after this, they spoke with him peaceably.[42]

NOTES ON IX

[1] 'and it came to pass . . . and . . .'.   [2] III, 36.   [3] VI, 24.
[4] Old accusative case ending; see also I, 7.   [5] Cf. II, 26.
[6] 'to him', VII, 2.   [7] VII, 15.   [8] Emphatic imperative.
[9] I, 2.   [10] II, 21.   [11] I, 13.   [12] 'heavy'.
[13] II, 49.   [14] II, 34.   [15] II, 51.   [16] Cohortative for emphasis.
[17] The imperfect with Waw conjunctive used with a cohortative effect. The
Lame<u>d</u> He verb cannot have an extension of the 1st imperfect for the cohortative, since the terminal radical has ceased to be a letter.
[18] III, 32.   [19] I, 10.
[20] The 3rd masculine singular imperfect Qal of לָקַח is יִקַּח, but the 3rd
masculine plural is יִקְחוּ, without the doubling daghesh forte. Since it is diffi-

cult to articulate a doubled vowelless letter, the doubling is often not pronounced and the daghesh forte (representing the doubling) is dropped.

[21] I, 12.   [22] 1, 5 and 5 (b).

[23] (a) Either לִפְנֵי בוֹאָם, 'before their coming'—the infinitive construct, or טֶרֶם יָבֹאוּ. (b) Though the English requires a past tense, the Hebrew uses the imperfect with טֶרֶם, probably because, by implication, the act is not yet completed.

[24] 'and they . . . (being) still'—עוֹד takes suffixes עוֹדֶנִּי, עוֹדְךָ, &c.

[25] הִנֵּה takes suffixes הִנְנִי, הִנְךָ, &c.   [26] II, 43.

[27] II, 1.   [28] The imperfect with jussive effect implied.

[29] אַנְשֵׁי מִקְנֶה, 'men of cattle'.

[30] The order is 'and said unto him Pharaoh'.

[31] Singular, I, 34.

[32] Either כַּטּוֹב, 'as the good (thing)' or כַּיָּשָׁר, 'as the right (thing)'.

[33] Of the verb קָרָא, which, in this case, is the same as קָרָה, 'met', 'happened', the infinitive construct with לְ is לִקְרַאת, 'to meet', 'towards' and, with suffix לִקְרָאתִי, 'to meet me', 'towards me', &c.

[34] Piel of כָּבֵד.   [35] He saw 'a man riding'.

[36] 'he knew that he is Joseph'.   [37] 'he kissed to him'.

[38] The imperfect Qal of בָּכָה is יִבְכֶּה and the shortened form with Waw consecutive is וַיֵּבְךְּ, unlike the usual Lamed He verb.

[39] By placing the noun before the verb, the subject is emphasized; '(it is) the Lord (who) hath sent'.

[40] The Hiphil of אָכַל, 'ate', namely, הֶאֱכִיל, 'caused to eat', has the meaning of 'fed'.   [41] 'which (are) to you'.   [42] 'in peace'.

X

I T came to pass,[1] when Moses heard that Pharaoh was[2] seeking his life,[3] that he arose and he fled from the land of Egypt and he went to the land of Midian and he dwelt there. And he took[4] the daughter of the priest of Midian unto himself[5] as[6] a wife and he kept his sheep. Now, on[7] a certain day, when Moses was[8] in the wilderness[9] with his father-in-law's[10] sheep, he[11] lifted up his eyes and he saw,[12] and behold, there was a fire before him. And he heard a voice calling unto him from the midst of the fire, saying: 'I am the God of Abraham. Come not nigh[13] unto Me, for this place is holy.'[14] And Moses fell upon his face to the ground[15] and he was exceedingly afraid.[16]

And the Lord spoke again[17] unto Moses and He said unto him:
'I have heard the cry of My people in Egypt and I have remembered My covenant with them. Go thou down to Egypt
and speak unto the elders of Israel in My name according to
all[18] which I shall say[19] unto thee. And it shall come to pass,
if they hearken not to thy words and they say: "Give us[20] a
sign that the Lord, our God, hath sent thee unto us", then[21]
thou shalt take water from the river[22] and pour it[23] upon the
ground, and the water shall become blood[24] before their eyes[25]
and they shall know that I have sent thee unto them.' And
Moses bowed himself[26] to the ground[15] and he said:[27] 'O Lord,
who am I that Thou shouldst send me unto the sons of Israel?'
And the Lord said unto him: 'Behold, the men who were[28]
seeking thy life are dead,[29] and thy brother Aaron will go with[30]
thee and he will also speak[31] in My name. The days of the
affliction of My people are full[32] and I shall bring them forth[33]
from the house of bondage[34] into the wilderness[15] and I shall
give[21] them My Torah[35], that[36] they may learn to walk in My
ways and to become[37] a kingdom of priests unto Me. And I
shall bring them into[38] the land which I have lifted up My
hand to their ancestors[39] to give unto them and they shall be
My people.[40] And thou shalt be a shepherd unto them and
thou shalt teach them to love that which is good[41] and to hate
that which is evil,[42] that[36] it may be well[43] with them in the
land which I have given unto them and that they may dwell
in it in peace. Go down, then, to Egypt[15] and do as[44] I have
commanded thee.'

NOTES ON X

[1] II, 29, and III, 2.   [2] He 'heard that Pharaoh *is* seeking'.

[3] II, 6, V, 4.   [4] I, 3.   [5] V, 39.   [6] I, 56.

[7] The idiom is וַיְהִי הַיּוֹם, 'and the day was'.

[8] 'in Moses's being', 'in the being of Moses'—infinitive construct of הָיָה.

[9] מִדְבָּר does not mean 'desert', but the wild area between the sown and un-
sown lands, where the bedouin can lead his sheep and goats to feed on the wild
outcrops of vegetation and where, occasionally, he may grow grain in the season.
There is a root דָּבַר which means 'led' and, with the Mem of location, suggests
a place to which herds may be led, see III, 27 (*a*).

[10] 'with the sheep which (were, i.e. belonged) to his father-in-law'.

¹¹ Following וַיְהִי we must continue with the Waw consecutive and imperfect.

¹² VIII, 15.   ¹³ The negative is אַל, I, 61 (a).

¹⁴ To bring out the idea of holiness, reverse to 'holy is . . .'.

¹⁵ Old accusative case ending.   ¹⁶ I, 61 (b), and II, 20, 46.

¹⁷ Either the direct translation with עוֹד, 'again', or שֵׁנִית, 'a second time', or the idiomatic use of the verb יסף in Hiphil as an auxiliary: וַיּוֹסֶף יהוה לְדַבֵּר, 'and the Lord added to speak', i.e. 'spoke again'.   ¹⁸ I, 47.

¹⁹ II, 36.   ²⁰ 'Give to' לְ.

²¹ I, 45.

²² The usual word for 'river', נָהָר, is never used for the Nile; this river is always הַיְאוֹר with the article and is the Hebrew form of the Egyptian *Io'r*.

²³ 'and thou shalt pour . . .': the object 'it' being understood.

²⁴ 'be(come) as (in Hebrew לְ, I, 56) blood'.

²⁵ Since the English preposition 'before' is represented either by לִפְנֵי, 'to the face of', or לְעֵינֵי, 'to the eyes of', we must modify the English expression to mean 'to their eyes', לְעֵינֵיהֶם. (To translate לִפְנֵי עֵינֵיהֶם (literally 'to the face of their eyes') would produce an absurd expression.)

²⁶ II, 61.   ²⁷ II, 49.

²⁸ 'the men the (ones) seeking', WHG 66.

²⁹ The masculine plural adjective מֵתִים (which is, really, the participle) would convey the sense of 'are dead men'. The perfect plural מֵתוּ, 'have died' has a stative quality and gives the true sense.

³⁰ I, 13.   ³¹ 'and he will speak, also he'.   ³² Perfect, V, 32.

³³ I, 25.   ³⁴ The Hebrew is 'the house of slaves'.

³⁵ The usual translation of תּוֹרָה as 'Law', following the Greek rendering νόμος, is not only inadequate (since much more than law is denoted by it), but does not convey the root-idea. The verbal root יָרָה means 'pointed', 'shot' (an arrow), 'directed', 'taught' (according to the context), so that the noun תּוֹרָה designates the body of teaching found in Scripture. We, therefore, no longer give a translation of this word, but use it as a term: Torah.

³⁶ Expand to 'in order that . . .'.

³⁷ 'to be'. Note the order of the words: 'to be unto Me a kingdom . . .'.

³⁸ I, 26.

³⁹ The plural of אָב is, curiously, אָבוֹת. This strange phenomenon—an obviously masculine noun having a feminine plural termination—may be explained rationally if we assume that this word was, originally, אָבוּת, i.e. a feminine singular noun with the וּת-ending, which is characteristic of abstract nouns and meaning 'ancestry'. Since the text was unpointed and this word, written אבות, implied 'ancestors', it was mistakenly regarded in later times as a plural form. With the 3rd plural suffix it is אֲבוֹתָם (and not אֲבוֹתֵיהֶם).

⁴⁰ I, 65.   ⁴¹ אֶת־הַטּוֹב, I, 39.   ⁴² אֶת־הָרַע, cf. I, 39.

⁴³ יִיטַב לְ, V, 26 (b).

⁴⁴ The Hebrew would, most probably, expand to 'according to all . . .', see I, 47.

XI

THE sons of Israel journeyed[1] in the wilderness of Sinai and they encamped at the border of the land of Moab. And the Lord spoke unto Moses, saying: 'Gather together[2] the sons of Israel and speak unto them the words which I shall put into thy mouth.'[3] And Moses did as the Lord commanded him[4] and he gathered all Israel together and he said unto them: 'Hear, O Israel, the statutes[5] and ordinances[6] which I speak in your hearing[7] this day, that[8] ye may learn to do them. The Lord, our God, made[9] a covenant with[10] us on Mount Sinai and He spoke unto you on the holy mountain[11] out of the midst of the fire, and I stood between the Lord and you[12] at that time, for ye were afraid[13] of the fire and ye went not up on the mountain. And it came to pass, when ye heard[14] the voice of the Lord coming forth out of the midst of the fire, that ye came unto me, even all the heads of your tribes and your elders, and ye said unto me: "The Lord, our God, hath shown[15] us His glory and we have heard His voice. This day we have seen that the Lord doth speak[16] with man[17] and that man liveth. Tell us,[18] we pray thee, that which the Lord commandeth us to do, and we shall do it."[19] And now, behold, the statutes and the ordinances are written[20] in the Book of the Covenant, in order that the generations who will come[21] after you[22] may read this Book[23] and learn to do the commandments[24] of the Lord, for the Lord hath chosen you of[25] all the peoples of the earth to be[26] a holy people unto him.' Then[27] Moses read the commandments of the Lord in the hearing[7] of all the people. And it came to pass, after these things, that the heads of the people drew near unto Moses and they said unto him: 'Behold, we are standing at the border of the land of Moab. Shall we send messengers unto the king of Moab, saying:[28] "Let us pass through[29] thy land"? And, if the king of Moab shall say: "Ye shall not pass through[30] my land", shall we go forth to meet them[31] in battle?'[32] And Moses answered and said:[33]

'I shall inquire of[34] the Lord, for we shall not be able[35] to
stand[36] against the sons of Moab, except that[37] the Lord command us to fight[38] against them.'

NOTES ON XI

[1] Begin, as usual, with the Waw consecutive and imperfect. The verb is נָסַע.

[2] V, 33.   [3] For this irregular noun with suffix, see WHG 288.

[4] I, 10 and 11.

[5] The plural of חֹק is חֻקִּים with the doubled ק.

Note (a) When the doubling of a letter (by daghesh forte in writing) cannot,
for some reason, be accomplished and the vowel preceding it is Qibbuṣ (ֻ u),
then this vowel is prolonged into Ḥōlem (˙ long ō). Qibbuṣ cannot be prolonged into Shūreq (וּ full û), because the presence of this full vowel in a word indicates that it was originally the letter ו which had quiesced. In the same way
Ḥireq (short i) is never prolonged into the full Ḥireq (י. î), but into Ṣērē (long ē).
To come back to our case, the double ʿAyin noun of the root חָקַק is, with suffix,
חֻקִּי &c. and, in the plural, חֻקִּים, with the doubling daghesh forte. However,
when the ק is the last letter of the word—and the terminal letter cannot be
doubled in articulation we are left with a hypothetical חֻק which becomes חֹק.
(b) Similarly כֹּל, 'all' (really 'whole', 'totality', I, 5 (a)), is from the root כלל
and, with suffix, is כֻּלִּי, &c., but without suffix it becomes כֹּל. (c) In the same
way, the Pual of the root ברך ('was blessed') is בֹּרַךְ (for בֻּרַךְ) in the perfect
and יְבֹרַךְ (for יְבֻרַךְ) in the imperfect, WHG 168.

[6] מִשְׁפָּטִים, the basic idea of מִשְׁפָּט being 'custom', 'usage', from which is
derived the idea of 'judgement', 'ordinance', also 'manner'.

[7] In Hebrew, we say 'in your ears', just as 'in your sight' is expressed as 'in
your eyes', I, 40.   [8] 'in order that . . .'.

[9] I, 53.   [10] I, 13.

[11] 'the mountain-of holiness', with the article attached to the second noun,
WHG 46 note, and I, 57.

[12] 'and between you', cf. VI, 29.   [13] WHG 211 (b) and VII, 31.

[14] 'as your hearing'—infinitive construct with suffix.

[15] The Hiphil of רָאָה, 'saw', namely הֶרְאָה, 'caused to see', produces the
derived idea 'showed'. Logically, it takes the direct object, e.g. 'he caused us
to see'.

[16] The imperfect, in its extended effect of 'frequentative future'.

[17] There are several words for 'man'. אָדָם refers to the species 'man(kind)'
and takes the article to denote a species. אֱנוֹשׁ suggests 'mortal man', and אִישׁ,
'man' in the sense of person and, sometimes, of a superior type.

[18] 'to us'. Use the emphatic imperative to suggest urgency.

[19] 'it' is not in the Hebrew, but is required by the English.

[20] Passive participle Qal masculine plural (WHG 84), כְּתוּבִים.

[21] I, 59.   [22] I, 60.   [23] In Hebrew one reads in a book.

[24] I, 36.

[25] (a) The verb בָּחַר is followed by the inseparable preposition בְּ. (b) To

emphasize the object of choice, it comes first in the order of words: 'for (in) you hath the Lord chosen'.

[26] The Hebrew is, simply, 'for (in English *as*) a holy people' and the English usage expands by inserting 'to be'.

[27] I, 45.   [28] I, 16.

[29] עָבַר means 'crossed over', 'passed through', and is followed by the inseparable preposition בְּ.

[30] The prohibition seems permanent; use לֹא, I, 61 (*a*).   [31] IX, 33.

[32] Use the article, like the French 'la guerre', 'to the battle'.   [33] II, 49.

[34] שָׁאַל בְּ means 'consulted (the oracle)'. Use the cohortative.

[35] The imperfect of the stative verb יָכֹל is יוּכַל, WHG 238D.

[36] The verb קָם (root קוּם) followed by לִפְנֵי.

[37] בִּלְתִּי אִם, 'except if'.   [38] I, 29.

XII

WHEN[1] the Lord, thy God, bringeth[2] thee into[3] the land which He hath sworn[4] to thine ancestors[5] to give unto[6] thee as[7] a possession, and thou seest great cities with lofty walls[8] around[9] them, say not[10] in thy heart: 'We cannot[11] prevail[12] against the peoples of Canaan, for they are mightier[13] than we and they have[14] horses and chariots and weapons[15] of iron in their hands.' Fear them not,[16] but[17] trust in the Lord, thy God, for He will do battle for thee and He will smite[18] them and deliver[19] their cities into thy hands.[20] And when thou comest[21] into[3] these cities, thou shalt utterly[22] destroy the temples of Baal and throw[23] down his altars, for they are an abomination unto[6] the Lord, thy God. Take heed[24] exceedingly and guard thy soul, lest thou depart[25] from the way of the Lord and go[25] after the gods of the nations whom the Lord driveth out before[26] thee. Do not[27] according to[28] their deeds, nor walk[29] in their ways, lest the anger of the Lord be kindled[30] against thee, and He send[25] evil plagues upon thee and cause thee to perish[31] from[32] the face of the earth. Behold, the commandments[33] and the ordinances[34] are written[35] in this Book, to teach[36] thee to do that which is pleasing[37] in the sight[38] of the Lord, in order that it may be well[39] with thee and with

thy children after[40] thee. Remember the generation of the
wilderness, who rebelled against[41] the word of the Lord and
the Lord did not permit[42] them to see the land into which[43]
thou art coming to possess[44] it. Keep the covenant which the
Lord, thy God, made[45] with[46] thee, that He may bless[47] thee
in all which thou doest.[25] And it shall come to pass, when the
Lord, thy God, giveth thee victory[48] over thine enemies, that
thou shalt deal kindly[49] with the stranger who is within thy
gates, and thou shalt remember that thou wast a stranger[50] in
the land of Egypt. Practise[51] righteousness and speak only the
truth, have compassion upon the widow and the fatherless, for
it is these things[52] which the Lord requireth from thee. And
if thy son asketh[25] thee, saying: 'Wherefore did the Lord drive
out the nations of the land before us?',[53] then thou shalt say
unto him: 'Because they were sinful to the Lord and they
acted wickedly[54] and spoke deceitfully[55] and oppressed the
fatherless. Therefore did the Lord destroy them off[32] the face
of the earth.'

NOTES ON XII

[1] Introductory 'when' is כִּי with the imperfect for the future and, though the
passage may be introduced by the familiar וְהָיָה, 'and it shall come to pass', it
is not essential.

[2] Imperfect, since the future is indicated.   [3] אֶל, 'unto'.

[4] I, 27.   [5] X, 39; WHG 288–9.   [6] I, 2.   [7] I, 56.

[8] חוֹמָה is a city wall, usually fortified, whereas קִיר is the wall of a building.

[9] 'around to them' (feminine plural, since 'city' is feminine).

[10] The negative אַל, since the negative command is not permanent, I,
61 (a).

[11] The perfect (of this stative verb)—יָכֹלְנוּ—means 'our being-able is complete', i.e. 'we are able'. On the other hand, the imperfect נוּכַל would mean 'we
shall be able'; see XI, 35.

[12] Either (a) the verb גָּבַר in Qal or Hithpael with עַל or (b) the verb קוּם
with לִפְנֵי, XI, 36.

[13] (a) The comparative degree is expressed by the ordinary verb or adjective
followed by מִן, WHG 136. (b) The plural adjective with the personal pronoun—
חֲזָקִים הֵמָּה מִמֶּנּוּ—would mean, literally, 'they are stronger (people) than we'.
However, by using the perfect of the stative verb חָזַק, i.e. חָזְקוּ, a completed
state-of-being is implied.

[14] 'to them . . .'. The singular 'horse' and 'chariot' is to be used, to suggest
(not numbers, but) classes of things—collectives.

¹⁵ כְּלִי, plural כֵּלִים, means 'vessel', 'instrument', 'weapon' and, in plural, 'goods', 'chattels', as indicated by the context.

¹⁶ The negative אַל, I, 61 (a) and (b).

¹⁷ Since a contrast or contrary suggestion is involved, use כִּי, (usually following a negative clause)—'but in the Lord shall ye trust'.

¹⁸ The Hiphil of נכה—הִכָּה (WHG 225) generally meaning 'smote' but, in this association, has the sense of 'defeated'. The root is not found in Qal in the Old Testament.   ¹⁹ I, 33.

²⁰ I, 34.   ²¹ Either as note 1 above or 'in thy coming'—infinitive construct.

²² Infinitive absolute before the finite verb, WHG 79. An alternative usage is 'and thou shalt destroy (perfect with Waw consecutive) them, even (גַּם) destroying (infinitive absolute).

²³ The Hiphil of נָפַל, 'fell', namely הִפִּיל, 'caused to fall', giving rise to the idea 'threw down' (WHG 143) is not used for demolishing structures. The proper word is נָתַץ in Qal.

²⁴ The sense is 'take care, watch yourself' and is expressed by the Niphal of שָׁמַר with the reflexive-middle effect. (If, in another context, the sense is 'pay attention', the Hebrew would be שָׂם לֵב.) Usually the Hebrew thought is fuller, namely 'take heed unto you(rselves)'—adding לָכֶם.

²⁵ Imperfect, since the reference is to the future.   ²⁶ II, 5.

²⁷ Here the prohibition is permanent; use the negative לֹא, I, 61 (a).

²⁸ 'as their deeds'.   ²⁹ The negative לֹא, as note 27 above, II, 43.

³⁰ V, 36.

³¹ Hiphil of אָבַד, 'perished', 'was lost'.

³² 'from upon the face of . . .', VI, 24.   ³³ I, 36.   ³⁴ XI, 6.

³⁵ XI, 20.

³⁶ Hiphil of the doubly weak verb יָרָה, in the infinitive construct with the inseparable prefix, i.e. לְהוֹרוֹת with direct object.

³⁷ 'good'.   ³⁸ 'eyes'.

³⁹ 'it shall be good for thee'—using the imperfect of יטב, V, 26 (b).

⁴⁰ I, 60.   ⁴¹ בְ.   ⁴² VI, 35.

⁴³ 'the land which thou art coming thither' (שָׁמָּה), I, 48.

⁴⁴ II, 22.   ⁴⁵ I, 53.   ⁴⁶ I, 13.

⁴⁷ Imperfect with Waw conjunctive giving a jussive effect.   ⁴⁸ I, 31.

⁴⁹ II, 52.

⁵⁰ To emphasize the status of 'stranger', put it first: 'a stranger wast thou'.

⁵¹ Simply 'do'.

⁵² אֵלֶּה (common gender). Since the feminine singular adjective implies 'thing' (II, 25 note), so the feminine plural denotes 'things'—like the Latin neuter.

⁵³ 'from our face'.   ⁵⁴ Simply, 'they did evil'—feminine singular adjective.

⁵⁵ 'they spoke falsehood'.

XIII

THESE are the words which the Lord spoke unto Moses before his death: 'O Moses, My servant, thou hast been a faithful shepherd[1] unto[2] My people, from the day I brought them forth[3] from the land of Egypt and until now.[4] Thou didst lead them[5] in this great wilderness for[6] forty years, according to[7] all which I commanded thee. But[8] they are a stiff-necked people,[9] and they rebelled against[10] Me, to provoke Me.[11] And Mine anger was kindled[12] against them, because they refused to hearken to thy voice and to do that which is good[13] and upright, and they went after strange[14] gods. Yea,[15] they made for themselves gods of gold which they worshipped[16] and they cried to one another:[17] "These are thy gods, O Israel, which brought you up[18] from the land of Egypt, from the house of bondage."[19] And I swore,[20] at that time, that the generation which did these evil things[21] should not enter[22] the land which I lifted up My hand to their ancestors[23] to give unto their seed, but that their children who would come[24] after them[25] would[26] possess it. And now, thy days are full[27] and thou art about[28] to die. Take, now, Joshua, thy minister, and place thy hands upon his head and bless him, for he will lead[5] the people into the land of Canaan and he will give it to[2] them as[29] an everlasting possession.[30] Say unto him: "Fear not,[31] O Joshua, for the Lord, thy God, will be with[32] thee, even as[33] He was with me, whithersoever[34] thou goest. Only take heed[35] exceedingly to walk in His ways and to keep His Torah according to all[7] which is written[36] in the Book of the Covenant. Depart not[37] from it, neither to the right nor to the left,[38] in order that thou mayest prosper in whatsoever[39] thou doest."[40] Then[41] thou shalt gather the people together,[42] both young and old,[43] upon this mountain, before thou goest up[44] on it, and thou shalt speak unto them the words which I shall put into thy mouth.[45] And it shall come to pass, when thou hast finished[46] speaking unto them, that thou shalt go up on the mountain and from the top of it thou shalt see the land of Canaan, but[8] thither thou shalt not come, for here shalt thou die.'

NOTES ON XIII

[1] See II, 4.   [2] I, 2.

[3] Hiphil of יָצָא, I, 25. Restore the Hebrew thinking; 'from the day of my bringing forth'—infinitive construct with suffix.

[4] The pausal form עָתָּה should be used at the end of a sentence; see WHG 21 and, for an analogous form, WHG 137 (b).

[5] Apart from the Qal נָהַג and the Piel נִהֵל, the Hiphil of the defective verb יָלַךְ—הָלַךְ, 'walked', 'went', namely, הוֹלִיךְ, 'caused to walk', 'go' produces the derived idea of 'led' (WHG 237–8). A simpler form of thinking is 'Thou didst go before them', suggesting 'Thou didst lead them'.

[6] 'for' is supplied by the English and is not in the Hebrew.

[7] I, 47.   [8] I, 45.   [9] 'a people stiff-of (construct of קָשֶׁה) neck'.

[10] XII, 41.   [11] Hiphil of כָּעַס, 'was angry', i.e. 'caused to be angry'.

[12] V, 36.   [13] אֶת־הַטּוֹב וְאֶת־הַיָּשָׁר, cf. I, 39.   [14] IV, 6.

[15] גַּם.

[16] 'and they worshipped them', either עָבַד or Hithpael of שָׁחָה (originally שׁחו) 'bowed down to them', II, 61.

[17] VI, 42.   [18] Hiphil of עָלָה ('went up'), 'caused to go up', 'brought up'.

[19] X, 34.   [20] I, 27.

[21] The feminine plural adjective implies 'things' (like the Latin neuter plural). For the singular, cf. II, 25.

[22] Following the formula for the taking of oaths, as given in III, 24, the Hebrew will be 'if they will enter (come) into'.

[23] X, 39.   [24] I, 59.   [25] I, 60

[26] 'they (personal pronoun) shall possess it', to emphasize 'they'.

[27] V, 32.   [28] 'thou art going (active participle Qal) to die'.

[29] I, 56.   [30] I, 57.   [31] The negative is אַל, I, 61 (a) and (b).

[32] I, 13.   [33] The Hebrew is 'as'; the English expands to 'even as'.

[34] בְּכֹל, literally 'in all'.   [35] XII, 24.

[36] 'the (thing) written'—passive participle Qal with the article—הַכָּתוּב, WHG 85.

[37] The prohibition here is permanent; use the negative לֹא, I, 61 (a).

[38] The Hebrew is 'rightwards or leftwards'—old accusative ending.

[39] בְּכֹל, 'in all'.   [40] Imperfect, since the future is implied.

[41] I, 45.   [42] V, 33.

[43] The Hebrew idiom is 'from a young (person נַעַר) and until an old (person זָקֵן)'.

[44] 'before thy going-up'—infinitive construct with suffix.

[45] WHG 288.   [46] 'as thy finishing (infinitive construct with suffix) to speak'.

XIV

MOSES gathered together[1] all the sons of Israel and he spoke
unto them, saying:[2] 'Ye[3] have seen all the wonderful things[4]
which the Lord, your God, hath done for you. Forty years He
led[5] you in this great and terrible wilderness[6] and He fed you[7]
with bread from the heavens and gave you water to drink[8]
from the rock. And now, I am old[9] and am about to[10] die. And
the Lord said unto me: "Thou shalt not cross[11] over the Jordan
with[12] the people, but[13] Joshua will bring them across[14] into
the land of Canaan, for I have chosen him,[15] to be a head[16]
over My people in thy place."[17] And now, behold, Joshua is
before you.'[18] And Moses called unto Joshua[19] and he spoke
unto him in the hearing[20] of all Israel and he said unto him:
'Be strong[21] and of good courage,[22] for thou wilt bring[23] the
people into the land at the border of which[24] we are standing.
The Lord will be with thee[12] and He will not forsake thee. He
will[25] fight for thee and He will deliver[26] thine enemies into
thy hands.'[27] And Joshua was filled[28] with the spirit of the
Lord, for Moses had laid his hands upon his head, and the
children saw that the spirit of the Lord had descended upon
him. Then Moses wrote all the words of the Torah in a book
and he commanded the priests, saying:[2] 'Take this Book of the
Torah[29] and place it in the ark of the covenant, that it may be
as[30] a witness against Israel, if they keep not the commandments[31] of the Lord.' And the priests did as[32] Moses commanded them and they took the Book of the Torah and they
placed it in the ark and they said: 'Let this Book be[33] as[30] a
witness against us, if we depart from the way of the Lord, our
God.' And Moses said unto the people: 'When I go up[34] on this
mountain, go ye not[35] after me[36] nor seek me, but cross over the
Jordan with[12] Joshua, for thus hath the Lord commanded
you.' And the people wept[37] there exceedingly[38] and they cried
in a loud[39] voice: 'O father of Israel, leave us not.'[35] And Moses
blessed[40] the people and he turned away from[41] them and he
went up on the mountain, as the Lord commanded him.

NOTES ON XIV

[1] V, 33.   [2] I, 16.

[3] Use the personal pronoun before the verb to emphasize 'ye'.

[4] XIII, 21. The Niphal participle of פלא, i.e. נִפְלָא, conveying an adjectival idea.   [5] XIII, 5.

[6] The Niphal participle of יָרֵא, namely נוֹרָא, '(a thing to be) feared', i.e. 'terrible'. Note the sequence of the Hebrew thought 'the wilderness, the great and the terrible (one), the this (one)'.   [7] IX, 40.

[8] The verb שָׁתָה, 'drank' is defective, the Hiphil being of the root שקה, namely הִשְׁקָה (WHG 238), and means 'he caused to drink', i.e. 'he gave to drink' and (in some contexts, would be translated) 'watered', 'irrigated'.   [9] II, 35.

[10] XIII, 28.   [11] לֹא for permanent prohibition, I, 61 (a).

[12] I, 13.   [13] XII, 17.   [14] Hiphil of עָבַר, namely הֶעֱבִיר, means 'caused to cross', i.e. 'brought across'.

[15] To emphasize the object of choice, reverse the order of words to 'for (in) him have I chosen', see XI, 25.

[16] 'to be a head' is the English elaboration of the Hebrew 'for (i.e. as) a head'.

[17] 'instead of thee', VII, 42 (b).   [18] II, 5.

[19] I, 22 (end of note).   [20] See XI, 7.

[21] Imperative Qal of the stative verb חָזַק, 'was strong', WHG 156.

[22] Imperative Qal of the stative verb אָמַץ, 'was firm', 'strong'; note that this is also a Pe 'Alep verb.

[23] I, 26 and 3 above.

[24] 'the land which we are standing at (ב or עַל) its border', cf. I, 48.

[25] Put the personal pronoun before the verb to emphasize 'he'.

[26] I, 33.   [27] I, 34.   [28] V, 31 (a) and 32.

[29] 'the Book of the Torah, the this (one—masculine singular demonstrative agreeing with the masculine singular noun 'Book').   [30] I, 56.

[31] I, 36.   [32] I, 10.   [33] Jussive form יְהִי.

[34] 'in my going-up'—infinitive construct with suffix, WHG 226.

[35] The negative is אַל, since it applies to an immediate situation.

[36] I, 60.   [37] The singular may be used with collective עַם, IX, 38.

[38] II, 46.   [39] III, 50.   [40] WHG 168 note.

[41] Either 'from with them' (VI, 24) or 'from at (עַל) them'.

XV

JOSHUA gathered together[1] all the sons of Israel and he spoke unto them, saying:[2] 'The Lord, our God, hath brought us across[3] this Jordan to give us[4] this land, as[5] He hath sworn[6] to our fathers.[7] And now, behold, we are standing opposite[8] the city of Jericho, which[9] shall be delivered[10] into our hands[11]

tomorrow. Hear ye, then, that which[12] I command you to do
before we draw[13] near unto the city to capture it.[14] Go ye
down to the Jordan[15] and bathe in the water of the river, that
ye may be cleansed. And in the morning ye shall approach[16]
the city and ye shall go round[17] its walls[18] all the day, until the
evening.[19] And the inhabitants of the city will say to each
other:[20] "Behold, the sons of Israel are as[21] many as the stars of
the heavens and as the dust of the ground, and who is able to
stand against[22] them?" And the fear of you[23] shall fall upon
them and they will have no[24] spirit to fight[25] against you.
Surely[26] ye have heard the words of the spies which they spoke
unto us, when they returned[27] hither from the city, saying:
"The heart of the inhabitants of the city hath melted[28] and
hath become as[29] water because of us."[30] And it shall come to
pass, when we approach[31] the city to take it,[32] if they come forth
to meet us[33] in peace, then ye shall not shed[34] any blood, but[35]
ye shall deal kindly[36] with them, as[5] Moses commanded us.[37]
But[38] if they call upon us for battle,[39] then shall ye all shout[40]
in a loud[41] voice: "For the Lord and for Joshua", and ye shall
go up into the city[15] and ye shall smite[42] them with the edge
of the sword.[43] Be ye strong[44] and of good courage,[45] for this
is the land which the Lord hath given us and He[46] will fight
for us and He will give us[4] victory[47] over our enemies. And it
shall come to pass, when we have taken[48] the city, that we shall
leave our wives and our children there, and we shall journey
on to Bethel, and we shall do to Bethel as[5] we have done to
Jericho. Return ye, now, unto your tents[49] and go not[34] forth
till the light of the morning.' And the elders of the people said
unto Joshua: 'All which thou hast commanded us to do we
shall do, for we know[50] that the word of the Lord is in thy
mouth.'[51]

NOTES ON XV

[1] V, 33.   [2] I, 16.

[3] Hiphil of עָבַר (XIV, 14), taking two accusatives, the one being 'us' ('caused
us to cross', with the verbal suffix) and the other being 'the Jordan' ('caused us
to cross the Jordan', preceded by אֶת־).

[4] 'to us'—לְ.   [5] I, 10.   [6] I, 27.   [7] X, 39.
[8] II, 11 (b).   [9] Rephrase 'and it (i.e. 'she') shall be . . .'.

[10] I, 33. [11] I, 34. [12] I, 38.

[13] 'our drawing near'—infinitive construct with suffix.

[14] Attach the suffix to the infinitive construct, WHG 131.

[15] Old accusative case ending. [16] קָרַב or root נגשׁ ('drew near').

[17] The verb סַב (double ʿAyin root סבב), see I, 6; WHG 231.

[18] XII, 8. [19] Use the pausal form, WHG 137 (e). [20] VI, 42.

[21] The Hebrew is 'are many, as . . .'. [22] XII, 11, and XI, 36.

[23] The construct state and the suffix sometimes reflect objective relationships, e.g. יִרְאַת־יהוה means 'fear in respect of Yahweh' (and not 'Yahweh's fear') and similarly יִרְאַתְכֶם means 'the fear in respect of you' (and not 'your fear').

[24] 'there shall not be in them a(ny) spirit'. [25] I, 29.

[26] VII, 20.

[27] 'in their returning'—infinitive construct with suffix.

[28] Niphal of the double ʿAyin verb מסס, WHG 233.

[29] I, 56.

[30] 'from our face'—מִפָּנֵינוּ; מִפְּנֵי is usually translated 'because of' (literally 'from the face-of').

[31] 'in our drawing-near unto'—infinitive construct with suffix.

[32] As in 14 above. [33] IX, 33.

[34] The negative is אַל referring to an immediate situation, I, 61 (a).

[35] XII, 17. [36] II, 52.

[37] The order of words is: 'as commanded us Moses'.

[38] Either וְאָם (I, 45) or 'and it shall come to pass, if . . .'.

[39] XI, 32.

[40] (a) The shouting is a battle-cry and expressed by the Hiphil of the root רוּעַ, WHG 200. (b) The wording in Hebrew is 'and ye shall shout, all of you'; see XI, 5, for the pointing of כֹּל with suffix. [41] III, 50.

[42] XII, 18.

[43] 'to the *mouth* of the sword', the sword being thought of as devouring its victims.

[44] XIV, 21. [45] XIV, 22.

[46] The personal pronoun with the imperfect emphasizes that *He* will fight.

[47] I, 31.

[48] 'in our taking (i.e. capturing) the city'—infinitive construct.

[49] II, 12. [50] II, 18. [51] WHG 288 for פֶּה with suffix.

XVI

JOSHUA called together[1] all the elders of the people and their judges and he said unto them: 'Ye have[2] seen the great things[3] which the Lord, our God, hath done for us,[4] from the day we crossed[5] over the Jordan to enter[6] this land until this day.

Because we have hearkened to His voice and we have done
according to all[7] which He commanded us and we have kept
the covenant which He made[8] with us, He gave us[9] victory
over our enemies and He blessed the fruit of our land and[10]
of our cattle. Take ye heed,[11] therefore,[12] lest the people turn
aside[13] from the way of the Lord, to go after the gods of the
nations among whom[14] we dwell. Remember ye the matter of
Achan, when he transgressed[15] the command of the Lord and
he took from the spoils at Ha'ai, and the anger of the Lord was
kindled[16] against us and we were not able to stand[17] against the
inhabitants of that city. And now, I am old[18] and I know not[19]
the day of my death. Choose ye, therefore,[12] from amongst
yourselves one[20] who will be a judge[21] and a ruler over you
after my death, that he may lead[22] the people in the way of the
Lord and that it may be well[23] with them. For, if ye do not
thus,[24] ye shall become divided into twelve tribes, each tribe[25]
being under its own leader,[26] and ye shall not be able to fight
against your enemies, each tribe[25] by itself.'[27] Then one of the
elders drew near and he said unto Joshua: 'We know[19] that
thou hast spoken the truth. Inquire, I pray thee, of the Lord,[28]
that He may choose[29] the one[20] who will be over us after thy
death, that we may know[30] that the Lord will be with[31] him,
even[32] as He hath been with thee, and we shall hearken unto
him, even as[32] we have hearkened[33] unto thee.' And Joshua
answered and said: 'Thou hast spoken well.[34] I shall inquire[35]
of the Lord and I shall declare[36] unto you that which is pleasing[37] in His sight.[38] Go ye, now, unto your tents[39] in peace.'
And Joshua fell down upon his face to the ground[40] and he
prayed unto the Lord and he said: 'O Lord, God of Israel,
if I have found favour in Thine eyes, deal kindly[41] with Thy
servant and choose Thou[42] a man who will lead[22] Thy people
after my death, that there may not be strife amongst them, to
their hurt.'[43]

NOTES ON XVI

[1] If you take it to mean 'summoned' it is קָרָא לְ, but if you take it to mean
assembled' it is הִקְהִיל, using Waw consecutive with the imperfect in either
case.   [2] The personal pronoun before the verb emphasizes 'ye'.

[3] The feminine plural adjective implies 'things', like the Latin neuter plural, cf. XIII, 21.

[4] The order of words is 'hath done for us, the Lord'.

[5] 'from the day-of our crossing'—infinitive construct with suffix, followed by the direct object with אֶת־.   [6] 'to enter (come) *into*'.

[7] I, 47.   [8] I, 53.   [9] 'to us'.

[10] Since there must be nothing between a word in the construct and the one upon which it is dependent, we must expand to 'and the fruit of our cattle'.

[11] XII, 24.   [12] I, 4.

[13] Imperfect, since it applies to the future.

[14] 'the nations who we dwell amongst them', I, 48.

[15] 'in his transgressing'—infinitive construct Qal, with suffix, of עָבַר which usually means 'crossed over' and, by extension, 'trespassed'.

[16] V, 36.   [17] XI, 36.   [18] II, 35.   [19] II, 18.

[20] XI, 25 (*a*) 'a person' is expressed by אִישׁ, see XI, 17.

[21] 'as (in Hebrew 'for') a judge and as (for) a ruler'.

[22] XIII, 5.   [23] X, 43.   [24] II, 25.

[25] The Hebrew idiom is 'a tribe, a tribe'.   [26] 'head'.

[27] לְבַדּוֹ 'he (i.e. it) alone', I, 58.   [28] XI, 34.

[29] 'in order that he shall choose' or the imperfect alone with jussive effect, using the Waw conjunctive.   [30] 'in order that . . .'.

[31] I, 13.   [32] XIII, 33.   [33] The sense is 'obey' and is expressed either by לְקוֹל or שָׁמַע בְּקוֹל (I, 46) or שָׁמַע אֶל.

[34] The Hebrew idiom is 'thou hast done well (Hiphil of יטב, 'thou hast caused it to be good', WHG 190) to speak', the first verb being used as an auxiliary.

[35] Use the cohortative to express exertion, see also XI, 34.

[36] Again use the cohortative with Waw conjunctive (root נגד in Hiphil).

[37] I, 39.   [38] Cf. I, 40.   [39] II, 12.

[40] אַרְצָה, old accusative ending.

[41] II, 52.   [42] XI, 25 (*a*).

[43] V, 43, using the feminine singular adjective (II, 25 note) or the idiom לְרַע לָהֶם 'for (it being) hurtful (evil) for them'.

XVII

AFTER[1] the death of Joshua there arose[2] a man of the tribe of Ephraim and his name was[3] Abimelech, and he was[3] a mighty warrior,[4] and the officers of the host made[5] him chief[6] over them. Now, on a certain day,[7] Abimelech gathered his companions together and he spake unto them, saying: 'Make me king[8] over the tribe of Ephraim, that we may be[9] as the peoples of the land of Canaan in which[10] we dwell. Then[11] go ye unto the tribes of Israel and speak unto them, each tribe[12] by itself,[13] and say unto them: "It is not good that ye should be[14] alone,[13] for ye are few and we are many. Serve ye, therefore, the king who[15] ruleth over us, that we may be strong[16] together." And it shall come to pass, if they hearken unto your voice and do according to all[17] which ye say unto[18] them, that ye shall choose from amongst them men[19] of valour to serve me.[20] But[21] if they answer[18] and say:[18] "What have we to do with you?"[22] then[11] ye shall go forth against them[23] with force.' And the words of Abimelech pleased[24] his companions exceedingly, and they answered and said: 'All which thou hast said unto us we shall indeed[25] do.' And they made a great feast[26] and they offered up[27] sacrifices upon the altar and they cried with one voice: 'May the king Abimelech live!'[28] And it came to pass, as they were eating[29] and drinking and making merry,[30] that a prophet of the Lord appeared[31] before them[32] and he spoke unto the people who were assembled[33] there and he said:[34] 'Wherefore have ye done this thing?[35] Are there no prophets among[36] the tribes of Israel that ye have not inquired of[37] the Lord? But[11] know ye that ye have done evil[38] in the sight[39] of the Lord and that this matter shall not prosper.' Then[11] the prophet turned away from them[40] and he departed and went on[41] his way. And the companions of Abimelech were sorely afraid[42] and they said to one another:[43] 'Who told[44] the man of God that which[45] was in our hearts[46] to do? The Lord hath surely[25] revealed hidden things[47] unto him. It is better[48] that we should return,[49] every man[50] to his house, and not provoke the Lord to anger[51] against us, for the prophet hath declared unto us that this matter shall not prosper.' And they separated[52] from one another[53] and they returned, every man[50] to his house.

NOTES ON XVII

[1] Begin with the introductory formula 'and it came to pass . . .'.

[2] 'and there arose . . .'.

[3] 'was' is required by the English. The Hebrew is 'and his name (being) . . . and he (being) . . .'.   [4] 'a mighty man-of war', גִּבּוֹר מִלְחָמָה.

5 The verb שָׂם (root שׂים), i.e. 'set', 'placed', WHG 197.

6 'for (in English 'as') a head'. 7 X, 7.

8 While the rendering 'place me for (in English 'as') a king over' would not be alien to Hebrew thinking, the more usual usage would be 'cause me to reign, to be king . . .', i.e. the Hiphil of the verb מָלַךְ.

9 Either 'in order that we shall be' or simply the perfect with Waw consecutive 'and (or then) we shall be' as a consequence.

10 'the land which we dwell in it (feminine)', cf. I. 48. 11 I, 45.

12 XVI, 25. 13 I, 58.

14 In Hebrew it is 'not good (is) your being'—infinitive construct of הָיָה.

15 'the (one) ruling'—active participle Qal with the article, WHG 66; see also VII, 15.

16 Cf. XII, 13 (b), and note 9 above. 17 I, 47.

18 Imperfect, since the future is implied. 19 XI, 25 (a).

20 Infinitive construct Qal with suffix, but if difficulty should be found in obtaining the correct pointing, keep the object (personal pronoun) separate.

21 I, 45. One may expand to 'and it shall come to pass, if they shall answer and shall say . . . that (in Hebrew 'and') ye shall . . .'.

22 Here we must employ the Hebrew idiom, which is 'What (is there) to us and to you?' 23 Say 'to meet them', IX, 33.

24 V, 26 (a) and (b).

25 The infinitive absolute before the finite verb expresses emphasis, WHG 79.

26 V, 34. 27 II, 38.

28 The jussive יְחִי (cf. XIV, 33)—meaning 'may (he) live' has the extended sense 'long live . . .'.

29 'as their eating and as their drinking'—infinitive construct with suffix, WHG 132 and 217. Alternatively, omitting the introductory clause, we may render 'and they (personal pronoun) eating and drinking' (participle).

30 The Hebrew idiom is: 'and as their heart was good', i.e. 'and as the being-good of their heart', כְּטוֹב לִבָּם—infinitive construct of the defective verb טוֹב, WHG 238B and 207. Alternatively, as above, one may use וְטוֹב, i.e. the participle with the conjunction.

31 II, 1. 32 II, 5.

33 'the people, the (ones) assembled'—Niphal participle plural with the article, in which the participle acts as an adjective qualifying the people; see end of V, 33. 34 II, 49.

35 Either literally or 'as this thing'; see end of II, 25.

36 Simply 'in'. 37 XI, 34.

38 Either the direct rendering: 'ye have done (an) evil (thing)' with the feminine singular adjective (V, 43) or, more idiomatically, הֲרֵעֹתֶם לַעֲשׂוֹת—'ye have caused evil for (i.e. in) doing', using the Hiphil of the double ʿAyin verb רַע (root רעע), see VII, 26, and XVI, 34, for analogy. Note also that the Hiphil of the normal double ʿAyin verb in the 2nd masculine plural perfect is הֲסַבֹּתֶם, but of the medial duplicated guttural verb it is הֲרֵעֹתֶם, since the guttural cannot be doubled the vowel before is prolonged. 39 'eyes'.

40 VI, 24. 41 'to his way'.

42 'they were afraid exceedingly', I, 61 (b). 43 VI, 42.

⁴⁴ 'told *to*'.　　⁴⁵ I, 38.　　⁴⁶ Singular as collective.
⁴⁷ Niphal participle feminine plural (of סתר), XIII, 21.　　⁴⁸ V, 27 (*a*).
⁴⁹ The full sentence reads: '(it is) good for us to return'.
⁵⁰ Simply אִישׁ (without כָּל־).　　⁵¹ XIII, 11.
⁵² VI, 43.
⁵³ 'a man from with (or beside עַל) his brother (or neighbour)'—notes 40
and 43 above.

XVIII

THE sons of Israel continued[1] to do that which was evil[2] in the sight[3] of the Lord and He delivered[4] them into the hands[5] of the Midianites[6] for[7] seven years. And when the Israelites[6] had sown[8] their fields and before[9] they had reaped their produce, the Midianites[6] came up and destroyed the produce of their land. And they cried unto[10] the Lord, because of[11] the Midianites,[6] and the Lord heard their cry and He sent a prophet unto[12] them. And the prophet came and spoke unto the elders of the people and he said unto them: 'Thus[13] saith the Lord, God of Israel: "I brought you[14] forth from the land of Egypt, out of the house of bondage,[15] and I led[16] you in this great and terrible wilderness[17] for[7] forty years and I brought you into[18] this good land and I drove out the inhabitants thereof before you[19] and I saved you[20] out of the hands[5] of your enemies. And I commanded you, saying: 'Fear not[21] the gods of the Canaanites,[6] in whose land[22] ye dwell.' But[23] ye hearkened not to My voice and ye went after your hearts[24] and after your eyes and ye served idols, the work of the hands[25] of man, and ye forgot the Lord, Who had shown kindness[26] to you. Therefore[27] have I delivered[4] you into the hands[5] of your oppressors and I hid[28] My countenance from you. But[23] now, if ye indeed[29] return unto Me with a pure heart, remove[30] from your midst the idols which ye worship and destroy them, and cleanse your hearts from your evil[31] doings. Then[32] shall I hear your cry and remember My covenant which I made[33] with your fathers."' And it came to pass, when the elders heard[34] the words of the prophet, that they said unto him: 'We have indeed[29] sinned against[35] the Lord, our God, as[36] thou hast said. We shall remove[37] the idols from our houses and destroy[37] them, and we shall return[37] unto Him. Pray, now, unto the Lord, that He may have mercy[38] upon us and deliver[39] us out of the hands[5] of our enemies for, except[40] He save us, we shall surely[29] perish from the face of[41] the earth.' And they commanded the people, saying: 'Let everyone[42] remove[43] the idols from his house and destroy[44] them in the sight[3] of the elders; and anyone[42] who will not do according to all[45] which we have said shall surely be put to death,[46] for this evil[47] hath come upon us, because we have worshipped strange[48] gods.'

NOTES ON XVIII

[1] The Hebrew idiom is '. . . added to do'; see end of X, 17.

[2] I, 39, and X, 42.   [3] I, 40.   [4] I, 33.   [5] I, 34.

[6] Following the note on I, 17, use מִדְיָן, the name of the country. Alternatively, one may say הַמִּדְיָנִי 'the Midianite' collectively. Similarly יִשְׂרָאֵל is used for 'Israelites' (but not הַיִשְׂרָאֵלִי), though הַכְּנַעֲנִי occurs, as well as כְּנַעַן, for 'the Canaanites'.

[7] 'for' is supplied by the English and is absent from the Hebrew.

[8] Rephrase 'and it came to pass, as the sowing-of Israel (i.e. as Israel's sowing—infinitive construct with prefixed כְ and followed by אֶת־ with the definite object) . . . and the Midianite(s) came up'.

[9] See IX, 23 (b).   [10] See I, 2.   [11] Either עַל (VII, 16) or, better, the fuller formula עַל אֹדוֹת.

[12] The order of words is 'sent unto (אֶל־ I, 2) them a prophet'.

[13] II, 25.   [14] I, 25.   [15] X, 34.   [16] XIII, 5.

[17] Note the order of the adjectives—'the wilderness, the great (one) and the terrible (one, XIV, 6), the this (one)'.   [18] I, 26.

[19] 'from your face'.   [20] Hiphil of נצל or ישע.

[21] I, 61 (a) and (b), and VII, 31.

[22] 'the Canaanite who, ye dwell in his land', cf. I, 48.   [23] I, 45.

[24] The singular, since the sense is 'your inclination'—collectively.

[25] In this case 'hands' is in the dual construct (WHG 38 note), for the sense is literally 'hands' (and not, as in note 5 above, 'power').

[26] II, 52.

[27] עַל־כֵּן or לָכֵן suggesting 'on that account', 'because of that'.

[28] Hiphil of סתר.

[29] Infinitive absolute for emphasis.

[30] The Hiphil of סָר (root סוּר) 'departed', namely הֵסִיר, means 'caused to depart', i.e. 'removed'.

³¹ The expression רֹעַ מַעַשִׁיכֶם, 'the evil of your doings', is more idiomatic that the direct translation.

³² 'then' means 'at that time', אָז. ³³ I, 53, and I, 13; also X, 39.

³⁴ Cf. III, 2. ³⁵ 'sinned unto (לְ)'. ³⁶ I, 10.

³⁷ The cohortative implies effort and eagerness.

³⁸ (a) Either 'in order that He shall have mercy' or the imperfect with Waw conjunctive, suggesting a jussive effect. (b) The Piel of רחם, namely רִחַם, means 'had mercy' followed by עַל; see the last section of WHG 169.

³⁹ In this context it means 'save', see 20 above.

⁴⁰ 'Except that' means 'if . . . not', i.e. 'if the Lord will not . . .'.

⁴¹ VI, 24. ⁴² 'everyone', 'anyone' is כָּל־אִישׁ, XVI, 20.

⁴³ Jussive; and see note 30 above. ⁴⁴ Jussive. ⁴⁵ I, 47.

⁴⁶ The Hiphil of the stative verb מֵת (root מות), 'died, was dead', namely הֵמִית, 'caused to die', conveys the derived idea 'put to death'. The Hophal imperfect (preceded by the infinitive absolute and see WHG 207) is to be used here—'will (surely) be put to death'.

⁴⁷ V, 43. ⁴⁸ IV, 6.

XIX

AFTER¹ the death of the judge the children of Israel returned unto the ways of the nations among whom² they dwelt and they served the gods of Canaan and they forsook the Lord, Who had dealt kindly³ with them. And the anger of the Lord was kindled⁴ against them and He delivered⁵ them into the hands⁶ of the Canaanites⁷ and they served them. Now, there was a woman,⁸ a prophetess, who⁹ judged Israel in those days. And she called unto¹⁰ Baraḳ, a prince of the tribes which dwelt¹¹ in the north, and she said unto him: 'Go, gather together all the warriors of Israel and bring them up¹² on this mountain, and go forth to meet¹³ the enemies of Israel in battle,¹⁴ for the Lord hath seen the affliction¹⁵ of His people and He will deliver⁵ the Canaanites into thy hands.'⁶ And Baraḳ answered and said: 'If thou wilt go with me, I shall go; but¹⁶ if thou goest not with me, I shall not go, for I know¹⁷ that whithersoever¹⁸ thou goest the Lord is with thee.' And she said unto him: 'I shall¹⁹ go with thee'; and she arose and went with him. And all the mighty men of the people were gathered together upon the

mountain, as the prophetess had commanded. And it came to
pass, as the morning star came up,[20] that they came down from
the mountain, all of them,[21] as a mighty river, and they fell
upon the Canaanites and they smote them[22] grievously[23] and
they pursued them to the wilderness.[24] In that day the Lord
gave a great victory to Israel and He saved[25] them out of the
hands[6] of their enemies. And it came to pass, after they had
returned[26] from smiting the Canaanites, and they were eating[27]
and drinking and making merry,[28] that the prophetess came
into the camp of the warriors and she said unto them: 'I hear
the sound of rejoicing in your camp and the songs which are
on your lips. I see the sacrifices which ye have made[29] upon
the altars and the booty which ye have taken[30] from the
Canaanites. And now, if ye have turned again[31] unto the Lord
in truth, swear[32] unto me that ye will[33] keep his commandments and cleave in His ways.' And they swore unto her on
that day to observe the covenant of the Lord and to do
according to all[34] which is written[35] in the Book of the Torah.

NOTES ON XIX

[1] Begin with 'and it came to pass . . . and the children of Israel returned . . .'.

[2] Cf. I, 48.   [3] II, 52.   [4] Cf. V. 36.

[5] I, 33.   [6] I, 34.   [7] XVIII, 6.

[8] The expression 'Now, there was a certain man' is וַיְהִי אִישׁ; use the corre-
sponding feminines here.

[9] Rephrase to 'and she, (a woman) judging'—the participle, acting as an
adjective descriptive of the prophetess—וְהִיא שֹׁפְטָה.

[10] End of I, 22.

[11] 'the (ones) dwelling'—active participle plural with the article: the participle serving as an adjective describing the tribes.

[12] Hiphil of עָלָה.   [13] IX, 33.   [14] XI, 32.

[15] The noun עֹנִי is a segholate, originally עָנְיְ; in the construct it is עֳנִי and
with suffix עָנְיִי, &c.   [16] I, 45.

[17] II, 18.   [18] XIII, 34.

[19] To make the reply emphatic, use either the cohortative or put the personal
pronoun before the verb.

[20] 'as the going-up-of the morning star'—infinitive construct—כַּעֲלוֹת.

[21] XI, 5 (b).   [22] XII, 18.

[23] In Hebrew 'a great smiting', מַכָּה גְדוֹלָה, using the noun cognate to the
verb.   [24] Old accusative case ending.

[25] XVIII, 20.

26 'after their returning'—infinitive construct with suffix; 'from smiting' is, similarly, a verbal noun—infinitive construct.

27 'and they, eating, &c.', using the active participle Qal.

28 See XVII, 30.   29 II, 38.

30 Use the verb שָׁלַל (cognate to the noun שָׁלָל) or the verb בָּזַז, adding לָכֶם, 'for you(rselves)'.

31 'turn again' is 'return'.   32 I, 27.

33 Rephrase 'to keep', for simplicity.   34 I, 47.   35 XIII, 36.

XX

THERE was a certain man[1] in Bethlehem of Judah, whose[2] name was Abiḥail. And he feared[3] the Lord with an upright heart and he kept His commandments, and he was greatly honoured[4] amongst the inhabitants of his city. And a son was born[5] unto him in his old age[6] and he called his name Jonathan, for he said: 'The Lord hath given me[7] a son.' And the boy grew up[8] and he became a man,[9] and he walked in the ways of his father and he did only that which was pleasing[10] unto the Lord; and his father loved[11] him. Now, on a certain day,[12] a captain of the king's host came to Bethlehem and he assembled[13] all the men of the city and he spoke unto them, saying: 'Hear ye the command of my master, the king of Israel, which he hath commanded you. Let all your young men gather together[14] at[15] this gate tomorrow at midday, and let them go after me to the camp of the armies of my master, the king, which is outside[16] Jerusalem. Let each one[17] bring with him provisions for three[18] days, for we are going forth into battle[19] against the enemies of Israel who have crossed over the border at the east.'[20] And it came to pass, in the morning, that Abiḥail gave his son provisions for three[18] days and he spoke unto him, saying: 'My son, behold, thou art going forth from my house into battle[19] and I know not[21] the day of thy return.[22] Remember, my son, the instruction[23] of thy father and forsake not[24] the teaching[25] of thy mother.[26] If wicked men[27] entice[28] thee, go not with them, but keep thy way far[29] from sinners, lest thou fall[28] into their snares. Let no false word[30] issue[31] from thy mouth, for lying and deceit are as a net spread out.[32] Put not thy pitcher in the well of those who lend[33] money, for its waters are bitter as gall and those who drink[34] thereof perish.[28] To thy fellow man speak peaceful[35] words and deal kindly[36] with him at the time of his distress.[37] May the Lord, thy God, be[38] with thee and keep thee from all evil and may He restore[39] thee unto me before I die.'[40] And Abiḥail embraced his son and he kissed[41] him and he sent him away[42] with the captain of the king's host, as[43] the king had commanded.

NOTES ON XX

[1] XIX, 8.   [2] III, 17.

[3] The sense is that he was a God-fearing man (not that he had feared), so the Hebrew is וַיְהִי יָרֵא 'and he was (one) fearing'—the participle acting as an adjective; see also VII, 31.

[4] Like the last note, the sense is that he was a much honoured man (not that he had been honoured)—וַיְהִי מְכֻבָּד—Pual participle.

[5] The verb יָלַד is an original Pe Waw (וָלַד) and the original initial radical appears in the Niphal perfect as a quiesced vowel-letter (נוֹלַד for נֶוְלַד), but in the Niphal imperfect as a full consonant, יִוָּלֵד, WHG 191.

[6] 'to his old age'.

[7] 'hath given to me the Lord a son'.

[8] II, 42.   [9] 'as (in Hebrew 'for') a man'.

[10] Rephrase: 'that which was good in the eyes of', I, 39, 40.

[11] V, 17. The style would be improved by putting the subject first: וְאָבִיו אֲהֵבוֹ (stative verb with suffix) giving the effect 'and (as for) his father, (he) loved him'. This is preferable to וַיֶּאֱהָבֵהוּ אָבִיו, since there is a change of subject.

[12] X, 7.   [13] V, 33.

[14] The imperfect serves as a jussive.   [15] 'in the gate'.

[16] The Hebrew is 'from outside to Jerusalem', cf. II, 11 (b).

[17] XVIII, 42. Note the shortened form of the Hiphil imperfect for the jussive. WHG 213.

[18] The numerals 3 to 10 are feminine nouns. 'Three', in Hebrew thinking, is 'a trio', so that 'three days' is 'a trio-of days', שְׁלֹשֶׁת יָמִים, WHG, 244.

[19] XI, 32.   [20] 'eastwards', קֵדְמָה.—with the old accusative ending.

[21] Cf. II, 18.   [22] 'thy returning'—infinitive construct (verbal noun).

[23] The noun מוּסָר suggests 'instruction' in the sense of 'moral correction and guidance'.   [24] I, 61 (a).   [25] X, 35.

[26] For precise Hebrew use the pausal form אִמֶּךָ.

[27] The masculine plural adjective implies 'men'.

[28] The imperfect, since future time is indicated.

[29] 'but (כִּי, XII, 17) make thy way far'—Hiphil of רָחַק.

[30] 'word of falsehood', see I, 57.   [31] i.e. 'come forth'.

[32] Passive participle Qal.

[33] 'the (ones) lending'—Hiphil participle masculine plural of לָוָה (which, in Qal, means 'borrowed' and the causative, 'caused to borrow', means 'lent').

[34] 'the (ones) drinking'—active participle masculine plural.

[35] 'words of peace', see I, 57.   [36] II, 52.

[37] I, 63, or, using the noun צָרָה. Note (a) This feminine noun comes from the double ʿAyin root צָרַר and, on that account, represents a hypothetical צָרָּה; the prolonging of the first vowel being due to the impossibility of doubling the letter ר following it. It is, on that account, considered as being virtually a *full* vowel, as opposed to a long vowel, since it is in lieu of a closed syllable. Thus, when an addition comes at the end, even though the accent moves on to the new syllable, the first vowel (being considered full) is not slurred over, but remains צָרָתִי, &c. There is a methegh in the first syllable, since it is two places back from the accented syllable. (b) Similarly, the adjective רַע comes from the double ʿAyin root רעע and the feminine singular רָעָה (representing רַעָּה) has a full vowel in the first syllable. When, as a feminine singular adjective, implying 'evil thing', it represents the abstract noun 'evil', 'harm', 'hurt', it is רָעָתִי, &c., with suffix.

[38] Jussive form יְהִי.   [39] I, 51.   [40] III, 32.
[41] IX, 37.   [42] III, 36.   [43] I, 10.

XXI

THERE was a certain man[1] of the tribe of Judah in the city of Hebron whose name was[2] Joseph, and he feared[3] the Lord exceedingly. And he had a young[4] son who[5] was born unto him in his old age[6] and his name was[2] Saul. And it came to pass, at the Feast[7] of the Passover,[8] that Joseph and his son went up to Jerusalem,[9] the holy city,[10] to make an offering[11] in the house of the Lord, as is written[12] in the Book of the Torah. And they came to Jerusalem[9] towards[13] evening and they lodged in the house of Jonathan, the nephew[14] of Joseph. And it came to pass, in the morning, that they went to the Temple of the Lord and they stood amongst those who had come[15] to Jerusalem[9] and they saw the service of the Lord at[16] the altar. And,[17] as the smoke went up[18] from the[19] altar to the heavens,[9] all the people fell upon their faces and they bowed themselves down[20] to the earth.[9] And,[17] when the people stood up,[21] the priests cried in a loud voice: 'O Lord, we have done that which[22] Thou hast commanded us. Bless, we pray thee, this great assembly, which hath come hither to serve Thee.'[23] And the spirit of the Lord came[24] upon Saul and he opened his mouth and he called unto the people who were gathered[25] there and he cried in a loud voice, in the hearing[26] of the priests, and he said:[27] 'Hear ye the word of the Lord which I speak unto you, O house of Judah. "Wherefore have ye come to My holy house[28] to offer[29] up the best of your flocks[30] and herds upon Mine altar?" saith the Lord. "Did I require this[31] of you?[32] Do I rejoice[33] in the sacrifices which ye offer up[29] daily?[34] Do ye good[35] to one another,[36] speak ye the truth to one another[36] and serve ye Me after this manner,[37] for it is this[31] which I require of you." '[32] And it came to pass, when the people heard[38] the words of the lad, that they said unto Joseph: 'Verily, thy son is a prophet and the word of the Lord is in his mouth.'[39] And Joseph was exceedingly[40] glad when he heard[41] the words of the people and he prayed unto the Lord and he said:[27] 'O Lord, give me[42] a sign that Thou hast chosen[43] my son to be[44] a prophet unto Thy people.' And Joseph said unto himself:[45] 'If the Lord will indeed[46] give me[42] a sign, then[47] I shall give him unto the Lord, that he may serve Him all the days of his life.'[48] And Joseph and his son stayed[49] in Jerusalem all the days of the Feast,[7] and[17] on the eighth day they arose and they returned to Hebron.[9]

NOTES ON XXI

[1] XIX, 8.   [2] Modify to 'and his name (being)'.   [3] XX, 3.
[4] 'small'.

[5] The participle (Niphal masculine singular of יָלַד with the article) הַנּוֹלָד, literally 'the (one) born', gives the subject ('son') an adjectival qualification or description.

[6] XX, 6.   [7] V, 34.   [8] הַפֶּסַח with the article.
[9] Old accusative ending.   [10] 'city of holiness', see I, 57.
[11] II, 38.   [12] XIII, 36.
[13] 'to the turning-of the evening', לִפְנוֹת עֶרֶב—infinitive construct.
[14] 'the son of his brother' (or 'sister', if the context suggests it).
[15] VIII, 16.   [16] Either בְ or עַל.

[17] Since a new element is introduced, begin with 'and it came to pass . . . and . . .'.

[18] 'as the going-up of the smoke'—infinitive construct of עָלָה.

[19] 'from *upon* . . .', VI, 24.   [20] II, 61.

[21] 'in the rising-up of the people'—infinitive construct of קָם (root קוּם).

[22] I, 38.   [23] If possible, attach verbal suffix, WHG 131.

[24] (a) The Hebrew phrasing is: 'and the spirit of the Lord *was*'. (b) Similarly 'and the word of the Lord *was*' is rendered in English as '*came*'. Note that רוּחַ is feminine.   [25] XVII, 33.

[26] 'in the ears of', cf. XI, 7.   [27] II, 49.

[28] Since (I, 57) 'a holy house' is expressed as 'a house of holiness', it follows that 'my holy house' will be 'my house of holiness'. Obviously, the suffix cannot be attached to the noun in the construct state; it is, therefore, attached to the noun following it—בֵּית־קָדְשִׁי—and refers to the whole concept (house-of-holiness) and not merely to the noun to which it is suffixed. To translate this phrase as 'the house of my holiness' is to miss the point of the Hebrew syntax on the construct-genitive relationship, in which the second noun has an adjectival effect on the first one in the construct state.

[29] Perhaps the best word to use here is the (infinitive construct) Hiphil of עָלָה, 'to cause to come up', i.e. 'to bring up'.

[30] I, 12.   [31] זֹאת, cf. II, 25.   [32] For better Hebrew it is necessary to expand to 'from your hand'.   [33] II, 24.

[34] The idiom is יוֹם יוֹם, that is 'day (by) day'.

[35] Hiphil of יטב, cf. VII, 26.   [36] VI, 42; 'one to the other'.

[37] מִשְׁפָּט, XI, 6.   [38] III, 2.   [39] WHG 288.

[40] II, 46.   [41] 'as his hearing'—infinitive construct with the suffix.

[42] '*to* me'.   [43] XI, 25 (a).

[44] Instead of 'to be . . .', use 'as (in Hebrew לְ, 'for') a prophet'.

[45] V, 40.   [46] Infinitive absolute before the finite verb.

[47] I, 45.   [48] II, 6.   [49] V, 29.

XXII

In[1] the days of the judges, before any king reigned[2] in Israel, there was a certain man[1] in the city of Bethlehem whose name[3] was Nabal. And that man was exceedingly rich and he had much flocks and herds,[4] menservants and maidservants and gold and silver,[5] beyond reckoning.[6] But[7] he was a man of evil spirit and he oppressed the poor, and the people of his city hated him and could not speak peaceably[8] with him. Now, on a certain day,[9] as Nabal was sitting[10] in his house, in the heat of

the day, robbers came in and they fell upon him and they bound him with cords. And they searched[11] his house and they found the gold and silver which was hidden[12] there and they took sacks which they had brought with them and they filled them with[13] the spoils and they departed. And it came to pass, in the evening, when the young men came[14] in from the fields that they saw their master lying upon the ground bound[15] with cords, and they hastened and they loosened the bonds. Then Nabal arose and he went forth from his house and he came to the gate of the city, where[16] the elders and the judges were sitting, and he related to them that which[17] had befallen him.[18] And he cried out in a loud voice: 'Woe to mine eyes which have seen[19] this evil day, for I have now become a poor[20] man', and he sat upon the ground and he wept.[21] Then[22] the chief[23] of the elders spoke unto him and he said: 'Thou knowest[24] that the people of this city do hate[25] thee, for thou hast hardened[26] thy heart against them and hast driven out lovingkindness and mercy from thy house. Yet, it shall not be said among the tribes of Israel that justice ruleth not[27] in Bethlehem. Therefore, the officers[28] of the city shall go forth and search out this matter well,[29] that they may find the men who have done this evil thing[30] and bring them[31] before the judges of this city, who[32] will judge them according to[33] the statutes which are written[34] in the Book of the Torah, which the Lord gave unto Moses. One justice shall there be for the rich and the poor, for him who is hated[35] as for him who is loved.[36] Return, now, unto thy house and, when[37] the officers have found these wicked men, we shall send to tell thee.'[38]

NOTES ON XXII

[1] Alter the order to 'Now there was a certain man in the days of . . .', XIX, 8.
[2] 'before the reigning of a king'—infinitive construct.   [3] XXI, 2.
[4] I, 12.   [5] III, 15.
[6] 'till there is not (any) reckoning (or number)', עַד אֵין מִסְפָּר.
[7] 'But (וְ, I, 45) he (being) a man . . .'.   [8] VII, 11.
[9] X, 7.   [10] 'as the sitting-of Nabal'—infinitive construct.
[11] חפשׂ in Piel, followed by בְּ, 'they searched in . . .'.
[12] 'the (thing) hidden'—Niphal participle with the article, WHG 66.

¹³ The stative verb מָלֵא means 'was full with' and takes a direct object. The Piel of some stative verbs has a causative effect; here מִלֵּא means 'he filled with'. Two accusatives follow this verb—וַיְמַלְאוּם שָׁלָל (with verbal suffix), the one accusative being the sack (which they filled) and the other the spoil (which they put in).

¹⁴ 'as the coming-in of the young men'—infinitive construct.

¹⁵ The Hebrew requires a slight expansion; 'and he (being) bound'—passive participle Qal.

¹⁶ 'the city which the elders . . . (were) sitting there', I, 48.

¹⁷ I, 38.   ¹⁸ literally, 'happened to', קָרָה ל.

¹⁹ Either the direct rendering or, alternatively, 'mine eyes, the (ones) seeing', הָרֹאוֹת—feminine plural active participle, serving as a descriptive (adjectival) word associated with 'eyes'.

²⁰ 'for now I have become (root הָיָה) as (in Hebrew 'for') a poor man'.

²¹ IX, 38.   ²² I, 45.   ²³ 'head'.   ²⁴ II, 18.

²⁵ The perfect; see end of II, 18.   ²⁶ Piel of כָּבֵד. As in note 13 above, the Piel makes the stative verb כָּבֵד, 'was heavy' into a causative 'caused to be heavy or hard, hardened'.

²⁷ Imperfect, II, 24, and VII, 15.

²⁸ Since the context implies civil, and not military, officers, the word is שֹׁטֵר.

²⁹ The Hiphil infinitive absolute of יטב, i.e. הֵיטֵב, 'making good', i.e. 'doing well', is used adverbially for 'well'.   ³⁰ V, 44.

³¹ The Hebrew requires 'will bring them near'—the Hiphil of קָרַב or נגש.

³² Modify to 'and they will judge'.   ³³ 'as', cf. I, 47.

³⁴ XI, 20.   ³⁵ 'for the hated (one)'—passive participle Qal.

³⁶ 'for the loved (one)'—passive participle Qal.

³⁷ Rephrase 'and it shall come to pass, in the finding of the officers (i.e. the officers' finding) the men . . . and we shall send'. Use the infinitive construct.

³⁸ 'tell to thee'.

XXIII

AFTER these things¹ the heads of the tribes of Israel gathered together² at Mizpah and they came unto the prophet Samuel³ and they said unto him: 'Thou knowest⁴ that the Philistines are mighty men of valour⁵ and that they rule over⁶ the cities of the plain to the west,⁷ and they are come up to fight against us and they seek to destroy us from⁸ the face of the earth. And it shall come to pass, if we go forth to meet them⁹ in battle,¹⁰ each tribe¹¹ by itself, that they will smite us¹² utterly, both young¹³ and old, both¹⁴ men and women. But, if all the tribes

of Israel go forth to meet them[9] as[15] one great army, then we
shall prevail[16] against them and we shall drive them out of the
land. And now, O man of God,[17] we require a king who will
rule over[6] us and who will lead us forth[18] into battle[10] against
the Philistines and who will deliver[19] us out of their hands,[20]
that[21] we may live and not die,[22] we and our wives and our
little ones[23] with us.' And it came to pass, when Samuel heard[24]
these words, that he was exceedingly wroth[25] and he said unto
them: 'Wherefore seek[26] ye a king like all the nations which
are round about[27] you? The Lord, your God, He is your king.
Keep ye His commands and walk in His ways, and He[28] will
do battle for you against your enemies and He will give you
victory.' But[29] the heads of the people hearkened not unto
Samuel and they said: 'Nay,[30] but[31] a king shall reign over us
and we shall become[32] one great people, instead of our being[33]
twelve tribes, each tribe dwelling in his inherited land.[34]
Choose, therefore, a valiant man[35] from amongst us who will
be king over us, for we know[4] that the one whom thou wilt
choose[36] will find favour in the sight[37] of the Lord.' And
Samuel answered and said: 'I shall inquire[38] of the Lord,
whether[39] this matter is pleasing in His sight[37] or not. Return
ye unto me in another[40] three days and I shall declare unto
you that which the Lord will reveal unto me.' And they said
unto him: 'We shall do as[41] thou hast said and we shall return
unto thee in another[40] three days.' And the prophet turned
away from them[42] and he went on[43] his way, and they also[44]
went on their[43] way.

NOTES ON XXIII

[1] One may begin with the conventional 'and it came to pass . . .'. or, simply,
without this introductory word, following the English: אַחַר הַדְּבָרִים הָאֵלֶּה.
[2] V, 33. [3] The order of words is 'Samuel, the prophet', cf. II, 26.
[4] II, 18.
[5] גִּבּוֹר is 'a mighty man'. To emphasize their valour, expand to 'mighty men
of valour (are) they'.
[6] VII, 15.
[7] Since the sea is on the west of Palestine, יָם is used for the 'west'. The old
accusative case ending is required.
[8] XII, 32. [9] IX, 33. [10] XI, 32. [11] XVI, 25, 27.

¹² The emphasis is best expressed in the following way: 'and they will smite us, even (גַּ) smiting (infinitive absolute)'; see XII, 18.

¹³ XIII, 43.   ¹⁴ 'from a man *and until* a woman', cf. XIII, 43.

¹⁵ The sense is '(being) one great army'; no preposition is required.

¹⁶ Apart from a more direct rendering (XII, 12), the text might be modified to 'and we shall be stronger than they', XII, 13 (a) and (b).

¹⁷ The vocative is expressed by the article, e.g. 'O king' is הַמֶּ֫לֶךְ. 'O man of God' is, then, אִישׁ־הָאֱלֹהִים. The reason might lie in the definiteness which the vocative implies.

¹⁸ XIII, 5.   ¹⁹ XVIII, 20.   ²⁰ I, 34.

²¹ 'in order that'.   ²² Imperfect.

²³ טַף, with suffix טַפֵּ֫נוּ as a collective.

²⁴ III, 2.   ²⁵ V, 36, and II, 20, 46.   ²⁶ Imperfect, II, 24.

²⁷ Cf. XII, 9.   ²⁸ Personal pronoun, to emphasize the subject 'He'.

²⁹ I, 45.   ³⁰ The negative לֹא.   ³¹ XII, 17.   ³² לְ, I, 56.

³³ Infinitive construct with suffix.

³⁴ 'his land-of inheritance', with the suffix attached (not to the construct, but) to the following noun—אֶֽרֶץ־יְרֻשָּׁתוֹ, cf. XXI, 28.

³⁵ 'a man of valour'; also XI, 25 (a).

³⁶ 'the man who thou wilt choose in him', I, 48.   ³⁷ I, 40.

³⁸ XI, 34.   ³⁹ III, 40.   ⁴⁰ 'in yet (בְּעוֹד) three days', XX, 18.

⁴¹ I, 10.   ⁴² VI, 24.   ⁴³ 'to his (their) way'.

⁴⁴ 'and they went, also they . . .'.

XXIV

IT came to pass, on the third day, that the elders of the tribes of Israel gathered together[1] at Mizpah to meet[2] Samuel, according to[3] the word which he had spoken unto them. And they saw the prophet coming up on the mountain towards the city[4] and they hastened forth to meet him[2] and to do him honour.[5] And,[6] when Samuel came nigh unto them, they said unto him: 'Peace unto thee, O man of God.'[7] And Samuel answered and said: 'May the Lord bless you, O shepherds of Israel.' And they said unto him: 'Didst thou inquire of[8] the Lord in the matter of the king whom we seek to reign over us?' And the prophet answered and said: 'Ye are a stiff-necked people,[9] as your fathers before you in the days of Moses. Know ye[10] the manner[11] in which your king will reign over

you? Behold, I shall tell you.[12] Ye shall be servants[13] unto him
and ye shall serve him for nought. Your sons, who are twenty
years old[14] and upwards, shall he take for his hosts and he will
send them forth[15] into battles which ye have not sought. Your
cattle, even the fattest thereof, shall ye deliver[16] up for his table
and your gold and your silver for his palace. Your fields and
your vineyards and your oliveyards he shall take for himself
and of that which remaineth[17] unto you shall ye deliver up[16]
a tenth part of its produce. And before the king there shall
arise a host of princes, officers and companions who[18] will
oppress you, if ye obey not[19] the commands of your king.
Grievous[20] taxes shall the king place upon you, that[21] he may
live in splendour, he and his wives and his companions with
him. And he will desire[22] great palaces for himself and for his
wives, and he will take you by force to build them for him,
even as Pharaoh, the king of Egypt, did[23] unto your fathers.
And any man[24] who raiseth[25] his voice against the king, by
reason of[26] the heavy burdens which he hath placed upon you,
shall surely be put to death,[27] for your life and your death shall
be in his hands,[28] to do according to[3] that which pleaseth[29]
him. Then[30] shall ye cry out unto the Lord, your God, because
of your king, but[31] the Lord will not hear your cry, for ye act[32]
in the stubbornness of your hearts[33] and ye heed not[34] good
counsel.'

NOTES ON XXIV

[1] End of V, 33.   [2] IX, 33.   [3] 'as'.
[4] Old accusative ending.   [5] IX, 34.
[6] 'And it came to pass, as the drawing-near of Samuel'—infinitive construct.
[7] XXIII, 17.   [8] XI, 34.   [9] 'a people stiff-of neck', XIII, 9.
[10] II, 18, and WHG 80 for the pointing of He interrogative before shewa.
[11] XI, 6.
[12] 'tell to you'. Use the cohortative for effort or determination.
[13] 'ye shall be unto him as (in Hebrew 'for') servants'.
[14] Age is expressed as 'a son of . . . years' for a male and 'a daughter of . . .
years' for a female. Modify the text to 'from twenty years old . . .'.
[15] III, 36.   [16] 'give'.
[17] 'from the (thing) left over'—Niphal participle of שָׁאַר with the article.
[18] Rephrase 'and they will oppress . . .'.   [19] 'hearken not unto'.
[20] 'heavy'.   [21] 'in order that'.   [22] 'covet', root חָמַד.

²³ 'as (that) which did Pharaoh unto . . .'. 'even' is supplied by the English.
²⁴ XVI, 20, and XVIII, 42.
²⁵ Imperfect, since the future is indicated.
²⁶ 'in (or 'on') the matter of' or, simply, 'from'.
²⁷ XVIII, 46.   ²⁸ I, 34.   ²⁹ 'good in his eyes'.
³⁰ XVIII, 32.   ³¹ Conjunction, I, 45.
³² Alter to 'for ye walk (or 'go')'—participle.
³³ Singular noun, as collective.
³⁴ 'Heed', in this instance, means 'pay attention to', for which the Hebrew
is שָׂם לֵב, 'set (one's) heart to'. Use the imperfect to denote recurrence, II, 24.

XXV

ALL the elders of the people came¹ to Shechem² to make Saul
king³ over Israel, for the Lord had chosen⁴ him to be⁵ king.
And Samuel, the prophet of the Lord, anointed Saul as⁶ king
over all Israel, as⁷ the Lord commanded him. Then⁸ Samuel
spoke unto the elders of the people and he said unto them:
'Behold, I have hearkened unto your voice, according to all⁹
which ye said unto me, and now, here is¹⁰ your king before
you. And it shall come to pass, if he will indeed¹¹ keep the
commandments of the Lord and will do according to all⁹
which is written¹² in the Book of the Torah, and if his heart
will be perfect with¹³ the Lord, his God, then⁸ the Lord will be
with¹³ him and He will give you victory over all your enemies
and he will set the fear of you¹⁴ upon all the nations of the
land.' And,¹⁵ when the heads of the people heard these words,
they cried with one voice: 'May the Lord, our God, be¹⁶
with¹³ our king, even¹⁷ as He was with¹³ Moses.' And they
made a great feast¹⁸ that¹⁹ day and they offered²⁰ up sacrifices
to the Lord and they were exceedingly²¹ glad. And Saul went
about²² among the people and the bearers of his arms²³ were
walking²⁴ behind him. And the people said to one another,²⁵
when they saw²⁶ Saul: 'Behold, the spirit of the Lord hath
rested upon the king.' And it came to pass, on the morrow, that
Saul called the heads of the people together²⁷ and he spoke
unto them, saying: 'Go ye through²⁸ the camp and speak unto

the men who[29] are going forth to meet[30] the Philistines in battle[31] and say unto them: "Fear not[32] your enemies against whom[33] ye are going forth to fight, for your king will lead[34] you into battle,[31] and he is a mighty man[35] of valour and the Lord is with[13] him. Be ye strong[36] and of good courage,[37] for to-day[38] the Lord will give us a great victory, and the nations which are round[39] about us will see and they will be afraid of[40] us and they will seek to make[41] a covenant of peace with[13] us." ' And the heads of the people did as[7] Saul commanded them and they spoke unto the warriors[42] according to[43] these words.

NOTES ON XXV

[1] Since, presumably, this would be a continuation of a preceding narrative, we should begin with the Waw consecutive 'and all . . .'.

[2] Old accusative case ending.   [3] See XVII, 8.   [4] XI, 25.

[5] 'as (in Hebrew 'for') a king'.   [6] As the preceding note.

[7] I, 10.   [8] I, 45.   [9] I, 47.   [10] 'behold'.

[11] Infinitive absolute before the finite verb.   [12] XIII, 36.

[13] I, 13.   [14] XV, 23.

[15] We may expand to 'and it came to pass', followed by 'as the hearing of . . .' —infinitive construct.   [16] Jussive; XIV, 33.

[17] 'even' is supplied by the English.   [18] V, 34.

[19] 'in that day'.   [20] II, 38.   [21] II, 46.

[22] Hithpael of הָלַךְ means 'went about, to and fro'.

[23] XII, 15.

[24] 'were' is required by the English. The Hebrew 'and the bearers . . . walking', by using the participle, gives the noun an adjectival or qualifying association. Note further that the word אַחַר (with the prepositional idea 'after, behind') takes the suffixes of a plural noun.   [25] VI, 42.

[26] 'as (or 'in') their seeing'—infinitive construct.

[27] XVI, 1.   [28] 'pass through (עָבַר) in the camp'.

[29] 'the (ones) going forth'—active participle Qal masculine plural with the article.   [30] IX, 33.   [31] XI, 32.

[32] I, 61 (a) and (b), and VII, 31.

[33] 'your enemies who ye are going forth to fight against them', I, 48.

[34] XIII, 5.   [35] XXIII, 5.   [36] XIV, 21.   [37] XIV, 22.

[38] הַיּוֹם without the accompanying demonstrative adjective; the article having a virtual demonstrative effect, like the English 'to-day'.

[39] XII, 9.   [40] VII, 31.   [41] I, 53. Note also the order of words 'to make with us a covenant'.

[42] 'the men of the host'.   [43] 'as'.

XXVI

THE warrior of the Philistines came forth[1] and he stood upon the mountain opposite[2] the camp of Israel and he called in a loud[3] voice, in the hearing[4] of the people, and he said:[5] 'Choose ye[6] from among your mighty men one[7] who will come forth and fight[8] with me. And it shall come to pass, if he will slay me, that we shall be servants unto[9] you; but[10] if I slay him, then[10] shall ye be servants unto us.'[11] And the elders came and told[12] Saul the words of the Philistine. Then[10] David drew near unto the king and said: 'My lord, O king,[13] let thy servant go forth[14] to meet[15] this Philistine, and I shall smite[16] him to the earth.'[17] And Saul said unto him: 'How art thou able[18] to fight[8] with him? Thou art but[19] a youth and he is a mighty warrior.[20] Go, return to thy father's house, for why shouldst thou fall by the sword before[21] mine eyes?' And David answered and said:[5] 'Thy servant was a shepherd[22] and I kept the sheep of my father. And, on a certain day,[23] an evil beast came from the wilderness and fell upon one of the sheep. And I arose and I took my sword in my hand and I slew the beast, and there was no one[24] with me. And now, if it pleaseth[25] the king, let me go forth to battle[8] with the enemy of Israel, and I shall cut off his head[26] and I shall bring it to thee, that the people may know that there is God in Israel.' And the words of David pleased[27] Saul exceedingly[28] and he said unto him: 'Go forth to meet[15] him, my son, and may the Lord, God of Israel, deliver[29] thine enemy into thy hands.'[30] And it came to pass, when David's brethren heard[31] that he was going forth to battle[8] with the Philistine, that they were exceedingly wroth[32] and they said unto him: 'Behold, all the men of valour in Israel fear[33] this mighty Philistine and thou thinkest[34] that thou art mightier[35] than they. Go back, therefore, to thy father's house and keep his sheep, for thou art a shepherd and not a warrior.'[36] And David answered and said: 'If I do not this thing, the heart of the people will melt[37] and they will flee from[38] the Philistines. The Lord, in whom[39] I trust, will give me victory over the Philistine and I shall smite[16] him to the earth.'[17]

NOTES ON XXVI

[1] XXV, 1. [2] II, 11 (b). [3] III, 50. [4] XI, 7.

[5] II, 49. [6] Expand to 'choose (ye) for you(rselves—לָכֶם).

[7] XI, 25 (a), XVI, 20. [8] I, 29.

[9] 'we shall be unto (לְ) you as (in Hebrew 'for') servants'. [10] I, 45.

[11] 'ye shall be unto us as servants', cf. note 9 above.

[12] 'told *to* Saul'. [13] XXIII, 17.

[14] The imperfect serves as a jussive. [15] IX, 33.

[16] XII, 18. [17] Old accusative case ending. [18] XII, 11.

[19] Rephrase 'surely (הֲלֹא, VII, 20) thou art a youth'. [20] XVII, 4.

[21] See X, 25.

[22] To emphasize his occupation, the order of words would be 'a shepherd was thy servant'. [23] X, 7.

[24] 'and no one being', וְאֵין אִישׁ, XVI, 20.

[25] Either 'if it is good in the eyes of' or 'if I have found favour in the eyes of'. [26] Add 'from upon him'.

[27] Either 'were good in the eyes of' or 'found favour in the eyes of'.

[28] II, 46. [29] Meaning 'give'. [30] I, 34.

[31] 'as the hearing-of the brethren of David'—infinitive construct, followed by 'that he going forth'—active participle Qal, giving a quality or attribute to the subject 'he'. [32] V, 36.

[33] The perfect of the stative verb יָרֵא often expresses the English present tense, since one can only speak of being afraid when that condition is completed; see also VII, 31. [34] VII, 14. [35] XII, 13 (a) and (b).

[36] 'man of war'. [37] XV, 28.

[38] Expand to 'from the face of'.

[39] (a) 'The Lord who I trust in Him', I, 48. (b) The perfect may be used, expressing the completed state of trusting. On the other hand, the imperfect suggests a frequentative effect—'keep on trusting'.

XXVII

THAT morning[1] Samuel arose early[2] and he went forth from his house to go to Bethlehem, and he came to the city[3] in the evening. And he asked the men of the place, saying: 'Know ye[4] a young man whose[5] name is David?' And they said unto

him: 'We indeed[6] know him and, behold, he[7] is in the field
at the east[8] of the city with his father's sheep.[9] Go thither, and
there wilt thou find him.' And Samuel went forth to the field
and he saw and, behold, a young man was[10] sitting upon a
great stone and watching the sheep. And it came to pass, as
Samuel drew near,[11] that David saw him and he came down
from[12] the stone and he ran to meet him[13] and he said unto
him: 'Peace unto thee, my lord. Sit down, I pray thee, with
me under this tree and eat bread with me.'[14] Then Samuel
knew that he was[15] David, and he sat down with him and they
ate together. And David asked him, saying: 'What is thy name?
Whence comest[16] thou and whither goest[17] thou?' And Samuel
said unto him: 'I am Samuel, the prophet of the Lord, and
He hath sent me unto thee to anoint thee king[18] of Israel, for
He hath rejected[19] Saul and He hath chosen thee to be[20] king
instead[21] of him.' And David said unto Samuel: 'Who am I and
what is my father's house, that I should rule over[22] this great
people?' And Samuel said unto him: 'Arise and come forth
with me, for thus hath the Lord commanded thee.' And David
said: 'Behold, I[7] am keeping my father's[9] sheep, and it shall
come to pass, when I go forth[23] with thee, that they will become a prey[24] to the beasts of the field. Let me send,[25] I pray
thee, to tell[26] my father that thou art come unto this city and
that thou hast commanded me to go forth with thee. If it
pleaseth[27] my lord, abide with us till the morning, for there is
place in my father's house to lodge and, in the morning, we
shall go forth as[28] thou hast said.' And David's words pleased[29]
Samuel exceedingly[30] and he said unto him: 'Do as[28] thou hast
said, for thy words please[31] me.' And David called the[32] lad
who was[33] with him and he sent him unto his father.

NOTES ON XXVII

[1] One may begin with 'and it came to pass, in that morning, that Samuel
arose early' or, simply, 'and Samuel arose early in that morning'.
[2] Hiphil of שכם.   [3] Old accusative case ending.
[4] II, 18, and WHG 80 for the pointing of He interrogative before shewa.
[5] 'a young man who David is his name', I, 48.
[6] Infinitive absolute before the finite verb (in perfect).   [7] IX, 25.

8 'from the east to the city', cf. II, 11 (a), and XX, 16.
9 Either 'the sheep of his father' or 'the sheep which (belong) to his father',
cf. IV, 51.   10 He saw 'a young man sitting'.
11 'as the drawing near of Samuel'—infinitive construct.
12 'from *upon* the stone', VI, 24.   13 IX, 33.
14 The order of words is 'and eat with me bread'.
15 He knew that 'he *is* David'.
16 Logically the perfect, since he had come.
17 Logically the imperfect, since the going is not completed.
18 'thee as (in Hebrew 'for') a king'.
19 The verb מָאַס is often followed by the inseparable בְּ (as is בָּחַר).
20 Simply, 'chosen (in) thee as a king'.   21 VII, 42 (b).
22 VII, 15.
23 'in my going forth'—infinitive construct, WHG 212 (c).
24 'as (in Hebrew 'for') a prey'.   25 Cohortative.
26 'to tell to . . .'.   27 XXVI, 25.   28 I, 10.
29 XXVI, 27.   30 II, 46.
31 Either 'are good in mine eyes' or 'have found favour in mine eyes'. For the
former mode of expression the perfect plural of טוֹב, namely טוֹבוּ, may be used,
since it is only when the condition (of this stative verb) is completed that one
can speak of (something) being good.
32 I, 22—end of note.   33 'was' is not in the Hebrew.

XXVIII

DAVID heard[1] that the king was[2] seeking his life,[3] and he escaped[4] in the night and he hid himself[5] in the mountains and
he abode[6] in a cave. And there gathered[7] unto him men from
the house of Judah who had fled from[8] the king's wrath, and
David became head[9] over them. And, when[10] Saul heard that
David had fled to the mountains, he took his servants and he
pursued him[11] all the day, and in the evening he came to the
place where[12] David and his men were hidden. And David was
told,[13] saying: 'Saul and his men have come hither to slay
thee.' And David answered and said: 'I trust[14] in the Lord,
my God, Who delivereth me out of the hands[15] of mine
enemies.' And it came to pass, in the night, that messengers
came and told[16] the king, saying: 'Behold, the Philistines are
gathered together[17] against us in the valley of Megiddo and the

elders of the people are saying that thou hast forsaken the people. Return, we pray thee, thou and thy warriors[17] with thee, and go forth to meet[18] the Philistines, lest the city be delivered[19] into their hands.'[15] And Saul did as the messengers said and he arose, he and his servants with him, and they went forth, to go to the plain of Megiddo. And, when[10] David heard that Saul and his men had departed to meet[18] the Philistines in battle,[20] he said unto the men who were[21] with him: 'Gird ye, every man his sword, for it is not good that we should abide[22] here in safety, while[23] our brethren are fighting against the Philistines. Let us depart[24] this night[25] and go to the field of the battle and it shall come to pass, when the hosts of the Philistines come forth[26] to meet[18] the sons of Israel, that we shall fall upon them from the rear[27] and they shall be smitten[28] before us.'[29] And they did as David commanded and they went forth and they journeyed all the night and in the morning they came to the mountain behind[30] the camp of the Philistines and they encamped there. And it came to pass, when the Philistines went forth[26] to fight the sons of Israel, that the men of David fell upon them from the rear[27] and they smote them utterly,[31] for they were not able to flee hither or thither,[32] for the hosts of Israel were before them[33] and the men of David behind them.[27] And, when Saul saw[34] that which David had done, he repented[35] of the evil[36] which he had thought[37] to do him.[38]

NOTES ON XXVIII

[1] XXV, 1.   [2] He heard that Saul '*is* seeking . . .'.   [3] II, 6.

[4] Niphal of מלט, WHG 103 and footnote *a*.

[5] Niphal or Hithpael of סתר or חבא.   [6] V, 29.

[7] V, 33.   [8] Expand to 'from the face of', which means 'on account of'.

[9] '*as* (in Hebrew '*for*') a head'.

[10] Expand to 'and it came to pass, as the hearing of . . .'.

[11] VI, 9.

[12] 'the place which David and his men were hidden there', I, 48.

[13] Alter to 'and it was told (Hophal of נגד) to David'.

[14] XXVI, 39 (*b*).   [15] I, 34.   [16] 'told to . . .'.

[17] גִּבּוֹר 'warrior'.   [18] IX, 33.   [19] I, 33.

[20] In Hebrew it is '*to the* battle'.

[21] 'were' is supplied by the English; in Hebrew it is 'the men who (being) with him'.

[22] Rephrase: 'not good (is) our abiding' (root יָשַׁב)—infinitive construct with suffix.   [23] Simply 'and our brethren . . .'.

[24] Imperfect serving as jussive.

[25] The demonstrative adjective is not necessary, XXV, 38.

[26] 'in the going forth of the hosts of the Philistines'—infinitive construct.

[27] מֵאָחוֹר adding, perhaps, לָהֶם.

[28] Apart from the Hophal of נכה (XII, 18), the Niphal of נגף may be used for routing.   [29] See note 8 above.

[30] 'from behind to', using מֵאָחוֹר, cf. II, 11 (b).   [31] XIX, 23.

[32] הֵנָּה וָהֵנָּה, literally 'hither and hither'.

[33] Instead of לִפְנֵיהֶם, one may say (לָהֶם) מִפָּנִים, 'in front'.

[34] 'and it came to pass, as the seeing of Saul . . .'—infinitive construct.

[35] Niphal of נחם followed by עַל, 'concerning', and sometimes by אֶל.

[36] V, 43.   [37] חָשַׁב, meaning 'planned', 'devised'.

[38] 'to do to him'.

XXIX

THERE was a certain man[1] in the city of Bethlehem in the land of Judah and his name was[2] Elhanan. And he feared[3] the Lord and he did only that which is pleasing in His sight.[4] He fed[5] the poor at[6] his table and he clothed[7] the naked; he upheld[8] the cause of the widow and the fatherless and strengthened[9] the hands of the weak. And the Lord blessed him and he was exceedingly rich[10] in gold,[11] in silver[11] and in cattle.[11] And he had three[12] sons who[13] walked in the way of the Lord and he loved[14] them. Now, on a certain day,[15] as Elhanan was sitting[16] at the entrance of his house in[17] the heat of the day, a messenger came unto him and fell down upon his face to the earth[18] and he cried: 'Alas! my master, misfortune[19] hath overtaken[20] thee, for a plague broke out[21] amongst thy cattle and they have all[22] died.' And Elhanan said: 'Who am I, that I should rebel against[23] the works of the Lord? Behold, He[24] hath given and He[24] hath taken away.' And, as Elhanan finished[25] speaking, another[26] messenger came, with rent garments,[27] and he cried: 'It were better that I had died than to have seen[28] that which hath befallen[29] thy three sons. For, behold, when they were returning[30] hither, after tending[31] the flocks, one of them said to the other:[32] "I am thirsty."[33] And he went down to the river and he drew water therefrom[34] and he drank[35] and he also gave to his brethren to drink[36] and they drank with him. And, when the three of them[37] had finished drinking, they fell to the ground dead.' Then Elhanan arose from[38] his seat and he rent his garments and he cast[39] dust upon his head and he sat down on the ground. And he lifted up his voice and he cried: 'O Lord, what is my sin and what is my transgression that Thou hast smitten thy servant? If I have sinned against[40] Thee take, I pray Thee, my life,[41] for Thou art a righteous judge.'[42] And the Lord heard the words of Elhanan and He said: 'My servant, Elhanan,[43] hath not sinned with his lips and his heart is perfect with Me.' And it came to pass, as Elhanan was sitting[16] upon the ground and mourning[44] for his sons, that other[26] messengers came and they told him, saying: 'Hear us, O our master, and rejoice, for thy sons are alive. They indeed[45] fell to the ground, when they drank[46] from the waters of the river, and we said: "Behold, they have died." But now they have risen up and, behold, they[47] are as heretofore.'[48]

NOTES ON XXIX

[1] XIX, 8.   [2] 'was' is not in the Hebrew, which is 'his name (being)'.

[3] XX, 3.   [4] I, 39, 40.   [5] IX, 40.   [6] 'upon'.

[7] Hiphil of לָבַשׁ, i.e. 'caused to dress'.

[8] The noun for a 'cause' is רִיב and the cognate verb רָב (root רִיב) is used with it for pleading a cause. See the ʿAyin Yod verb in WHG 197.

[9] The Piel of the stative verb חָזַק, 'was strong', see XXII, 13, 26.

[10] The normal translation would be either וַיְהִי עָשִׁיר (using the adjective) or וַיֶּעֱשַׁר (using the stative verb). Another form of expression is וְהוּא or וַיְהִי כָּבֵד, 'and he was heavy'.

[11] The article is used with classes or species.

[12] For the syntax of the numerals, see WHG 244.

[13] Rephrase 'and they walked'.   [14] V, 17.   [15] X, 7.

[16] 'as the sitting of Elhanan'—infinitive construct.

[17] The expression found in Genesis xviii. 1 is כְּחֹם הַיּוֹם, 'as . . .'. It may be that חֹם is used as an infinitive construct—'as the being hot of the day', the root being the double ʿAyin חמם.

[18] Old accusative case ending.   [19] 'evil', V, 43.

²⁰ Though the Hiphil of נָשַׂג, namely הִשִּׂיג, means 'overtook', the simpler mode of expression 'hath come upon thee' gives the sense.

²¹ Root פָּרַץ.   ²² 'they died, all of them', see XI, 5 (b).   ²³ בְּ.

²⁴ The personal pronoun before the verb emphasizes the subject 'He'.

²⁵ 'and it came to pass, as the finishing of Elhanan *to* speak *and* another . . .'. Note: the Piel of כָּלָה 'was at an end', namely כִּלָּה, has a causative effect— 'caused to be at an end', i.e. 'brought to an end', 'finished', cf. XXII, 13, 26.

²⁶ עוֹד.

²⁷ 'and his garments (being) rent'—passive participle Qal.

²⁸ The sentence must be rephrased in terms of Hebrew thinking to something as follows: 'better my dying than my seeing'. Both verbal nouns are represented by the infinitive construct (with suffix). Note also the comparative degree 'better' is טוֹב מִן, cf. V, 27.

²⁹ XXII, 18.   ³⁰ 'in their returning'—infinitive construct with suffix.

³¹ 'after *their* tending'—infinitive construct of רָעָה with suffix.

³² VI, 42.   ³³ The verb צָמֵא 'was thirsty' is a stative. The perfect is to be used here, since one can only speak of being thirsty when that condition is completed; see also WHG 211 (c).

³⁴ 'from it'.

³⁵ The Qal imperfect of שָׁתָה is יִשְׁתֶּה and the shortened form, with Waw consecutive, is וַיֵּשְׁתְּ, cf. IX, 38, with בָּכָה.

³⁶ XIV, 8.

³⁷ 'and it came to pass, as the finishing of (note 25 above) the three of them to drink'. Note that, when the numeral שְׁלֹשֶׁת, a segholate noun of the קֹדֶשׁ pattern, takes a suffix, the original form שְׁלָשְׁתְ (on the pattern of קָדְשׁ) receives it—שְׁלָשְׁתָּם, the vowel being Qameṣ-Ḥaṭup.

³⁸ 'from *upon* his seat', VI, 24.   ³⁹ VII, 40.   ⁴⁰ 'unto'.

⁴¹ II, 6.   ⁴² 'a judge of righteousness', I, 57.

⁴³ 'Elhanan, my servant', cf. II, 26.   ⁴⁴ VII, 44.

⁴⁵ Rather than the infinitive absolute before the finite verb, it is better to introduce the clause with an adverb like אָמְנָם, 'indeed', 'in truth', cf. IV, 36.

⁴⁶ 'in their drinking'—infinitive construct.

⁴⁷ Attach suffix to הִנֵּה, IX, 25.

⁴⁸ The idiom is תְּמוֹל שִׁלְשֹׁם, 'yesterday, the day before yesterday'.

XXX

IT came to pass, after these things, that David inquired¹ of the Lord, saying: 'Shall I go up² into one of the cities of Judah?' And the Lord said unto him: 'Go up to Hebron.'³ And David took his wives and his sons and his daughters and all which he possessed⁴ and he departed to go to Hebron.³

And David sent messengers unto the inhabitants of Hebron, saying: 'The Lord,[5] our God, hath commanded me to come to Hebron[3] and, behold, I[6] am coming unto you, I and my men with me. Open, therefore,[7] your gates unto me, when I come,[8] for I am your kinsman.'[9] And it came to pass, when David and his men came[10] to Hebron,[3] that the elders of the city opened the gates unto them[11] and they said unto David: 'Blessed be thy coming[12] unto us. Be thou a prince[13] and a judge over us.' Then[14] David sent messengers unto all the cities of Judah, saying: 'Thus saith your kinsman,[9] David:[15] "Behold, your master, Saul,[16] is dead and the hosts of Israel are scattered[17] over the face of the land, as sheep[18] without[19] a shepherd, and the Philistines have dominion[20] over the plains in the west.[21] And the Lord said unto me:[22] 'Be thou a shepherd unto My people and I shall be with thee.' And now, if it pleaseth[23] you, come ye to Hebron[3] and make me king[24] over the land of Judah." ' And David's words pleased[25] the men of Judah and they came to Hebron[3] and they anointed David as king[26] over them, according to[27] the word which the Lord had spoken through[28] His prophet, Samuel. And it came to pass, on the morrow, that David called together[29] the heads of the house of Judah and he said unto them: 'When ye return[30] unto your cities, choose from among your young men those[31] who are stout of heart and send them unto me, that they may become officers[32] of the hosts of Judah, for the Philistines who dwell[33] in the cities of the plain will surely[34] come forth to do battle with us. But[14] it shall come to pass, if we are men of valour and trust in the Lord, our God, that we shall smite[35] them out of the land, and we shall dwell here in peace and safety.' And the heads of the people said unto him:[36] 'All that thou hast said unto us we shall do. May the Lord be[37] with thee in whatsoever[38] thou doest.'[39]

NOTES ON XXX

[1] XI, 34.   [2] WHG 80 for the pointing of the He interrogative before a guttural.   [3] Old accusative case ending.   [4] I, 5.
[5] To emphasize the subject, 'the Lord', it should be placed before the verb.

⁶ IX, 25.   ⁷ I, 4.   ⁸ 'in (or 'as') my coming'—infinitive construct.   ⁹ 'brother'.

¹⁰ 'in the coming of . . .'—infinitive construct.

¹¹ Note the order of words: 'opened to them the gates'.

¹² Infinitive construct with suffix—a verbal noun.

¹³ 'as (in Hebrew 'for') a prince and as a judge'.   ¹⁴ I, 45.

¹⁵ The order of words is: 'thus saith David, your brother', II, 26.

¹⁶ 'Saul, your master, is dead', as note 15 above.

¹⁷ Participle Pual of פּוֹר or Niphal of פּוּץ, giving an adjectival or descriptive effect—'are scattered (people)'.

¹⁸ 'as *the* sheep', XXIX, 11.

¹⁹ Recast in Hebrew thinking 'as the sheep which there is not to them (i.e. have not) a shepherd'. Note that צֹאן, being a collective, may be followed by a plural.

²⁰ VII, 15.   ²¹ XXIII, 7.   ²² 'said to me the Lord'.

²³ XXVI, 25.   ²⁴ XVII, 8.   ²⁵ XXVI, 27.

²⁶ לְ, I, 56.   ²⁷ I, 47.

²⁸ בְּיַד, literally, 'by the hand of', 'through the agency of'.

²⁹ V, 33.   ³⁰ 'in your returning'—infinitive construct.

³¹ The demonstrative plural will not convey the sense or make correct Hebrew. Either expand to 'choose . . . men, stout-of (construct plural) heart' or, better, 'choose (the ones) stout of heart'.

³² 'as (Hebrew לְ) officers'.

³³ 'the Philistines, the (ones) dwelling'—Qal active participle masculine plural, as descriptive adjective.

³⁴ Infinitive absolute before the finite verb.   ³⁵ XII, 18.

³⁶ 'said to him the heads . . .'.   ³⁷ Jussive, XIV, 33.

³⁸ VII, 47.   ³⁹ Imperfect, since the future is implied.

XXXI

WHEN¹ Solomon finished² building the sanctuary of the Lord, he called his counsellors before him and he commanded them, saying: 'Gather together³ all the inhabitants of Jerusalem before the temple of the Lord on the day of the Feast.'⁴ And they did as⁵ the king commanded them and a great multitude assembled³ on that day before the sanctuary, and with them the priests, the⁶ Levites, the⁶ judges and the officers.⁷ And the king appeared⁸ before⁹ the assembly and he commanded the priests to offer up¹⁰ the sacrifices upon the altar. And the High Priest¹¹ drew near and he made sacrifice upon the altar, in the presence[9] of all the people. And it came to pass, as the smoke went up[12] from[13] the altar to the heavens,[14] that the king spread out his hands[15] and he prayed unto the Lord in a loud voice, in the hearing[16] of the whole assembly of the people and he said: 'O Lord, God of Israel, look down[17] from Thy holy habitation[18] and bless[19] this people, who have built this great house for Thy glorious name.[20] And[21] when they come[22] into Thy holy house[23] to pray unto Thee, when they are in distress,[24] hear their supplication and be gracious[25] unto them. For Thou art gracious and merciful and forgivest the sins of Thy people which they have sinned against[26] Thee.' Then[27] the king turned unto the people and he blessed[19] them, saying: 'May the Lord bless[28] you and keep[29] you. May He increase[30] your herds[31] and your flocks[31] and the produce of your land and may He grant[32] you peace in this good land,[33] that ye may dwell[34] in it in safety, and none shall make you afraid.'[35] And,[1] when the king finished[2] speaking, the Levites drew near and they divided themselves[36] into two companies,[37] and they stood facing one another;[38] the one was[39] playing musical instruments[40] which were[41] in their hands and the other was[39] singing. And they sang this song unto the Lord: 'It is good to praise the Lord, for His lovingkindness endureth[42] for ever. There is none like the Lord, our God, Who made[43] the heavens and the earth and the seas and all which is in them, and there is none like His people, Israel,[44] upon the earth. Praise ye the Lord, Who hath granted[45] peace in the land and Who watcheth[46] over the house of Israel.'

NOTES ON XXXI

[1] Begin, as usual, with 'and it came to pass . . .'.   [2] XXIX, 25.

[3] V, 33.   [4] V, 34.   [5] I, 10.   [6] Supply conjunction.

[7] XXII, 28.   [8] II, 1.

[9] It means 'in the sight of', so לְעֵינֵי is appropriate.   [10] II, 38.

[11] 'the great priest'.   [12] XXI, 18.   [13] XXI, 19.

[14] Old accusative case ending.

[15] כַּף (dual כַּפַּיִם) is better than יָד, since it refers to the palms of the hands.

[16] 'in the ears of', cf. XI, 7.

[17] Emphatic imperative—either שׁקף or נבט in Hiphil.

[18] Following note XXI, 28, 'a holy habitation' is expressed as 'a habitation

of holiness', מְעוֹן קֹדֶשׁ, so 'thy holy habitation' will be 'thy habitation of holiness', מְעוֹן קָדְשְׁךָ, with the suffix attached to the word following the noun in the construct. [19] WHG 168.

[20] Following note XXI, 28, 'a glorious name' is 'a name-of glory', שֵׁם כָּבוֹד, and 'thy glorious name' is 'thy name of glory', שֵׁם כְּבוֹדֶךָ.

[21] 'and it shall come to pass'.

[22] 'in (or 'as') their coming'—infinitive construct.

[23] Cf. XXI, 28 and note 18 above. [24] I, 63.

[25] The double ʿAyin verb חָנַן means 'was gracious to' and takes a direct object, WHG 231, 232. [26] 'to thee'. [27] I, 45.

[28] Imperfect serving as jussive.

[29] Imperfect with Waw conjunctive serving as jussive.

[30] The Hiphil of רָבָה 'was much', 'were many' produces the derived idea 'caused to be much', 'many', i.e. 'increased', 'multiplied'. Note the form of the shortened imperfect for jussive, WHG 219.

[31] I, 12. [32] Root שִׂים (perfect שָׂם). For the jussive form, see WHG 197.

[33] Note the order of thinking: 'the land, the good (one), the this (one)'—the demonstrative referring to 'the good land'.

[34] Either 'in order that . . .' or, simply, the perfect with Waw consecutive. Note also 'in safety' is לָבֶטַח (and not בְ).

[35] The idiomatic phrase is 'and none making (you) tremble'—Hiphil of חָרַד, 'you' being understood. [36] VI, 43, Niphal of פרד or חָלַק.

[37] For the sake of clarity expand to 'and they became (root הָיָה) into (לְ) two companies', מַחֲלְקוֹת.

[38] 'facing one another' may be expressed as 'face to face' or 'a man opposite his neighbour', VI, 42.

[39] 'the one playing . . . and the one singing'. In both cases the participle acts as a verbal adjective and 'was' is supplied by the English.

[40] Following I, 57, 'musical instruments' will be 'instruments of music'. Note one plays *with* an instrument; see also XII, 15.

[41] 'which (being) in their hands'; 'were' is needed in English. Since 'hands' are meant literally, one uses the dual as plural, WHG 38 note.

[42] 'for ever (is) his lovingkindness'. 'Endureth' is supplied by the English.

[43] Either verbatim or the participle masculine singular in the construct, 'the maker of', עֹשֵׂה.

[44] The order is 'like Israel His people', II, 26.

[45] As note 43 above, either literally or the participle masculine singular 'the (one) granting'; see note 32 above and WHG 66.

[46] 'the (one) watching'.

XXXII

Now, on a certain day,[1] I stood by[2] the priests in the temple of the Lord as they were offering[3] up sacrifices upon the altar and I saw, and behold, an assembly of people were[4] standing at[5] the entrance of the temple and they had[6] gifts in their hands. And I asked one of the priests, saying: 'For whom are these gifts?' And he said unto me: 'These gifts are for us, for we require them from the people.' And it came to pass, in that night, that the word of the Lord came[7] unto me in a dream. And I heard a voice calling unto me, saying: 'Wherefore liest thou upon thy couch, while[8] thou knowest that My priests have forsaken My Torah and they walk after[9] the ways of the gods of Canaan? They have forgotten the covenant which I made[10] with them and they do that which is evil[11] in My sight; the widow and the fatherless they have put into bondage[12] to serve them. Therefore[13] say unto them: "Thus saith the Lord: 'I have heard the cry of My people, who call unto Me out of their sorrow and I shall deliver[14] them out of your hands.[15] And I shall visit you with My fierce wrath[16] and I shall raise up instead of you other priests who will keep My statutes and ordinances. Cease, then,[17] to do evil,[18] lest I destroy[19] you from[20] the face of the earth.'"' And I awoke[21] from my sleep and I knew that the Lord had chosen me[22] to be[23] His servant and to declare His words to the oppressors of Israel. And it came to pass, in the morning, as the priests were coming[24] into the temple, as was their custom,[25] that I stood at the entrance and called unto them in a loud voice and I spoke unto them the words which the Lord had put into my mouth. And they were exceedingly wroth[26] with me and they drew near unto me to drive me out of the temple. But the power[27] of the Lord came[7] upon me and I was not afraid of[28] them and I said:[29] 'Take ye heed[30] of that which I have said unto you, for a king whom[31] the Lord shall choose shall arise to sit upon the throne of Israel and he will destroy[19] you, if ye continue[32] to do evil.'[18] And the priests were not able to touch me,[33] and they were exceedingly afraid and they said not a word, for they knew that the Lord was[34] with me.

NOTES ON XXXII

[1] X, 7.

[2] Either אֵצֶל or עַל־יַד, 'by the hand of' (cf. the English 'at hand').

[3] 'and they, offering . . .', II, 38.

[4] He saw 'an assembly of people standing'. 'Were' is required by the English.

[5] 'in'. [6] The Hebrew thought is, simply, 'and gifts in their hands'.

[7] XXI, 24. The preposition is אֶל, since speech is implied, I, 2.

[8] Either 'in thy knowing'—infinitive construct, or 'and *thou* knowest', with the personal pronoun before the verb to emphasize 'thou'. See also II, 18.

[9] In Hebrew 'in'. [10] I, 53. [11] X, 42, and I, 40.

[12] The Hiphil of עָבַד 'served', i.e. 'caused to serve', 'enslaved'.

[13] XVIII, 27. [14] XVIII, 20. [15] I, 34. [16] VII, 32.

[17] I, 45. [18] VII, 26. [19] Hiphil of אָבַד, 'caused to perish'.

[20] VI, 24. [21] The verb יקץ is a stative and a Pe Yod. The imperfect is יִיקַץ. [22] XI, 25 (*a*).

[23] 'chosen (in) me for him(self) as (לְ) a servant'.

[24] 'in the entering of . . .'—infinitive construct.

[25] 'as their custom', XI, 6.

[26] V, 36. [27] I, 34. Note that יָד is feminine.

[28] VII, 31; WHG 211 (*b*). [29] II, 36. [30] XXIV, 34.

[31] '(there) shall arise a king who the Lord shall choose (in) him'.

[32] 'if ye shall add' (Hiphil of יסף, X, 17).

[33] נָגַע is followed by בְּ.

[34] 'they knew that the Lord *is* with me'.

XXXIII

I N[1] the third year of the reign of Uzziah[2] a plague broke forth[3] in the land and a great multitude of the people died, both men and women,[4] both young and old.[5] And the king was sorely distressed[6] and he rent his garments and he sat upon the ground and he cast[7] dust upon his head and he mourned[8] for the dead. And he called[9] his priests, his counsellors and his judges and he spoke unto them, saying: 'Wherefore hath this evil[10] come upon us? What is our sin, that the Lord hath smitten[11] us and hath poured out His wrath against[12] us? For, behold, there is not a house in the land in which[13] there is no lamenting, and the dead are numerous, beyond reckoning.'[14] And it came to pass, as the king finished[15] speaking and before the[16] priests could answer him, that a prophet of the Lord appeared[17] and he said unto the king: 'Hear the word of the Lord, which He hath spoken against[12] thee. Thou art affrighted[18] at the calamity which hath befallen[19] this land and thou wailest as a mother bereaved of[20] her children. Surely thou[21] knowest wherefore the vengeance of the Lord hath come upon thy people!' But,[22] if thou wilt say: "I know not",[23] then go thou round[24] the city, traverse[25] the land, in its length[26] and its breadth; ascend[27] the mountains and go down into the valleys, and thou wilt see thy people worshipping[28] the gods of Canaan. Art thou blind,[29] that thou seest not[30] the temples of Baal which are full?[31] Art thou deaf[29] that thou hearest[30] not the songs of the priests of Ashtoreth? Have they not informed thee[32] that an Ashera hath been set up[33] under every green[34] tree and at[35] every well of water? Cease, then, lamenting and speak not vain words,[36] but[22] get thee up[37] and go forth and cleanse[38] the land from the evil in its midst. Throw down[39] the temples of Baal which the people serve and remove[40] the false priests[41] therefrom. Restore[42] the prophets of the Lord, that they may teach the people to turn aside from their evil paths[43] and turn again[44] unto the Lord, their God. For then[45] He will have mercy upon them and He will repent[46] of the fierceness of His anger and the plague in the land will cease.' Then the prophet finished speaking and he turned away[47] and went forth from the palace.

NOTES ON XXXIII

[1] Though one may begin with the usual 'and it came to pass . . .', one finds the narratives in 2 Kings opening with 'in the . . . year of . . .', without the introductory וַיְהִי.

[2] This phrase may be expressed either as 'in the year of three (feminine) of (in Hebrew לְ) Uzziah, the king' or, more fully, 'and it came to pass, in the days of Uzziah, in the year of three of (לְ) his reigning'—infinitive construct with suffix.   [3] XXIX, 21.   [4] XXIII, 14.   [5] XIII, 43.

[6] The verb צַר (root צָרַר), meaning 'was narrow', 'straitened', is a stative and (following WHG 231) the imperfect Qal is יֵצַר but, with Waw consecutive, the accent is retracted one syllable (WHG 92 (c)) and the Paṭaḥ in the last syllable is depressed to Seghol וַיִּצֶר. The Hebrew idiom is 'and it was straitened to him exceedingly'—('sorely' being an elegant translation).

⁷ VII, 40.　　　　　⁸ VII, 44.　　　　　⁹ I, 22.　　　　　¹⁰ V, 43.

¹¹ The verb נָגַף is used to express the idea 'plagued'.

¹² Either עַל or ב.　　　　¹³ 'a house which there is not in it'.

¹⁴ XXII, 6.　　　　¹⁵ Cf. XXIX, 25.

¹⁶ The English is an expansion of 'before the priests answered', using טֶרֶם with imperfect (IX, 23 (b)).　　　　¹⁷ II, 1.

¹⁸ The sense includes fear and panic, for which the Niphal of בהל serves.

¹⁹ XXII, 18.

²⁰ Qal passive participle feminine singular of the stative verb שָׁכֹל or the feminine singular adjective שַׁכּוּלָה.　　　　²¹ VII, 20, and II, 18.

²² I, 45.　　　　²³ II, 18.　　　　²⁴ The verb סַב (סָבַב).

²⁵ 'Pass (through) in the land.' The difference between עֲבֹר אֶת־הָאָרֶץ and עֲבֹר בָּאָרֶץ is that the former implies crossing to the other side, while the latter suggests passing from place to place.

²⁶ 'to its length and to its breadth'. Both nouns אֹרֶךְ and רֹחַב (the latter having Paṭaḥ in the second syllable, owing to the guttural) are segholates of the קֹדֶשׁ type. Since they were originally אָרֶךְ and רָחְב, they will be אָרְכָּהּ and רָחְבָּהּ with the suffix. Note the mappiq in the ה of the 3rd feminine singular suffix.

²⁷ 'go up upon'.

²⁸ Qal of עָבַד or Hithpalel of שחה, II, 61, with ל.

²⁹ The adjective before the personal pronoun emphasizes the defect.

³⁰ If you read the sense as referring to the past, use the perfect. If, however, the sense seems to suggest continuity, use the imperfect.

³¹ Either 'the full (ones)'—Qal active participle masculine singular with the article or the relative with the plural perfect אֲשֶׁר מָלְאוּ (pausal form), since one can only speak of anything being full when that condition is completed.

³² 'told to thee'.　　　　³³ Hophal of קָם (root קום).

³⁴ רַעֲנָן.　　　　³⁵ XXXII, 2.　　　　³⁶ 'words of vanity', cf. I, 57.

³⁷ 'arise to thee', or 'for thyself', followed either by the imperative or the perfect with Waw consecutive 'and thou shalt go forth'.

³⁸ The perfect Piel with Waw consecutive. The Qal טָהַר means 'was clean' (stative) and the Piel makes it a causative, cf. XXII, 13, 26.

³⁹ נָתַץ is used for destroying buildings.　　　　⁴⁰ XVIII, 30.

⁴¹ 'priests of falsehood', I, 57.　　　　⁴² I, 51.

⁴³ Either 'their ways, the evil (ones)' or 'the evil of their ways', using the noun רֹעַ, cf. XVIII, 31.　　　　⁴⁴ 'return'.

⁴⁵ XVIII, 32.　　　　⁴⁶ XXVIII, 35, i.e. Niphal of נחם. As an alternative, giving the same sense, the verb שָׁב (root שׁוב) with the meaning 'turned back' may be used.

⁴⁷ Add 'from with them' or 'from at (עַל) them'.

XXXIV

THERE was a certain man[1] whose name was[2] Abinadab and he was dwelling[3] in Jerusalem. And the spirit of the Lord came[4] upon him and he went forth to the gate of the city and he lifted up his voice and he prophesied[5] unto the people. And he said:[6] 'Hearken unto me, ye who have done evil;[7] close not[8] your ears, ye sinful people.[9] For, behold, the Lord hath appeared[10] unto me and hath commanded me to speak unto you the words which He hath put into my mouth. Therefore[11] I say unto you: "Woe unto you, for the Lord hath seen the evil works[12] of your hands, and the wickedness of your hearts is revealed before Him. Except[13] ye turn aside from your wickedness and cling no more[14] to deceit and wrongdoing, He shall surely visit you with His fierce wrath.[15] And He will deliver[16] you into the hands[17] of your adversaries and ye shall be brought into slavery[18] and ye shall be afflicted, even[19] as ye have afflicted the poor and the weak. And, when ye have had the fulness[20] of your sorrows, ye shall cry unto the Lord, by reason of[21] your anguish, but[22] He will hide[23] His countenance[24] from you and will not see[25] your distress. Then[26] shall ye know that He is the God of justice."' And it came to pass, when Abinadab finished[27] speaking these words, that the king's officers[28] gathered around[29] him and they smote him and they said unto him: 'Why dost thou prophesy[30] evil against[31] us? Surely[32] we bring up our burnt offerings[33] upon the altar of the Lord, even the best[34] of our cattle, according to the commands of the priests, and wherefore sayest[30] thou that we provoke Him to anger?[35] Cease, therefore,[36] speaking idle words,[37] lest we drive thee forth from the land.' And Abinadab answered and said:[6] 'The Lord rejecteth[38] the sacrifices which ye offer up daily[39] and He requireth[40] not the gold and the silver which ye bring into His temple. The Lord seeketh a pure heart, the practice[41] of righteousness and the bestowing[42] of kindness. Behold, your priests have led you astray[43] and your prophets have prophesied[5] falsely,[44] but[22] know ye that the path of the wicked leads[45] to Sheol, for the vengeance of the Lord shall overtake them.'

NOTES ON XXXIV

[1] XIX, 8. [2] III, 17.

[3] Since this phrase is meant to be descriptive of the man, use the Qal active participle יֹשֵׁב הוּא‎וְ—'and he (being one) dwelling'. [4] XXI, 24.

[5] The Niphal or Hithpael of נבא. [6] II, 49.

[7] The Hebrew expression is: '(ye) doers of evil'—Qal active participle masculine plural construct.

[8] The special verb for closing the ears is אָטַם; see also I, 61 (a), for the negative. [9] '(O) sinning people'—Qal active participle masculine singular with עַם. [10] II, 1. [11] XVIII, 27.

[12] 'the evil (רֹעַ) of the works of your hands'.

[13] 'if . . . not', using the imperfect of the verb, since the future is implied.

[14] 'and ye shall not cling any more' (עוֹד). The verb דָּבַק is followed by בּ.

[15] VII, 32. [16] I, 33. [17] I, 34.

[18] The Hiphil of עָבַד, 'served', i.e. 'caused to serve', means 'enslaved', 'brought into slavery', and the Hophal, then, has the meaning 'was enslaved', 'was brought into slavery'.

[19] XIII, 33.

[20] The sense is 'when your sorrow is full for you' expressed as 'in the being-full for you your sorrow'—infinitive construct, see V, 31.

[21] Either, simply, 'from' or XVIII, 11. [22] I, 45.

[23] XVIII, 28. [24] The plural noun פָּנִים.

[25] The sense is 'take notice of', 'pay attention to', expressed by רָאָה ב or שָׂם לֵב ל. [26] XVIII, 32. [27] XXIX, 25. [28] XXII, 28.

[29] The sense is 'closed in on him', with the verb סַב (סָבַב).

[30] The imperfect, to indicate a continuous process. [31] XXXIII, 12.

[32] VII, 20. [33] The noun is עֹלָה 'something brought up'; use, therefore, the cognate verb עָלָה in Hiphil, II, 38.

[34] The sense is 'the choicest'—the definite construct (of מִבְחָר) for the superlative degree, WHG 136.

[35] XIII, 11. [36] I, 4. [37] XXXIII, 36.

[38] See XXVII, 19. Use the perfect, since the state of rejecting is a completed one.

[39] XXI, 34.

[40] Here the imperfect is to be used, since the state of (not) requiring is continuous.

[41] 'the doing of . . .'—infinitive construct as verbal noun.

[42] (a) Infinitive construct as verbal noun of the verb גָּמַל; (b) 'kindness' in the sense of 'kind deeds' is expressed by the plural of חֶסֶד—i.e. 'kindnesses'.

⁴³ The Hiphil of תָּעָה, 'went astray', 'wandered', namely 'caused to go astray', i.e. 'led astray'.   ⁴⁴ In Hebrew it is 'falsehood'.

⁴⁵ The English may be regarded as amplification of the Hebrew 'the path of the wicked is to Sheol (Sheolwards)'—with old accusative ending.

XXXV

THE word of the Lord came[1] unto the prophet Jeremiah, saying: 'Take the yoke of an ox and place it upon thy neck and go forth into the streets of Jerusalem, that[2] all who pass by[3] may see thee. And when thou comest[4] to the entrance of My holy temple,[5] take up thy position[6] there and call out in a loud voice in the hearing[7] of the people, saying: "Look, O sons of Judah, and see. For, even[8] as I bear this yoke upon my neck, so shall ye bear the yoke of the king of Babylon. Seek not[9] to do as the other peoples, who thought[10] to break off[11] the yoke of Babylon from themselves[12] and perished from the face[13] of the earth. And, when the king of Babylon cometh[14] hither, go ye forth to meet him[15] with words of peace and bring him offerings[16] in your hands, that[2] ye may live under his dominion and not die." '[17] And Jeremiah did as the Lord commanded him and he went forth and he stood at the entrance of the sanctuary of the Lord and he spake all the words which the Lord had put into his mouth. And, it came to pass, as he finished[18] speaking, that one of the prophets of Baal drew near unto him and he took hold[19] of the yoke which was[20] on the neck of Jeremiah and he broke it in twain,[21] in the sight[22] of the people. And he lifted up his voice and he said: 'Hear ye me, O sons of Judah. Even[8] as I have broken this yoke, so shall ye throw off[11] the yoke of the Babylonians.'[23] And he said unto Jeremiah: 'Wherefore speakest[24] thou thus[25] unto the people, to weaken[26] their spirit and to lead them away[27] from the counsel of their leaders?[28] But know thou,[29] that if thou speakest any more[30] words such as these,[31] we shall surely slay[32] thee.' Then Jeremiah spoke unto the people and he said: 'Heed[33] not the words of this man, for he speaketh not the truth. Behold, he is a false prophet[34] and he leadeth you astray with false words.[35] Surely[36] it is better[37] to live in this land under the yoke of Babylon than to die in battle, when[38] the Lord is not with you!' And, when he finished[39] speaking, he turned away from[40] the people and went on his way.[41]

NOTES ON XXXV

[1] XXI, 24. Begin with Waw consecutive.　　　[2] 'in order that . . .'.

[3] 'the (ones) passing'—Qal active participle masculine plural with the article.

[4] 'as thy coming'—infinitive construct.　　　[5] See XXI, 28.

[6] Hithpael of יצב, as opposed to the (inactive) עָמַד, 'stood'.

[7] See XI, 7.　　　[8] XIII, 33; 'as my bearing'—infinitive construct with suffix.

[9] The negative is אַל, since the objection is to an immediate situation.

[10] VII, 14.　　　[11] The appropriate verb is פְּרַק.

[12] 'from *upon* themselves', cf. VI, 24. The order of words is: 'to break off from upon themselves the yoke of . . .'.

[13] 'from *upon* the face of . . .', cf. VI, 24.

[14] 'as the coming of'—infinitive construct.　　　[15] IX, 33.

[16] מִנְחָה is used also for a 'gift'.　　　[17] Imperfect, 'ye shall not die'.

[18] 'as his finishing'—infinitive construct followed by לְ.

[19] Qal of אָחַז or Hiphil of חָזַק followed by בְּ.

[20] 'which (being) upon . . .'.　　　[21] '(in)to two (masculine)'.

[22] 'to the eyes of'.　　　[23] Cf. I, 17, and add 'from upon you' to complete the Hebrew thought.　　　[24] XXXIV, 30.　　　[25] II, 25.

[26] The Piel of the (stative) verb רָפָה, 'was weak', makes it a causative 'weakened', XXII, 13, 26.　　　[27] XXXIV, 43.　　　[28] 'heads'.

[29] 'know for thyself', cf. XXXIII, 37.

[30] 'if thou addest to speak', X, 17.　　　[31] 'as these words'.

[32] XVIII, 46.　　　[33] XXIV, 34.

[34] 'a prophet of falsehood', cf. I, 57.

[35] 'words of falsehood', I, 57.　　　[36] VII, 20.

[37] 'better your living . . . than your dying'—infinitive construct, V, 27 (a).

[38] simply 'and'.　　　[39] 'as his finishing'—infinitive construct.

[40] As in XXXIII, 47.　　　[41] XXIII, 43.

XXXVI

IT came to pass, after these things, that a messenger came to the king and he told[1] him, saying: 'Behold, the hosts of the

Babylonians[2] are drawing near unto the city, to fight against[3] it, and it will be delivered[4] into their hands.[5] Flee, therefore, for thy life,[6] thou and all thy household,[7] and hide[8] in the cave which has been prepared[9] for thee in the wilderness of Judah. Thy food shall be brought to thee daily[10] and thou shalt abide[11] there till[12] the Lord shall have mercy upon us and drive the Babylonians out of the land.' Then the king arose and he went forth from his palace and he went up on the wall,[13] at the[14] northern gate, and he saw the hosts of Babylon encamped[15] upon the mountain opposite[16] the city. And it came to pass, when the captain of the hosts of the Babylonians saw[17] the king standing upon the wall[13] of the city, that he lifted up his voice and he called[18] unto him and he said: 'O king of Israel, thinkest[19] thou that thou canst prevail[20] against these mighty armies? Where are all the great kings who refused to open the gates of their cities unto[21] us and where are their cities? Thou surely knowest[22] that their corpses were given to the birds of the heavens and their cities were made[23] heaps of desolation. Therefore I say unto thee: "Take upon thyself the yoke of my lord, the king of Babylon, and live in peace in this land, and seek not to rebel against[24] him."' Then the king rent his garments and he sent unto the prophet, saying: 'Pray unto the Lord for us,[25] for we are delivered[4] into the hands[5] of our enemies.' And the prophet came unto the king and he said unto him: 'Because thou trustest[26] in the Lord, this evil[27] shall not come upon thee. For, behold, the Lord will send His angel into the camp of the Babylonians and he will smite them grievously[28] and they will flee from this place.' And the king arose early[29] in the morning and he went up on the wall[13] of the city and he looked[30] at the camp of the Babylonians and, behold, it was[31] empty. Then the king lifted up his voice and he sang[32] this song:

It is better[33] to trust in the Lord
　Than to trust[34] in the sons of man,
He hath commanded and so it was,[35]
　He hath spoken and it was accomplished.[36]

Let us, therefore,[37] praise[38] the Lord,
Let us give thanks[39] to His glorious name.[40]

NOTES ON XXXVI

[1] 'told *to* . . .'. [2] See I, 17. [3] I, 29. [4] I, 33.

[5] I, 34. [6] II, 6; V, 4. [7] II, 21. [8] XXVIII, 5.

[9] The Hiphil of כוּן (not used in Qal) means 'prepared' and the Hophal 'was prepared'. The Hophal participle with the article, meaning 'the (one) prepared', is idiomatic Hebrew; see WHG 201.

[10] XXI, 34. [11] V, 29. [12] Since a preposition cannot be directly associated with a verb, the relative is placed between—עַד־אֲשֶׁר, cf. I, 10. [13] XII, 8.

[14] XXXII, 2; rephrase 'the gate of the north'.

[15] The verb חָנָה means 'encamped' or 'was encamped' in Qal.

[16] II, 11 (*b*). [17] 'as the seeing of the captain . . .'—infinitive construct.

[18] I, 22. [19] VII, 14. [20] XI, 35, 36.

[21] The order of words is '. . . open to us the gates'.

[22] VII, 20, and II, 18.

[23] Rephrase 'have become'—plural perfect of הָיָה.

[24] XII, 41. [25] 'pray for us unto . . .'. [26] II, 37 (*a*).

[27] V, 43. [28] XIX, 23. [29] XXVII, 2.

[30] For the verb, cf. XXXI, 17.

[31] He saw 'it *is* empty'—'was' is required by the English.

[32] The ʿAyin Yodִ verb שָׁר (root שׁיר) is יָשִׁיר in the imperfect, but with Waw consecutive, and the accent retracted, it is וַיָּשַׁר. [33] V, 27 (*a*).

[34] 'than (מִן) trusting (infinitive construct)'.

[35] Instead of the literal rendering, use the pausal וַיְהִי, 'and it was, became', which conveys the exact sense. [36] 'and it was done'.

[37] I, 4. [38] Cohortative.

[39] Imperfect serving as cohortative. [40] See XXXI, 20.

XXXVII

THESE are the words of the epistle which the prophet Jeremiah[1] sent from Jerusalem unto the elders and the priests and unto all the people whom Nebuchadnezzar had carried away captive[2] to Babylon.[3] 'Thus saith the Lord of hosts, the God of Israel, unto all the captivity:[4] "Build ye[5] houses and dwell in them and plant ye gardens and eat the fruit thereof. Take unto yourselves wives and beget[6] sons and daughters, and multiply in your land of captivity[7] and be not diminished. And seek ye the welfare of the land whither[8] I have caused you to be carried away captive,[2] for therein[9] lieth[10] your welfare. For lo! after seventy years have been accomplished[11] for Babylon, I shall remember you, O my people, and I shall bring you back[12] to the land of your fathers. For ye[13] will seek Me and I[13] will be found, and I will gather you from all the nations and from all the places whither[8] I have driven you and I shall plant you again in this land. Therefore,[14] fear not,[15] O Jacob, nor be dismayed,[16] O Israel, for I shall save thee from afar, and thy seed from their land of captivity.[7] Behold, the day will come when[17] I shall make a new covenant with the house of Judah, and I will put my Torah in their hearts.[18] And they shall no more say to one another:[19] 'Know the Lord', for they shall all[20] know Me, from the least[21] of them to the greatest[22] of them, for I shall forgive their iniquity and their sin shall I remember no more. And Jacob shall again be at ease[23] and none shall make him afraid.[24] For a new king shall arise and rule[25] over all these lands and he will permit[26] the sons of Judah to return to Jerusalem[3] and to rebuild[27] the house of the Lord there. And men of stout heart[28] will arise, and their wives and children with them, and they will go forth and return to Jerusalem[3] and they will rebuild[27] the desolate city and the temple. And those who will remain[29] in Babylon will support their hands with gifts and with money, that[30] their work may prosper. And a new Jerusalem will be built and it shall be called the righteous city,[31] for righteousness[32] shall rule[25] over the hearts[18] of men.'''

NOTES ON XXXVII

[1] 'Jeremiah, the prophet', cf. II, 26.

[2] Hiphil of גָּלָה, 'was exiled', 'went into exile', namely הִגְלָה, means 'caused to be exiled', i.e. 'brought (or carried) into exile', 'made captive', 'brought into captivity'. Another root is שָׁבָה in Qal.   [3] Old accusative ending.

[4] The abstract noun גָּלוּת (as the English 'captivity') often implies the people in exile. Another form is גֹּלָה, which appears to be a feminine singular adjective 'a captive (thing)'.

[5] The plural imperative implies 'ye', but add לָכֶם 'for yourselves'.

⁶ The Qal יָלַד, 'bore (a child)', obviously refers to a woman, while the Hiphil הוֹלִיד, 'caused to bear', i.e. 'begot', refers to a man.

⁷ 'land of captivity' is אֶרֶץ גָּלוּת and 'your land of captivity' is אֶרֶץ גָּלוּתְכֶם, cf. XXI, 28.

⁸ 'the land which . . . thither'.   ⁹ 'in it'.

¹⁰ '(is)'; 'lieth' is supplied by the English.

¹¹ 'full', V, 31—'after the being-full of seventy years'—infinitive construct.

¹² I, 51.   ¹³ Use the personal pronoun before the verb for emphasis.

¹⁴ XVIII, 27.   ¹⁵ The negative אַל for an immediate situation, I, 61 (a).

¹⁶ The verb is the double 'Ayin חתת, WHG 231 (stative).

¹⁷ 'and'.   ¹⁸ Singular as collective.   ¹⁹ VI, 42.

²⁰ XI, 5 (b).

²¹ 'from their small (one) to (עד)   ²² their big (one)'.

²³ The quadriliteral verb שַׁאֲנַן.   ²⁴ XXXI, 35.

²⁵ VII, 15.   ²⁶ VI, 35.

²⁷ 'to build'; re-building being understood.

²⁸ 'men, stout of heart' (the adjective אַמִּיץ).

²⁹ 'the (ones) remaining'—Niphal participle of שאר with the article.

³⁰ 'in order that'.   ³¹ 'city of righteousness', I, 57.

³² By placing the noun before the verb, emphasis is laid on it.

XXXVIII

THE prophet arose[1] and he went forth from the cave wherein[2] he was hidden and he went to Jerusalem,[3] a journey[4] of three[5] days, and he came to the city[3] by[6] the way of the northern[7] gate. And one of the king's officers saw him walking about[8] in the broad places[9] of the city and he drew near unto him and he said unto him: 'O man of God,[10] what doest thou[11] here? Surely[12] thou knowest that which the king commanded thee, saying: "Thou shalt not be seen[13] again in the streets of Jerusalem, for on the day that thou showest thyself[14] in this city, thou shalt surely[15] die." Wherefore, then, hast thou returned hither?' And the prophet answered him and said: 'The Lord[16] hath sent me unto the king and I cannot rebel[17] against the word of the Lord. Bring me, therefore,[18] into the presence of[19] the king.' And the king's officer did as the prophet bade him and he brought him into the king's chamber. And, when[20] the king saw the prophet standing before him, he was exceedingly wroth[21] and he said: 'Wherefore hast thou returned to trouble Israel? Did I not command thee not[22] to see my face again? Behold, thy blood is on thine own[23] head.' Then the[24] prophet said unto him: 'Thus saith the Lord, God of Israel: "Behold, I chose thee[25] from among thy brethren to be king[26] over My people, and I commanded thee to deliver them out of the hands[27] of their despoilers, to execute[28] justice, to sweep away evil from the midst of the land and to establish[29] a righteous kingdom. But thou didst incline[30] thy heart unto the oppressors of My people and thou didst make a[31] covenant with them, and thus thou didst increase[32] the wealth of thy house. Behold, the day of the Lord cometh, and He will exact vengeance[33] from thee and He will cast thee down[34] from the throne upon which thou sittest. Yea, He will remove[35] thy heart of understanding[36] and He will give thee the heart of a beast, and thou shalt dwell in the wilderness and thou shalt eat grass all the days of thy life."' And it came to pass, when the king heard[37] the words of the prophet, that he was greatly afraid[38] and he fell upon his face to the ground[3] and he cried: 'Verily,[39] I have sinned against[40] the Lord. Entreat Him,[41] I pray thee, that He may have mercy[42] upon me.'

NOTES ON XXXVIII

[1] Begin 'and the . . .'.   [2] 'the cave which he was hidden there' (or 'in it'), I, 48.   [3] Old accusative ending.   [4] 'a way'.

[5] XX, 18.   [6] 'by' is supplied by the English.   [7] XXXVI, 14.

[8] XXV, 22.   [9] The feminine plural רְחוֹבוֹת means 'broad *places*'.

[10] XXIII, 17.   [11] 'what (is there) for thee . . .?'   [12] VII, 20.

[13] The negative is לֹא for permanent prohibition; see also X, 17.

[14] The Niphal of רָאָה, with its passive-reflexive effect, means 'was seen', 'appeared', 'showed oneself'. The Hithpael of this verb may also be used. Note the construction: 'in the day of thy showing thyself'—infinitive construct.

[15] VI, 19.

[16] By placing the subject before the verb, the sender is emphasized.

[17] Cf. XII, 11, 41.   [18] I, 4.

[19] 'before', i.e. 'to the face of'.

[20] 'and it came to pass, as the seeing of the king . . .'—infinitive construct.

[21] V, 36.

²² לְבִלְתִּי with infinitive construct. This form, with an archaic ending, seems to mean 'non-existence' and appears to be an infinitive construct of a root בָּלָה ('withered', 'was worn out').

²³ 'own' is understood in the Hebrew, but supplied by the English.

²⁴ I, 45.   ²⁵ XI, 25 (a).

²⁶ XXVII, 20.   ²⁷ I, 34.   ²⁸ Simply, 'to do'.

²⁹ Either the Hiphil of קוּם or the Polel (representing Piel, WHG 201) of כוּן. The former has the derived idea 'made to stand' and the latter 'made firm'.

³⁰ The sense is transitive: 'made to incline', i.e. Hiphil of נָטָה, WHG 224.

³¹ I, 53.   ³² Hiphil of רָבָה, 'was much', 'many', XXXI, 30.

³³ V, 41.

³⁴ Hiphil of נָפַל. Rephrase: 'He will cast thee down from *upon* the throne which thou sittest upon it', VI, 24; I, 48.   ³⁵ XVIII, 30.

³⁶ 'a heart of understanding' is לֵב בִּינָה; 'thy heart of understanding' is לֵב־בִּינָתֶךָ, cf. XXI, 28.   ³⁷ Cf. III, 2.   ³⁸ I, 61 (b).

³⁹ IV, 36.   ⁴⁰ 'unto'.   ⁴¹ 'to him'.   ⁴² XVIII, 38.

XXXIX

THE word of the Lord came[1] unto me, saying: 'Son of man, what seest thou?' And I lifted up mine eyes and I beheld a field, and upon the face of it were[2] sheep, but[3] they[4] were scattered[5] all around[6] and they wandered hither and thither,[7] for there was no[8] shepherd with them to keep them. And I saw, and behold, a wild beast[9] came forth from the wilderness and it fell upon one of the sheep to rend it asunder.[10] And, when[11] the sheep cried out to its shepherd to deliver it out of the mouth of its adversary, there was no[12] answer, and it was torn to pieces.[13] And my soul was troubled at[14] the sight of mine eyes and I said: 'I pray thee,[15] O Lord, where is the shepherd? And to whom do these sheep belong,[16] that he should require them from the hand of the shepherd?' And the Lord answered me and said: 'The sheep are the poor of My people,[17] and the shepherd who careth[18] not for their well-being[19] is[20] the king who sitteth[21] upon the throne of Israel, and the sheep are Mine.[22] Go thou forth, therefore,[23] to meet the shepherd of Israel, who hath transgressed[24] against Me and against My people, as he returneth[25] to Jerusalem[26] from his winter palace[27] in Jericho, and say unto him: "How long[28] wilt thou not take heed[18] of the distress of My people? They call unto thee for help, but thou turnest[29] thy neck upon them. They cry unto thee in their anguish, but thou closest[30] thine ears, so as not to[31] hear their cry. But know, O king,[32] that the Lord heareth their wailing and seeth their evil plight.[33] He is a God of justice and He will require the innocent blood[34] of His flocks[35] from thy hand.'" And it came to pass, as the Lord finished[36] speaking unto me, that I arose and went forth to meet the king, as[37] He had commanded me. And the king saw me standing in the way and he said unto me: 'Whither goest[38] thou, O man of[32] God?' And I opened my mouth and I spake all the words which the Lord had spoken unto me. And the king was exceedingly wroth[39] with me and he said:[40] 'Get thee gone[41] from my presence and see not my face again[42] for, on the day that thou appearest[43] before me, thou shalt surely die.'[44] And I turned away from[45] him and I went on my[46] way, to return to the city.[26]

NOTES ON XXXIX

[1] XXI, 24.

[2] 'were' is not in the Hebrew, 'the sheep *being* . . .'.   [3] I, 45.

[4] Though צֹאן is collective and singular, the plural may be used following it.

[5] Note the difference between וַיָּפֻצוּ, 'and they were scattered', suggesting activity, and וְהֵמָּה מְפֻצָרִים, 'and they were (ones) scattered', suggesting a state or condition. The latter seems more suitable in this context; see also XXX, 17.

[6] '*from* around'.   [7] XXVIII, 32.

[8] וְאֵין, 'there (being) no . . .'.   [9] 'an evil beast'.

[10] 'asunder' is an extension required by the English.

[11] 'and it came to pass, in the crying (out) of the sheep . . .'—infinitive construct.   [12] Modify to 'no one answering', with the participle.

[13] The emphatic ending is expressed as 'and it was torn, even being torn'— infinitive absolute.   [14] לְ.   [15] II, 17.

[16] 'to whom (are) these sheep?'

[17] Expand to 'my people (are) they'.   [18] XXIV, 34.

[19] שָׁלוֹם.   [20] '*he* is'.

[21] 'the (one) sitting'—Qal active participle and article.

[22] 'to me (are) they'.   [23] I, 4.

[24] There are three verbs representing three types of sin, namely: חָטָא, from the root idea of 'missed the mark', 'erred'; עָבַר, 'crossed over', i.e. 'trespassed'; and פָּשַׁע, 'rebelled', suggesting defiance. Of the nouns denoting sin, חֵטְא or the

feminine חַטָּאת and פֶּשַׁע correspond to the first and third verbs, while the noun cognate to the second verb is found only in late Hebrew. However, there is a third word for sin, namely עָוֹן, usually translated 'iniquity', which is cognate to a verbal root עָוָה meaning 'was crooked'.

25 'in his returning'—infinitive construct.   26 Old accusative ending.

27 'a winter palace' is הֵיכַל חֹרֶף, 'his winter palace' is הֵיכַל חָרְפּוֹ, cf. XXI, 28. Note that חֹרֶף is a segholate noun, originally חָרְף, which survived with the suffix. Expand the following phrase to 'which is in Jericho'.

28 Usually expressed as 'till when?', עַד מָתַי.

29 Hiphil of פָּנָה, since it implies 'caused to turn away'. To bring out the effect more sharply use the personal pronoun—'but thou (i.e. as for thee), thou turnest . . . from their face'. The imperfect suggests continuity of the act.

30 XXXIV, 8, and as previous note.   31 *from* hearing'; this, in effect, means 'so as not to hear'.   32 XXIII, 17.   33 I, 63.

34 The plural דָּמִים refers to bloodshed.   35 I, 12.

36 Cf. XXIX, 25.   37 I, 10.

38 Imperfect, suggesting continuity.   39 V, 36.

40 II, 49.   41 'Go for thyself', לֶךְ לְךָ; 'from my presence' is, in Hebrew, 'from my face'.

42 The negative is לֹא for permanent prohibition; 'thou shalt not add to see', cf. X, 17.

43 'in the day of thy appearing (being seen)'—infinitive construct with the suffix; see II, 1.

44 Infinitive absolute before the finite verb.   45 VI, 24.

46 Cf. XXIII, 43.

XL

THE man of God arose and he went forth from the house wherein[1] he was lodged[2] and he stood at the entrance of the city gate, where[3] the people were coming in and going forth. And he lifted up his voice and he called unto the people and he said: 'Gather yourselves[4] unto me and hear the word of the Lord which He hath revealed unto me.' And a great multitude gathered[4] around him[5] and he opened his mouth and he said: "Thus saith the Lord: "If[6] a robber dig[7] under thy house, that[8] he may steal that which is thine,[9] wilt thou not fall upon him and drive him forth from thy house? And if thou canst[10] prevail against him, wilt thou not deliver[11] him unto the judges of thy city, that[8] they may judge him according to[12] the ordinances which are written[13] in the Torah? But,[14] when[6] thou seest[7] a robber digging under thy neighbour's house, while[15] he is on a journey,[16] thou sayest[17] in thy heart: 'Wherefore shall I watch over my neighbour's house and over his goods?'"[18] Therefore[19] thus saith the Lord: "Because thou didst not pity thy neighbour and didst not restrain the hand of the robber, to save that which belongeth[20] to thy neighbour, behold, a band of robbers will fall upon thy house and, when thou criest[21] out in thy distress,[22] none[23] shall hear thy voice and none will come to thy help."' And it came to pass, as the prophet finished[24] speaking, that a young man came forth from amongst those assembled[25] and he said: 'O man of God,[26] thou hast done well[27] to speak to us thus.[28] For, behold, it has indeed[29] been told to us that our brethren, who dwell[30] on the borders[31] of the wilderness, are delivered[11] into the hands[32] of their oppressors. The tribes of the wilderness have come upon them and they have taken as spoil[33] all which they have.[34] Their young men have fallen in battle[35] and their women and little ones[36] have been taken into captivity.[37] We have done evil[38] in abiding[39] here, while our brethren are[40] in distress,[41] for we have said: "This evil[42] is far from us; it shall not come upon us." Therefore I say: "Let every man gird on his sword and follow[43] me, and let us go forth to meet[44] the tribes of the wilderness in battle[35] for, if we do not this thing,[45] they will surely come[29] upon us and they will do to us even[46] as they have done to our brethren."'

NOTES ON XL

[1] 'the house which he (was) lodged there', I, 48.

[2] This is not a passive; the verb is לָן (root לי"ן), 'lodged'.

[3] 'the gate of the city which the people (were) going in and going out in (i.e. through) it', I, 48; 'were' is not expressed, since it does not mean 'had been'. The participle describes the people.

[4] V, 33.   [5] The preposition is עַל, 'on', 'at'.

[6] כִּי (and not אִם) in this case, for it implies a suggestion of 'when', XII, 1.

[7] Imperfect, since future time is indicated.

[8] 'in order that' or, simply, 'to steal'.   [9] 'which (is) to thee'.

[10] XI, 35, and XII, 12.   [11] 'give', as required by the sense.

[12] I, 47.   [13] XIII, 36.   [14] I, 45.

[15] 'and he . . .'.   [16] XXXVIII, 4.

[17] The imperfect implies frequency.   [18] XII, 15.

[19] XVIII, 27.   [20] 'which (is) to . . .'.

[21] 'in thy crying'—infinitive construct.   [22] XX, 37 (a).

[23] XVI, 20. Note: אִישׁ is 'a person'; 'no one' is expressed by the negative: לֹא יִשְׁמַע אִישׁ.   [24] XXIX, 25.

[25] 'the (ones) assembled'—Niphal participle masculine plural with the article.

[26] XXIII, 17.   [27] Hiphil of יטב, 'caused to be good'.

[28] II, 25.   [29] Infinitive absolute before the finite verb.

[30] 'the (ones) dwelling'.   [31] Usually in the singular.

[32] I, 34.   [33] The verb בַּז (root בָּזַז) means 'took as spoil'.

[34] 'which (is) to them'.   [35] XI, 32.   [36] XXIII, 23.

[37] Either the Hophal of גָּלָה or Niphal of שָׁבָה (XXXVII, 2). Another possibility is 'went into captivity', הָלְכוּ בַשֶּׁבִי (with pausal ending).

[38] XVII, 38.   [39] 'in our abiding'.   [40] 'and . . .'.

[41] Use the article.   [42] V, 43.   [43] Simply 'go after me'.

[44] IX, 33.

[45] Either literally or זֹאת, the feminine singular implying 'thing'.

[46] 'even' is required by the English but is not in the Hebrew thought.

XLI

IT came to pass, in the third year after the earthquake, that the word of the Lord came[1] unto me, saying: 'Arise and go forth to Jerusalem,[2] My holy city,[3] and go up on the Mount of Olives and look down[4] upon the city beneath thee. And thou wilt see a company of men coming towards[5] thee and bearing a dead man who has fallen in battle[6] to bury him. And thou shalt draw near unto them and thou shalt speak unto them the words which I shall put into thy mouth.' And I did as the Lord commanded me and I went up on the Mount of Olives and I saw the city spread[7] out beneath me and its appearance was as a fortress within its walls.[8] And upon the walls stood[9] the watchers with[10] weapons of war in their hands and in the city there was a great noise[11] like the sound of thunder, and the heavens were illumined[12] as with lightning, and a heavy smoke went up from the city towards the heavens.[2] And I saw,

and behold, a company of men were[13] coming up on the mountain towards me[5] and they were[14] bearing a dead man for
burial, and at their head was an old man, weeping as he went.[15]
And I drew near unto them and the spirit of the Lord came[1]
upon me and I opened my mouth and I said: 'O inhabitants
of Jerusalem, thus saith the Lord: "I have indeed[16] heard the
cry of Jerusalem which cometh unto Me and I have seen the
affliction within its gates. Strangers from afar have come and
they seek to destroy My holy city,[3] for the fear of Me[17] is not
in their hearts and they have profaned My holy name.[3] The
young men are slain[18] in battle[6] and the babes are asking for
bread. But I say unto these strange peoples: 'Cease to do evil[19]
unto My people, for I shall be silent no longer.[20] Return ye to
the lands whence ye[21] came, lest I pour out Mine anger against
you and cause you to perish from[22] the face of the earth. And,
when ye come again[23] to Jerusalem,[2] come ye to serve Me, for
Jerusalem shall be a holy city[24] unto all the nations of the
earth. No longer[25] shall it be called the city of slaughter, but[26]
a city of peace. The violence within it shall cease and tranquillity shall dwell therein: I, the Lord, have spoken.'"'

NOTES ON XLI

[1] XXI, 24.   [2] Old accusative ending.   [3] Cf. XXI, 28.
[4] XXXI, 17.   [5] IX, 33.   [6] XI, 32.
[7] Passive participle feminine singular of פָּרַשׁ.   [8] XII, 8.
[9] The sense here is taking up a position, the Niphal of יצב (also Hithpael) as
opposed to the inactive עָמַד, see WHG 192 note.
[10] 'and . . .'.   [11] שָׁאוֹן, meaning 'tumult', 'din'.
[12] Niphal of אוֹר, 'was light', i.e. 'became lit up'. The Niphal imperfect of
the normal 'Ayin Waw verb קָם is יָקוֹם, but since the first radical in אוֹר is a
guttural the imperfect is יֵאוֹר.
[13] 'a company of men coming'—'were' is required by the English.
[14] 'and they bearing'—'were' is required by the English.
[15] The Hebrew idiom is 'and he went, going and weeping'—the latter two
verbs being infinitive absolute. The first is not meant to be understood as
'walking', but in the auxiliary sense of 'keeping on . . .', and may be used with
inanimate objects.
[16] Infinitive absolute before the finite verb.   [17] See XV, 23.
[18] The adjective חָלָל meaning 'pierced'; perhaps 'have fallen, pierced'.
[19] See VII, 26.   [20] See X, 17.

[21] 'the lands which ye came from there', I, 48.   [22] VI, 24.
[23] 'And as (or 'in') your coming again'—infinitive construct.
[24] I, 57.   [25] 'she shall not be called again'.   [26] XII, 17.

XLII

In that night I lay upon my couch and sleep wandered[1] from mine eyes. And it came to pass, in the middle of the night, that I called[2] a musician that he should play[3] before me and,[4] as he played, my spirit was quietened and a deep sleep[5] fell upon me and I slept.[6] And I dreamed a dream and behold, an angel of God appeared[7] unto me and he touched[8] mine eyes and he said unto me: 'Son of man, open[9] thine eyes and see that which the Lord showeth[10] thee.' And I opened[9] mine eyes and behold, I was[11] standing in a great garden, wherein[12] there were fruit trees[13] without number.[14] And in this garden there were[15] many paths and they all led[16] to two mighty trees which were in the midst of the garden, the like of which[17] I had not seen. Upon the one tree there were many branches and leaves, but there was no fruit thereon.[18] The other[19] tree was exceedingly[2] pleasing[20] to mine eyes, for upon it was an abundance of fruit.[21] And I saw and behold, a man drew near unto this tree and in his hand was[22] an axe and he smote[23] the tree, as if[24] to cut it down. And mine anger was kindled[25] against that man and I cried out and I said: 'O wicked man,[26] wherefore destroyest[27] thou this tree which giveth forth[28] its fruit to the sons of man? Cease to do this evil[29] and cast away the axe from thy hand.' And the man turned unto me and he said: 'Thou seest these two great trees in the midst of the garden. The one upon which[30] there is no fruit is[31] the tree of knowledge, of which[32] the sons of man have eaten to satiety and have left nothing[33] but[34] the leaves. The other[19] tree, whereof[35] the fruit gladdeneth[36] thy heart, is the tree of lovingkindness, but[37] they have rejected[38] it and have left its fruit upon it, that it may rot.[39] Because they desire[40] not the fruit of the tree of lovingkindness, I shall cut it down[41] and I shall pluck up its roots, for it availeth not.[42] Oh, would that[43] the sons of man had eaten also from this tree, for knowledge[44] and lovingkindness[44] are the two pillars upon which[45] the kingdom of man resteth.'[46] And it came to pass, as he finished[47] speaking, that my soul was greatly affrighted[48] and I awoke.[49] And I understood that which the Lord had revealed unto me and I knew that He had chosen me[50] to be a prophet unto Him and to declare His words to the sons of man.

NOTES ON XLII

[1] The verb is גָדַד. The imperfect Qal is יָדֹד, but the form יָדַד is found also.

[2] I, 22.   [3] 'to play'; the English expands.

[4] 'and it came to pass, as his playing'—infinitive construct with the suffix.

[5] תַּרְדֵּמָה means 'deep sleep'. Note the order of words: 'and fell upon me a deep sleep'.

[6] יָשֵׁן, 'was asleep', 'slept', is a stative verb and a Pe Yod; the imperfect is יִישַׁן.   [7] II, 1.   [8] XXXII, 33.

[9] The special verb for opening the eyes is פָּקַח.   [10] XI, 15.

[11] 'behold I (a person) standing'. The participle describes the subject; see IX, 25.   [12] Rephrase 'and in it (there being) . . .'.

[13] 'trees of fruit', cf. I, 57.   [14] XXII, 6.

[15] '(there being) many paths'. In Hebrew הָיוּ would suggest 'there had been'. The English requires 'were'.

[16] 'and all of them (XI, 5 (b)) leading' (XIII, 5—participle).

[17] 'which like them . . .'.   [18] i.e. 'upon it'.   [19] 'second'.

[20] Cf. IV, 47.   [21] 'fruit to abundance', לָרֹב.

[22] 'in this hand (there being) an axe'.   [23] XII, 18; WHG 225.

[24] 'as if' is implied by the Hebrew and expressed by the English.

[25] V, 36.   [26] See XXIII, 17. The masculine singular adjective רָשָׁע by itself means 'a wicked man'; similarly חָכָם by itself means 'a wise man', 'a sage', and זָקֵן 'an old man', an elder'.

[27] Imperfect, since the act is not completed.

[28] The Hebrew usually has, simply, 'which giveth'. Use the participle with the article as a verbal adjective—'the tree, the (one) giving'.   [29] V, 43.

[30] 'the one which there is not fruit upon it', I, 48.

[31] Insert 'it is . . .'.

[32] 'which the sons of man have eaten of it'.

[33] The Hebrew phrasing would be 'until without (בִּלְתִּי) leaving (Hiphil infinitive construct of שָׁאַר) to it anything (מְאוּמָה)'.

[34] The contrast after the negative statement implied by the English 'but' is expressed by כִּי אִם when a noun follows and by כִּי only when a verbal idea follows.   [35] 'the other tree which its fruit . . .'; see note 19 above.

[36] Piel of שָׂמַח, 'was glad', produces the idea 'made glad', cf. XXII, 13.

³⁷ Use the personal pronoun to emphasize 'they'; see also I, 45.

³⁸ XXVII, 19.

³⁹ 'and it will rot', using the imperfect with Waw conjunctive as a jussive.

⁴⁰ The perfect, since one can only speak of desiring when that condition is complete. Add 'for them(selves)'.

⁴¹ 'I shall *indeed* cut it'; infinitive absolute before the finite verb, or 'I shall cut it', 'even cutting'—infinitive absolute.

⁴² Hiphil of יעל (originally וֹעל). The imperfect suggests continuity.

⁴³ VII, 42 (*a*).   ⁴⁴ The article is used with abstract nouns.

⁴⁵ 'the pillars which . . . resteth upon them', I, 48.

⁴⁶ Niphal participle of כון, namely נָכוֹן, means 'is made firm'.

⁴⁷ XXIX, 25.   ⁴⁸ XXXIII, 18.   ⁴⁹ XXXII, 21.

⁵⁰ 'chosen in me (XI, 25 (*a*)) unto Him as (ל) a prophet'.

XLIII

WHEN I saw¹ the works of the sons of man, my spirit was troubled² within me, and the Lord had not revealed His word unto me. And it came to pass, in that night, that I prayed unto the Lord and I said:³ 'O Lord, my God, show me⁴ that which shall befall⁵ the sons of man at the end of the days.' And I lay down⁶ upon my couch and a deep sleep⁷ fell upon mine eyelids and I slept.⁸ And I dreamed a dream and, behold, in my dream, I was⁹ standing before a very great mountain, the top of which¹⁰ reached¹¹ unto the heavens.¹² And upon the mountain were¹³ many paths and they all led¹⁴ to the top thereof. And I saw a great multitude of men ascending upon these paths without respite¹⁵ and they bore¹⁶ heavy burdens upon their shoulders. And I was astounded¹⁷ at this wondrous sight and I heard a voice saying:¹⁸ 'The mountain which thou beholdest is the likeness of the whole earth¹⁹ and the paths thereon²⁰ are the paths of life²¹ and they lead¹⁴ to tranquillity and rest. The burdens which thou seest upon the shoulders of those who are ascending²² are their evil deeds and these they must²³ bear till they²⁴ reach the end of the path at the top of the mountain.' And my spirit was affrighted²⁵ when I heard²⁶ these words and I cried out in the anguish of my soul: 'How long,²⁷ O Lord, shall the sons of man be afflicted thus?'[28] Then I heard the voice speaking unto me again, saying:[29] 'Until[24] they learn to walk in the ways of righteousness, to love justice, and to practise[30] lovingkindness with one another.[31] In that day, the Lord will remove[32] the burdens from their[33] shoulders and they will walk with upright stature.[34] And the mountain shall become a plain[35] and the top thereof[36] shall be in the midst of it and the paths shall become straight.[37] And no man[38] shall lift up a sword against his fellow man, nor shall there be any strife amongst them and the earth shall be called[39] the garden of the Lord and the sons of man His children.' Then I awoke[40] from my sleep and, behold, it was[41] a dream. And I arose from[33] my couch and I fell upon my face to the ground[12] and I prayed unto the Lord and I said:[3] 'I give thanks[42] unto Thee, O Lord, for Thou didst not forsake Thy servant and Thou hast revealed unto me that which I shall declare unto the sons of man. Send me,[43] O Lord, and I shall speak[44] in Thy name, for I am filled[45] with the spirit of understanding.'

NOTES ON XLIII

[1] 'in my seeing'—infinitive construct with suffix.   [2] Niphal of פעם.

[3] II, 36.   [4] XI, 15.

[5] Though the usual formula is קָרָה ל (XXII, 18), one also finds the verb קָרָא (with a terminal 'Alep) followed by a direct object; see also IX, 33.

[6] IV, 16.   [7] XLII, 5.   [8] XLII, 6.

[9] 'I standing'—'was' is required by the English.

[10] 'its head'.

[11] The verb is the Hiphil of נָגַע, 'touched', namely הִגִּיעַ, 'caused to touch', i.e. 'reached'. The sense is 'its head reaching'—participle.

[12] Old accusative ending.

[13] The verb הָיוּ would suggest 'there had been'; the sense is '(there being) many paths'.

[14] Consistent with above, the sense is 'leading'—participle; see XI, 5 (b) for 'all of them', and XIII, 5 for the verb.

[15] Either a direct translation or the syntactical use of the infinitive absolute of הָלַךְ, i.e. הָלֹךְ וְעָלֹה, 'keeping on ascending', XLI, 15.

[16] 'and they bearing', as in notes 9, 11, and 14 above.

[17] The reflexive of the double 'Ayin verb שָׁמַם. Two adjustments are to be noted in the form. Since the middle radical is already doubled (as the third radical) the form of the reflexive is not Hithpael (with the doubling of the medial radical, as הִתְגַּדֵּל), but Hithpolel (as, from the root גָּלַל, 'rolled', it is

הִתְגּוֹלֵל). Furthermore, since the first radical is a sibilant, the ת of the prefix הִת is transposed with the first radical, producing הִשְׁתּוֹמֵם, WHG 120 note. Similarly, the reflexive of סָבַב is the Hithpolel הִסְתּוֹבֵב.

[18] Participle, since it qualifies 'voice'.

[19] Adjust to 'of the earth, the whole of it', XI, 5.   [20] 'on it'.

[21] II, 6. Expand to 'the paths of life (are) they'.

[22] 'the (ones) ascending'—active participle Qal masculine plural with the article.

[23] The effect is brought out by phrasing the clause 'they shall bear, even bearing'—with the infinitive absolute.

[24] 'until *that* they shall reach', cf. I, 10.   [25] XXXIII, 18.

[26] 'as my hearing'—infinitive construct with suffix.   [27] XXXIX, 28.

[28] II, 25.   [29] As opposed to note 18 above, here it is לֵאמֹר, I, 16.

[30] 'to do'.   [31] 'one with the other', VI, 42.   [32] XVIII, 30.

[33] 'from upon', VI, 24.   [34] The abstract noun קוֹמְמִיּוּת, root קוֹם.

[35] 'as (in Hebrew 'for') a plain'.   [36] As note 10 above.

[37] The verb יָשַׁר, 'was straight', is a stative and the Piel makes it a causative or transitive (XXII, 13, 26), i.e. 'caused to be straight', i.e. 'made straight'. The Pual is, thus, appropriate—'will be made straight'.

[38] The negative לֹא before the verb gives אִישׁ (XI, 17) the sense 'no one'

[39] Adjust to 'to the earth (it) shall be called'.   [40] XXXII, 21.

[41] '(it being) a dream'.   [42] Imperfect.

[43] Add 'I pray thee'.

[44] To suggest eagerness use the cohortative with Waw conjunctive.

[45] Perfect, V, 32.

XLIV

THE word of the Lord came[1] unto me, saying: 'Son of man, wouldst thou indeed see[2] that which shall befall[3] the sons of man in the days which shall come?[4] Behold, I shall show[5] thee.' And I was borne on high[6] on the wings of the wind and I saw beneath[7] me lofty mountains and deep valleys and mighty rivers flowing[8] towards the sea.[9] And the Lord set me upon a cloud and He said unto me: 'Open[10] thine eyes and look down[11] upon the earth and see what[12] the sons of men[13] are doing.' And I opened[10] mine eyes and I beheld a city situated[14] upon the slope[15] of a mountain and the appearance thereof[16] was fair, as a precious stone in a kingly crown.[17] And there was peace and tranquillity all around it[18] and my heart rejoiced within me. Then suddenly I heard a loud noise, as the sound of a swarm[19] of bees, and I saw a host of mighty birds, whose flesh[20] was of iron, and they flew towards the city.[9] And they swooped down upon it and they rained down[21] fire and brimstone upon it. And the earth quaked and was cleft asunder[22] and there were[23] mighty sounds as of wrathful thundering[24] and flames of fire as of devouring lightning. And a terrible cry came up from the city and its inhabitants went down alive into the bowels of the earth. And great pillars of smoke arose towards the heavens[9] and there remained of this city only[25] a mound of ruins and a dreaded silence. And a great terror seized me and the hair of my head stood on end[26] and my heart trembled within me and was turned[27] to stone. And I cried out in the bitterness of my soul: 'Wherefore hath this destruction come upon the sons of men?[13] What is their sin that thou wouldst utterly cut them off[28] from[29] the face of the earth?' And the Lord answered and said: 'Behold, I have given wisdom and understanding into the heart of man, that[30] he may live by them; but he hath rejected[31] the way of life and he hath fashioned for himself weapons of death. Therefore by his own cunning shall he perish. Yet,[32] if he chooseth[33] the way of life, to love his neighbour and to practise[34] justice, then shall I turn My countenance unto him and make the light of peace shine[35] upon him. Behold, I have given him good[36] and evil,[36] life[36] and death;[36] let him choose[37] goodness[36] and life.'[36]

NOTES ON XLIV

[1] XXI, 24.

[2] The shade of meaning expressed by the English 'wouldst thou . . .' is implied by the imperfect in the context. The infinitive absolute before the finite verb expresses emphasis.

[3] XLIII, 5, and I, 38.

[4] 'the days, the (ones) coming'—participle.   [5] XI, 15.

[6] 'in (or to) the height' with the noun מָרוֹם, root רוּם, with the preformative מ, III, 27.   [7] VII, 42 (b).   [8] The verb is הָלַךְ.

[9] Old accusative ending.   [10] XLII, 9.

[11] XXXI, 17.   [12] 'that which', I, 38.

[13] 'sons of man', since the word 'man' means 'mankind', XI, 17.

[14] 'dwelling'—thus giving the city a personality.

[15] מוֹרָד, from the root יָרַד, 'descended', with preformative מ, III, 27, i.e. 'place of descent', 'slope'. [16] 'its appearance'.

[17] 'a crown of kingship', I, 57. [18] XII, 9.

[19] עֵדָה, literally 'community', means 'swarm' when referring to bees.

[20] Rephrase to 'and their flesh (being) iron'.

[21] Hiphil of מטר, 'caused to rain', i.e. 'sent down rain'.

[22] 'asunder' may be expressed by לִשְׁנַיִם, 'in twain', or considered to be implied in the verb itself.

[23] Rephrase to 'and behold, mighty sounds'.

[24] Use the verb זָעַם, which contains the idea of foaming and raging.

[25] An alternative to a direct rendering is a negative formulation, thus: 'there remained not . . . but (or except) (XLII, 34) a mound of ruins'.

[26] The verb סָמַר means 'stood on end', 'bristled'.

[27] The Hebrew is, simply, 'and it became (root הָיָה) as (in Hebrew לְ)'.

[28] The Hiphil of כָּרַת is used in the sense of destroying life.

[29] 'from upon', VI, 24. [30] 'in order that he shall . . .'.

[31] XXVII, 19. [32] אַךְ, implying 'surely', 'only'.

[33] XI, 25 (a). [34] 'to do'.

[35] The Hiphil of אוֹר, 'was light', namely הֵאִיר, means 'caused to be light', 'gave light', 'illumined', 'made shine'.

[36] The article is used for abstract nouns.

[37] The jussive is implied by the imperfect in the context.

XLV

IN[1] that night the prophet arose secretly[2] and he fled from the city to the wilderness[3] and he hid himself[4] in a cave and he abode there, for he said unto himself:[5] 'Let me not see[6] the distress of my brethren.' And the Lord spoke unto him and said: 'Son of man, what doest thou here?'[7] And the prophet answered and said: 'Lord, God of all flesh, Who knowest[8] the thoughts of every man and Who seest[8] the works of their hands, I have forsaken the habitation of the wicked to seek peace and tranquillity. For, behold, in the cities there is violence and oppression. Righteousness is forsaken[9] as a widow and truth as an orphan. Evil have they raised on high[10] and wrongdoing have they crowned with glory. The judges have corrupted their ways and they honour the face of the rich. They take unto themselves the food of the needy and the garments of the poor do they rob.[11] And if[12] there is found one[13] who raiseth[14] his voice against this evil, they seize[15] him and cast[16] him into the pit.[3] And if it be told[14] that there is one[13] who seeketh[17] justice, they put him to death[18] by the sword.[19] Woe to mine eyes which have seen[20] these things;[21] woe to mine ears which have heard[22] deceit and lying. And now, O Lord, take, I pray thee, my life[23] from me, for the sorrow is too great to[24] bear.' And the Lord spoke unto him, saying: 'Son of man, thou hast done evil[25] in fleeing from the city. Was it not for this[26] that I sent thee unto the rulers of the people? Go, return to the city[3] whence[27] thou hast come and be not silent,[28] but[29] teach the ways of My Torah. Strengthen[30] the hands of the weak and bind the wounds of the sick. Speak words of comfort to the widow and give of thy bread to the fatherless. Gather together[31] the few upright men who are left[32] in the city and bid them go after thee and do as thou doest.[33] For iniquity shall not rule for ever[34] over the hearts of men.[35] And,[36] when they see[37] thy works of mercy,[38] they shall be ashamed of their deeds and they will repent[39] of the violence of their hands. Arise, then, and return unto the city[3] in the light of the day, and do according to all[40] which I have commanded thee.'

NOTES ON XLV

[1] One may, if one wishes, begin with 'and it came to pass . . . that the prophet arose'.   [2] בַּסֵּתֶר or בַּלָּט or adverbially חֶרֶשׁ.

[3] Old accusative ending.   [4] XXVIII, 5.   [5] IV, 35.

[6] The imperfect serves as cohortative, since the Lamed He verb cannot have a lengthened form (the terminal radical being silent). The negative is אַל.

[7] XXXVIII, 11.

[8] 'the (one) knowing . . . the (one) seeing'—the participle with the article.

[9] Qal passive participle.   [10] XLIV, 6.

[11] Add 'unto themselves'.

[12] XL, 6; the imperfect is to be used.   [13] XI, 17.   [14] Imperfect.

[15] Imperfect of the Pe 'Alep verb (WHG 162) אָחַז.

[16] Hiphil of שלך. For emphasis reverse the order: 'into the pit they (shall) cast him'—imperfect.

[17] The Hebrew is 'a man seeking'.   [18] XVIII, 46.

[19] Use the pausal form, WHG 137 (e).   [20] 'the (ones) seeing', XXII, 19.

[21] XII, 52.

[22] As in note 20 above we may rephrase 'the (ones) hearing'.

²³ II, 6.   ²⁴ 'great more than (מִן of comparison) bearing'.
²⁵ Hiphil of רעע (cf. VII, 26) followed by ל with infinitive construct.
²⁶ Feminine singular implying 'this thing'.
²⁷ 'the city which thou hast come from there', I, 48.
²⁸ The verb חָרַשׁ, meaning 'was deaf', 'was dumb', is a stative and is used for maintaining silence. The negative is אַל with imperfect.
²⁹ XII, 17, 'but thou shalt teach'.   ³⁰ XXIX, 9.   ³¹ V, 33.
³² XXXVII, 29.   ³³ Imperfect.   ³⁴ 'not for ever shall . . .'.
³⁵ The singular אָדָם meaning 'mankind'.
³⁶ 'and it shall come to pass . . .'.
³⁷ 'as their seeing'—infinitive construct with suffix.
³⁸ The plural of חֶסֶד means 'kind deeds', 'works of mercy'.
³⁹ 'turn back', root שׁוּב.   ⁴⁰ I, 47.

XLVI

THE king of Babylon made[1] a great feast[2] for all his princes and he commanded his servants to bring forth[3] the vessels of gold and silver[4] which he had taken from the house of the Lord in Jerusalem, to show them to all who had assembled[5] in his palace. And it came to pass, while they were eating and drinking[6] and making merry,[7] that they saw a hand writing upon the wall, and they were exceedingly afraid.[8] And the king called his wise men[9] and he said unto them: 'Tell me[10] the words which are written[11] upon this wall, and if ye are not able[12] to tell me,[10] death will be your judgement.' And one of the wise men drew near unto the king and he said: 'Behold, there is among the servants of my lord a prophet of the Hebrews whom the king hath taken into exile[13] and he knoweth how[14] to interpret hidden things.[15] If it pleaseth[16] the king, let us call him hither, that he may read the words which are written[11] upon this wall.' And the king commanded them to do so, and they went and they brought[17] in the Hebrew prophet before the king. And the king said unto him: 'Art thou able[18] to read the words which are upon this wall, for they were not written by the hand of a man?' And the prophet said unto him: 'Behold, the interpretation of the words. Thou hast lifted up thy heart and wast not afraid[19] to sin against[20] the Lord, God of Israel, and thou didst bring forth[3] the vessels of His holy house[21] to jest with them before thy princes. Therefore the Lord hath removed[22] thee from being king[23] over this people and He hath given thy throne to another, who will rise up against thee.' And,[24] when the prophet finished[25] speaking, he turned away from[26] the presence of the king and he went forth. And the king was sorely afraid[8] and he said: 'Bring back[27] the prophet of the Hebrews, that he may tell us that which we shall do, for there hath not been a thing such as this,[28] from the day Babylon was founded[29] till now.' And they brought the prophet back[27] and he spoke unto the king and he said: 'O king, if thou desirest to do that which pleaseth[16] the Lord, my God, place the holy vessels in a room in thy palace and keep them there till the day my people is restored[30] unto its land and the house of the Lord rebuilt.'[31]

NOTES ON XLVI

[1] Begin with Waw consecutive.   [2] V, 34.   [3] I, 25.

[4] 'The vessels of gold and the vessels of silver', see WHG 46 note.

[5] See XVII, 33.   [6] XVII, 29.   [7] XVII, 30.

[8] I, 61 (b), and II, 20.   [9] I, 22, and XLII, 26 (b).

[10] 'to me'.   [11] See XIII, 36.   [12] XI, 35.

[13] XXXVII, 2.   [14] 'how' is supplied in English.

[15] Feminine plural participle Niphal of סתר, the feminine plural implying 'things'.

[16] See IV, 47.   [17] I, 26.   [18] XII, 11.

[19] WHG 211.   [20] In Hebrew 'to'.   [21] XXI, 28.

[22] XVIII, 30.

[23] 'from reigning'—infinitive construct, since מָלַךְ means 'reigned', 'was king'.   [24] Expand to 'and it came to pass . . .'.

[25] XXIX, 25.

[26] 'from *with* the presence (i.e. 'face') of', VI, 24.   [27] I, 51.

[28] Contract to 'there hath not been as this', II, 25.

[29] 'from the day of the being-founded of Babylon'—infinitive construct Niphal of יָסַד (originally וָסַד, WHG 191).

[30] 'the day of the being-restored of my people'—infinitive construct Hophal of שוב, following note 27 above.

[31] 'and in the being-built of the house of the Lord'—infinitive construct Niphal. Alternatively, one might render 'and the house of the Lord shall be rebuilt', placing the noun first.

XLVII

THERE arose[1] a new king over Babylon, who remembered not
the events which happened[2] in the days of his father, and his
heart was haughty[3] and he called[4] his servants and he said
unto them: 'I am your god; build ye temples unto me in all
the cities of my kingdom and set ye up[5] therein images in[6] my
likeness, and command ye the people to bow down[7] before my
image, in the manner[8] in which they have served the gods of
Babylon heretofore.'[9] And it came to pass, as he finished[10]
speaking, that a voice, loud and terrible, was heard, calling:
'Who art thou, O one born[11]of a woman, that thou wouldst
make thyself[12] a god? Art thou not flesh and blood, as the
meanest[13] amongst the servants of thy kingdom? And now,
hear the judgement which the Lord, God of the whole earth,
hath proclaimed[14] against[15] thee. Before[16] thy temples are
built, thy cities will be laid[17] in ruins. Before[16] thy servants
worship[18] thine images, they will fall in battle.[19] For, behold, a
mighty host approacheth[20] Babylon and will lay siege[21] against
the city and will burn it[22] in fire.[23] Thou and thy nobles will
be taken into captivity[24] in a strange land and thy kingdom
will be turned[25] into mounds of desolation.' And it came to
pass, when the king heard[26] these words, that he was sorely
afraid,[27] and he went down from[28] his throne and he put off[29]
his royal garments and he sat upon the ground. And he said
unto his counsellors: 'Know ye[30] a man in whom[31] is the spirit
of God, the Lord of the whole earth, that I may inquire[32] of
him that which will find favour in the sight[33] of the Lord? For
I fear[34] the voice which spoke unto me.' And one of his counsellors said unto him: 'My Lord, O king,[35] there is amongst
us a Hebrew who doth minister[36] unto thee at thy table, and
his name is Daniel, and he is filled with[37] the spirit of wisdom.'
And the king commanded and they hastened and they
brought[38] Daniel into the presence of[39] the king and they told
him[40] that which had happened. And Daniel said: 'I am the

servant of the Lord, God of all the earth, and He hath revealed His word unto me, saying: "Behold, Babylon shall be laid waste, for even[41] as they have done to the nations which are on her borders, so shall it be done unto her. And, because the king's heart is haughty, I am hastening to accomplish[42] this thing." '[43]

NOTES ON XLVII

[1] Begin with Waw consecutive.

[2] The Hebrew thought is much contracted: 'the (things) happening', i.e. the feminine plural (implying 'things') active participle Qal of קָרָה. The English expands to 'the events which happened'.

[3] i.e. 'was high' expressed either by (a) the verb רָם (root רוּם) or (b) the verb גָּבַהּ. Note that, in the latter verb, there is a mappiq in the terminal radical, indicating that the letter is (not a silent vowel-letter, but) a fully sounded consonant, WHG 17. The imperfect is יִגְבַּהּ, again with mappiq.   [4] I, 22.

[5] The Hiphil (a) of קָם (root קוּם), 'arose', i.e. 'caused to rise up', 'raised up', or (b) of יָצַב, 'stood in a position', i.e. 'caused to stand' or 'set up in a position', see WHG 192 note.

[6] 'as my . . .'.   [7] II, 61.   [8] XI, 6.   [9] XXIX, 48.

[10] 'as his finishing'—infinitive construct with suffix, see XXIX, 25.

[11] Either (a) the passive participle Qal construct of יָלַד, i.e. יְלוּד, or (b) the construct of the passive adjective יָלִיד, i.e. יְלִיד.

[12] The Niphal of עָשָׂה, with passive-reflexive effect, WHG 226.

[13] 'smallest'; the superlative is expressed by the article, WHG 136.

[14] Hiphil of שָׁמַע, 'heard', namely 'caused to hear', i.e. 'published', 'proclaimed'.   [15] The preposition is עַל, see VII, 16.

[16] See III, 32.   [17] 'shall become (root הָיָה) as (in Hebrew 'for') . . .'.

[18] 'serve' or 'bow down before', II, 61.   [19] XI, 32.

[20] 'drawing near *unto*'.   [21] The verb צָר (root צוּר).

[22] The simplest verb is שָׂרַף.   [23] 'in *the* fire'.

[24] Either Qal of גָּלָה or the Hophal, XXXVII, 2.   [25] As note 17 above.

[26] III, 2.   [27] 'exceedingly afraid', I, 61 (b); II, 20, 46.

[28] 'from *upon* his throne', VI, 24.

[29] (a) The Qal of פָּשַׁט or Hiphil of סָר (root סוּר), XVIII, 30. (b) In Hebrew 'he put off from upon him(self) . . .', see VI, 24. (c) 'royal garments' is, in Hebrew, 'garments of kingship', בִּגְדֵי מַלְכוּת I, 57; 'his royal garments' is, then, בִּגְדֵי מַלְכוּתוֹ, see XXI, 28.

[30] II, 18, and WHG 80 for pointing He interrogative before shewa.

[31] 'who the spirit of God is in him', I, 48.

[32] The cohortative with Waw conjunctive expresses urgency.

[33] I, 40.   [34] VII, 31.   [35] XXIII, 17.

[36] Piel of שׁרת.   [37] V, 31 (a).   [38] I, 26.

[39] 'before'.   [40] 'told *to* him', VII, 2.

[41] simply 'as (that) which'. 'Even' is supplied by the English.

[42] 'to do'.   [43] II, 25 note; or direct translation.

XLVIII

SON of man, lift up[1] a banner unto the peoples and proclaim[2] freedom unto the captives,[3] for Mercy hath raised[4] its voice and Justice hath stretched forth[5] its arm. The rod of the tyrant is broken and the yoke of the oppressor hath been thrown off.[6] The taunt of the taskmaster hath ceased and the mouth of the scoffer is shut.[7] The sword of the redeemer hath devoured and the feet of the avenger hath trampled down. The Lord hath executed[8] vengeance upon His enemies and those who rose[9] against Him hath He brought low.[10] Rejoice, O ye heavens,[11] and be glad, and thou, O earth,[11] break forth with[12] shouts of joy;[13] for evil hath been swept away from the land and righteousness brought back[14] from captivity. Yet turn thee,[15] son of man, unto the peoples of the west and say unto them: 'The Lord hath not forgotten the days of your tranquillity, when ye beheld[16] wrongdoing and oppression in the earth and ye said in your hearts:[17] "This evil[18] is of afar; it shall not come upon us. Wherefore shall we go forth to stay the hands of the evildoers,[19] when[20] it is well with us?" And ye closed[21] your eyes lest[22] ye see, and ye stopped[23] your ears lest[22] ye hear, and ye placed a bolt upon the gates of your hearts, lest pity enter therein. Go ye, therefore, forth into the lands of desolation and deal kindly[24] with the remnant of the people. Feed[25] the hungry, clothe[26] the naked, bind up the wounded, succour the needy, comfort the widow and protect the fatherless. For only thus shall the shame of this generation be rolled away[27] and the cry of innocent blood be stilled.[28] Acknowledge[29] your transgression and do ye good,[30] for the Lord is of much[31] mercy.' Then set thy face unto the afflicted ones of the people and say unto them: 'Be ye comforted, O My people, for help from afar doth come. Your cities shall be rebuilt[32] and your fields shall again be ploughed. And I shall send My blessing upon the fruit of your land and upon the increase[33] of your cattle and ye shall eat bread in satiety.[34] Yet shall the laughter

of the young men and the maidens be heard in the broad
places[35] of your cities and the song of the reaper in the field.
Be ye strong[36] and of good courage, for peace[37] and righteousness[37] shall reign over the hearts[17] of man.'

NOTES ON XLVIII

[1] Either Qal of נָשָׂא or Hiphil of רָם (root רום), 'was high', i.e. 'caused to be
high', 'lifted up', 'raised up'.

[2] XLVII, 14.   [3] Qal passive participle masculine plural of שָׁבָה,
WHG 217.

[4] As note 1 above, the first verb generally preceding an utterance.

[5] נָטָה is used with both זְרוֹעַ, 'arm', and יָד, 'hand', though שָׁלַח is also used
with the latter.   [6] XXXV, 11.

[7] סָתַם means 'stopped up' an opening.

[8] Either the verb עָשָׂה with the noun 'vengeance' or the Niphal of נקם, meaning 'hath avenged himself'.

[9] 'the (ones) rising up'—active participle masculine plural Qal with the
article.

[10] Hiphil of the stative verb שָׁפֵל, 'was low', i.e. 'caused to be low', 'brought
low'.   [11] XXIII, 17.   [12] The verb is פָּצָה and takes a direct object.

[13] רִנָּה means 'joyful shouting'.   [14] Hophal of שָׁב (root שׁוב), I, 51.

[15] Imperative of פָּנָה followed by לָךְ, 'for thyself'.

[16] 'in your beholding', i.e. 'seeing'—infinitive construct with suffix.

[17] Singular as collective.   [18] V, 43.

[19] 'doers of evil'—Qal active participle masculine plural construct.

[20] 'and (it) being well', וְטוֹב.   [21] עָצַם is used for closing the eyes.

[22] Idiomatically the phrase would be 'from (as a negative) hearing, seeing'.

[23] XXXIV, 8.   [24] II, 52.

[25] Hiphil of אָכַל, 'ate', i.e. 'caused to eat', 'fed', IX, 40.

[26] XXIX, 7.   [27] The verb is גלל.   [28] Niphal of דמם.

[29] The sense is 'confess', i.e. Hithpael of ידה (originally ודה), הִתְוַדָּה.

[30] Hiphil of יטב, 'caused to be good', i.e. 'did good'.

[31] 'much of mercy'.   [32] בָּנָה in this context means 're-built'.

[33] 'fruit'.   [34] 'to satiety'.   [35] XXXVIII, 9.

[36] XIV, 21.   [37] Use the article for an abstract noun.

XLIX

IN the third month of the second year after the war of the
nations the word of the Lord came[1] unto me, saying: 'Dost
thou remember[2] the day on which[3] the righteous nations

girded on the sword of vengeance and they went forth into battle[4] against Mine enemies? The princes of these peoples gathered[5] together and took counsel together,[6] in order to cast down[7] the evil[8] which held dominion over[9] the face of the earth. And they made[10] a covenant and they swore[11] to one another[12] to pursue[13] peace[14] and lovingkindness.[14] And their assembly was pleasing[15] in My sight,[16] for they were My rod of correction[17] to chastise those who had rebelled[18] against Me. And I delivered[19] the evildoers[20] into their hands[21] and they smote them grievously[22] and brought them low,[23] and they laid their cities waste and made[24] them into heaps of ruins.[25] And they continued[26] to perform[27] great deeds,[28] for they brought succour to the captives,[29] they fed[30] the hungry, they bound the wounds of the sick and they gave freedom to those who were enslaved.[31] And the people of the earth sang a song of praise to those who had delivered[32] them and they said: "Wickedness hath been crushed to the earth[33] and it shall not raise[34] its head again.[35] Peace shall reign upon the earth and justice shall rule over[36] the sons of man." But see what[37] the rulers of the earth are doing! They speak[38] no more of peace, for there is war in their hearts.[39] They speak falsely[40] against each other[12] in their assemblies and they covet that which is not theirs.[41] Go thou, therefore,[42] into their assembly and admonish them, lest the fruits[43] of deliverance be turned to wormwood and they die of their own[44] folly. Wherefore should[45] they fear for their safety, when[46] the power of evil is broken? Wherefore should[45] men be hungry, when[46] the earth is full of[47] My bounty? Surely[48] they are sated with[49] the work of destruction, that they prepare themselves again for war![4] Behold, the sons of man are weary in spirit and they seek tranquillity and safety. They have cleansed[50] the earth, that it be not defiled again; they have enthroned[51] peace that it should abide.[52] Recall[53] unto them the words of the covenant which they made[10] with each other,[54] that they may do according to that which[55] they have sworn.[11] Then[56] shall My spirit continue[26] to dwell amongst them and shall not depart from their midst.'

NOTES ON XLIX

1 XXI, 24 (b).   2 II, 18 (b).   3 'the day which . . . in it'.

4 XI, 32.   5 V, 33.

6 Niphal of יָעַץ (originally וָעַץ), WHG 191, with a reflexive sense, though the Hithpael is also used.

7 XII, 23.   8 V, 43.

9 'the (one) ruling over'—Qal active participle, VII, 15.

10 I, 53.   11 I, 27.   12 'one to the other', VI, 42.

13 VI, 9.   14 XLVIII, 37.   15 V, 26 (b).   16 I, 40.

17 'a rod of correction' is שֵׁבֶט מוּסָר; 'my rod of correction' is שֵׁבֶט מוּסָרִי, cf. XXI, 28.

18 'the (ones) rebelling'—the participle serving as an adjective.

19 'gave'.   20 XLVIII, 19.   21 I, 34.   22 XIX, 23.

23 XLVIII, 10.   24 The verb שָׂם (root שִׂים), WHG 197.

25 A familiar expression is 'mounds of desolation'.

26 'added to', X, 17.   27 Simply 'to do'.

28 The feminine plural adjective גְּדוֹלוֹת implying 'things' obviates the need for a noun to express 'deeds'.   29 XLVIII, 3.

30 IX, 40.   31 'to (the ones) who were enslaved'—Hophal, XXXIV, 18.

32 'to (the ones) who delivered, i.e. saved . . .'. An alternative is 'to their deliverers', i.e. the participle masculine plural with suffix.

33 Old accusative ending.   34 XLVIII, 1.

35 Either simply עוֹד or rephrase 'shall not add to (raise)', X, 17.

36 VII, 15.   37 I, 38.

38 The imperfect, suggesting that they do not keep on talking. Also note 35 above.   39 XLVIII, 17.

40 'falsehood', 'one against the other'.   41 'not to them'.

42 If you read the sense as being that of an emphatic adverb, use נָא, I, 4. If, however, you feel it means 'on that account', begin the line with לָכֵן.

43 Singular.   44 'own' is supplied by the English.

45 Imperfect.   46 'and'.   47 V, 31 (a), 32.   48 VII, 20.

49 שָׂבַע (like מָלֵא, V, 31 (a)) means 'was sated with' and takes a direct object.

50 The verb טָהַר, 'was clean', is a stative. The Piel makes it causative or transitive—טִהַר, 'he cleansed', cf. XXII, 13, 26.

51 'caused to reign over them'.

52 The idea of enduring is conveyed by עָמַד or קָם (root קוּם).

53 The Hiphil of זָכַר, 'remembered', namely 'caused to remember', produces the idea 'reminded'. Since the sense is 'cause them to remember', the direct object follows.

54 'one with the other', VI, 42.   55 I, 10.   56 XVIII, 32.

L

SON of man, thy spirit is troubled[1] at[2] the evil which thou
seest in the land and the rulers of My people heed[3] not thy
words of correction.[4] Thou seekest to flee from[5] thy brethren
to the wilderness,[6] for thou sayest[7] in thy heart that thou canst
not prevail against[8] the evildoers.[9] Yet, if thou wilt not desist
from speaking the words which I put into thy mouth and wilt
not flee from[5] the deeds which I have sent thee to do, then the
prophets who will come[10] after thee will reprove them, even[11]
as thou hast done. And the day shall surely[12] come when[13] men
will turn away[14] from their evil ways and they will turn[15] unto
Me with a pure heart. For My children shall not be wicked
for ever, nor will they harden[16] their hearts[17] against mercy to
the end of the days. For, behold, a time cometh when[13] My
spirit shall rule over the hearts of men and they will say:
'Happy are we[18] who know[19] the ways of the Lord, our God,
and who keep[20] His Torah.' In those days, no man[21] shall hate
his fellow man, nor will he do any evil unto him, for everyone
shall seek only the well-being of his neighbour. No one[21] will
remove the border stones[22] from his neighbour's field, nor
place a snare before a blind man. The widow and the orphan
shall no longer beg for bread,[23] but they shall eat daily[24] from
the king's table. The judges of the people shall become their
counsellors, for there shall be no strife amongst them and there
shall be none to condemn.[25] And they shall say to one
another:[26] 'Come,[27] let us go to the house of the judge, that we
may hear from him words of wisdom, for understanding is
better[28] than gold and knowledge more precious[28] than wealth.'
In those days there will be no hunger in the land for bread,[23]
but for the knowledge of the Lord. And the heavens will send
down[29] rain in its season and the earth will bring forth[30] its
fruit in abundance[31] and the trees will be bowed down with
the fruit thereon. Let not thy heart be melted,[32] nor thy hands

be weakened, for thy words shall yet avail[33] and that which I
have spoken unto thee shall come to pass.

NOTES ON L

[1] XLIII, 2.   [2] VII, 16.

[3] XXIV, 34. Since the negative action is continuous the imperfect may be used,
though the sense might equally be 'have not heeded', requiring the perfect.

[4] 'words of correction' would be rendered דִּבְרֵי מוּסָר and 'thy words of
correction' דִּבְרֵי מוּסָרְךָ, XXI, 28.

[5] 'from the face of'.   [6] Old accusative ending.   [7] As note 3
above.   [8] XI, 35, 36.   [9] XLVIII, 19.   [10] I, 59.

[11] 'even' is supplied by the English.

[12] Infinitive absolute before the verb.   [13] 'and . . .'.

[14] The sense is 'depart', i.e. סָר (root סוּר).

[15] 'return' is implied, i.e. שָׁב (root שׁוּב).   [16] XXII, 26.

[17] XLVIII, 17.

[18] (a) the idiomatic expression is '(O) our happinesses', the plural of the
segholate noun אֶשֶׁר with suffix—אַשְׁרֵינוּ. (b) Similarly, 'happy is the man' is
'(O) the happinesses of the man', אַשְׁרֵי הָאִישׁ.

[19] 'the (ones) knowing'—Qal active participle plural with the article.

[20] 'the (ones) keeping'—Qal active participle plural with the article.

[21] 'a man shall not'.   [22] 'stones of the border', I, 57.

[23] Use the article.   [24] XXI, 34.

[25] Hiphil of רָשַׁע, meaning 'to pronounce in the wrong'. Similarly the Hiphil
of צָדַק means 'to pronounce in the right'. These meanings point to the basic
notions of the adjectives צַדִּיק and רָשָׁע as being 'the one who is in the right' and
'the one who is in the wrong', in the forensic sense.

[26] 'one to the other', VI, 42.   [27] In Hebrew 'go ye', imperative.

[28] XII, 13 (a).

[29] Either Hiphil of יָרַד, 'went down', i.e. 'caused to go down', 'brought down',
'sent down', or the Hiphil of the verb מטר, 'caused it to rain', XLIV, 21.

[30] I, 25.   [31] XLII, 21.   [32] XV, 28.   [33] XLII, 42.

LI

THE[1] prophet opened his mouth and he called unto the people
and he said: 'Thus saith the Lord, God of Israel, unto the
captivity,[2] who were taken into exile[3] to Babylon:

"Fear not,[4] My servant Jacob,
Nor be dismayed,[5] My first-born Israel:

For the days of thine affliction are full[6]
   and the time of thy redemption is come.
A star shall arise in the east,[7]
   and shall illumine[8] the whole[9] earth;
The clouds of blackness[10] shall be scattered,
   and the shadows of darkness shall be no more.
The Lord hath perceived[11] thy distress[12]
   and is moved to pity[13] for thee.
Rise up, then, out of the dust
   and put off[14] thy garments of mourning.[15]
For as light[16] followeth upon darkness,[16]
   so shall gladness come after thy sorrow.
For He hath smitten, yet[17] will He heal;
   He hath destroyed, yet[17] will he rebuild.[18]
And those thrust[19] afar shall be gathered together,[20]
   And those uprooted[21] shall be planted again.
Then shall they break forth[22] into joyful shouting[23]
   and they shall sing this song:
'I will give thanks to the Lord at all times,[24]
   And shall sing praises[25] to His name continually.
I will declare[26] His lovingkindness in the broad places[27]
   and His faithfulness in the congregation of peoples.
For He hath gladdened[28] my heart with His deeds,
   I exult in the work of His hands.[29]
The heavens declare the glory of God,
   And the firmament showeth His greatness.
The earth is the Lord's and the fulness thereof,[30]
   The world and they that dwell[31] in it.
The gods of the nations are things of nought,[32]
   But the Lord reigneth for ever supreme.[33]
Happy is the people whose God is[34] the Lord,
   The nation He hath chosen as His inheritance.' " '[35]

NOTES ON LI

[1] Begin with Waw consecutive.   [2] XXXVII, 4.
[3] Hophal of גָּלָה or Niphal of שָׁבָה, XXXVII, 2.   [4] I, 61 (a), (b).
[5] XXXVII, 16.   [6] V, 32.   [7] *'from* the east'.

8 XLIV, 35.

9 Either direct rendering or 'the earth, all of it', XI, 5 (b).

10 צַלְמוּת; this noun, unpointed צלמות in manuscripts, was mistaken as a composite word צֵלְמָוֶת, 'shadow of death', but it is an abstract noun of the root צָלַם, 'was dark'.

11 i.e. 'taken note of', expressed by רָאָה ב.   12 XX, 37.

13 The Hebrew idiom is 'His mercies became warm', נִכְמְרוּ רַחֲמָיו.

14 XVIII, 30. If you use the emphatic imperative for 'rise up', use it also for 'put off'. The Hebrew would add 'from upon thee'.

15 'garments of mourning' is בִּגְדֵי אֵבֶל; 'thy garments of mourning' will be בִּגְדֵי אֶבְלְךָ, cf. XXI, 28.   16 Use the article.

17 Simply the conjunction. The English rightly supplies 'yet'.

18 XXXVII, 27.

19 'the (ones) thrust'—Niphal participle plural of נדח.

20 V, 33. Pausal form.

21 'the ones uprooted'—Niphal participle plural of עָקַר.

22 XLVIII, 12.   23 XLVIII, 13.

24 Singular—'in every time'.

25 Piel of הלל, שבח, or זמר. Use the cohortative.   26 Cohortative.

27 XXXVIII, 9.   28 Piel of the stative שָׂמַח, 'was glad', cf. XXII, 13.

29 (Dual as) plural, WHG 38.   30 'its fulness'.

31 'the (ones) dwelling'—Qal active participle masculine singular. Note: In poetry we sometimes find the construct plural followed by the inseparable preposition.

32 'vanity'.   33 עֶלְיוֹן, usually translated 'most high'.

34 'the people who the Lord (is) his God', I, 48.

35 'chosen for Him(self) as (לְ) an inheritance', cf. I, 65, 66.

LII

A. UNTO[1] Thee, O Lord, I lift[2] up my soul,
   for in Thee alone[3] is my salvation.
Give ear,[4] I pray Thee, to my prayer,
   make haste to answer my supplication.
How long,[5] O Lord, wilt Thou forsake me?
   why shall I perish before Thine eyes?[6]
By day[7] and by night I hope unto Thee,
   for Thou art merciful and compassionate.
Teach me, O Lord, Thy way,
   lead me[8] in the path of righteousness.

Send Thy light and Thy truth,
    they will gladden the soul of Thy servant.
Make the light of Thy countenance shine[9] upon me,
    that I may rise[10] from the depths of darkness.
Let me behold Thy lovingkindness and truth,
    that they may guide me in the path of uprightness.
I shall praise Thy name at all times,[11]
    and declare Thy greatness before all.
For Thou art my rock in distress,
    my fortress and my deliverer.

B. Sing unto the Lord, O house of Jacob,
    O sons of Israel sanctify His name.
He hath wrought great things[12] for His people,
    He hath multiplied[13] His wonders amongst us.
From the land of Egypt He brought us forth,[14]
    He delivered us out of the house of bondage.[15]
Forty years He led[8] us in the wilderness,
    in a parched and desolate land.
From the heavens He fed us[16] with bread,
    and from the rocks He gave us water to drink.[17]
He scattered our enemies before us,
    and brought us[18] into this good land.
Let us, then, praise[19] the Lord,
    for His lovingkindness endureth[20] for ever.

NOTES ON LII

[1] I, 2.   [2] Imperfect for continuous action.
[3] I, 58.   [4] Hiphil of either אוּז or קשׁב. Use the cohortative.
[5] XXXIX, 28.   [6] X, 25.   [7] The adverbial form יוֹמָם.
[8] XIII, 5.   [9] XLIV, 35.
[10] Use the cohortative with Waw conjunctive.
[11] Use the singular: 'in every time', 'season'.
[12] Feminine plural adjective, implying 'things', II, 25 note.
[13] XXXI, 30.   [14] I, 25.   [15] X, 34.   [16] IX, 40.
[17] XIV, 8.   [18] I, 26.   [19] Cohortative.
[20] 'endureth' is supplied by the English. The Hebrew is 'for ever (is) His lovingkindness'.

LIII

A. VIOLENCE[1] hath come upon the earth
   And the days of peace are forgotten.[2]
  Judgement[1] hath gone forth against[3] the sons of men,[4]
   For the fear of God is not in their hearts.
  In the heavens and the earth is death and destruction,
   And upon the mighty waters wrath is poured out.
  Weapons of death have they fashioned for themselves,
   Even[5] chariots of iron which move swiftly,[6]
  Devouring all living beings with fire,[1]
   Both[7] man and beast as burnt offerings.
  They soar into the heavens as birds,[1]
   They swoop down as an eagle upon its prey.
  In the seas they swim as the sea-monsters,
   In the paths of the waters they lie in wait,
  To cleave asunder the ships bringing food,
   For with hunger have they made a covenant.
  If a man goeth forth into the broad places,[8]
   He is slain suddenly from above.
  And if he abideth within his house,
   It is thrown down[9] and it falleth upon him.
  And, when the sound of the trumpet is heard,[10]
   He awaketh[11] from his sleep and ariseth from[12] his
    couch,
  He descendeth into the pit which he hath digged,
   And there he abideth till the light of the morning.

B. Hear, O Lord, the voice of our little ones,[13]
   For they are innocent and have done no evil.
  Not for our sakes wilt thou have mercy on the earth,
   But for the sake of our babes, which are without
    blemish.
  The spirit of man is evil from his youth,
   But when he turneth[14] unto thee Thou dost cleanse[15]
    him.

Turn[16] Thy countenance unto us, O Lord,
　　For we come before Thee with a contrite[17] heart.
How long, O Lord, shall we call unto Thee in vain?
　　For now we are cleansed[18] of our wickedness.
Remove[19] from us the heart of stone,
　　Give us, O Lord, a heart of flesh,
That we may walk in the way of life.

NOTES ON LIII

[1] The article is used for abstract ideas and classes of things.
[2] Use the pausal form.　　　　　　　[3] Either עַל or ב.
[4] The singular אָדָם for 'mankind'.
[5] 'even' is supplied by the English usage.
[6] 'which hasten (Piel participle of מהר) to go'.
[7] The English 'both' may be omitted as 'man and beast' would imply 'both'.
Alternatively, one may make use of גַם . . . גַם.
[8] XXXVIII, 9.　　　　　　[9] XII, 23.
[10] 'in the being-heard of the sound . . .'—infinitive construct Niphal.
[11] XXXII, 21.　　　　[12] 'from *upon*', VI, 24.　　　　[13] XXIII, 23.
[14] The idea is '*returneth*'.　　　　[15] XLIX, 50.
[16] This is causative. The sense seems to be 'cause Thy countenance to turn'.
[17] 'broken'—Niphal participle.　　　　[18] Niphal.
[19] XVIII, 30.

LIV

Evil waters have encompassed me
　　And there is no escape for me.
I am gone down into the depths of the sea,
　　And none attendeth[1] to my distress.[2]
Vanity are the days of (mortal) man,[3]
　　As nothing is his wealth when he is[4] alone.
Yesterday I was pronounced happy,[5]
　　But to-day there is none to comfort me.
Many were gathered at my house,
　　When my table was filled[6] with dainties.
Those who blessed me[7] do mock[8] at me
　　and those who praised[9] me do revile[8] me.

They have requited[10] me evil for[11] good,
    They call me sinner, rejected.[12]
But I shall not sin with my mouth,
    And no evil thought is in my heart.
The Lord trieth the firm in spirit,
    But He will not forsake him for ever.
While there is yet[13] life[14] within me,
    I shall not leave off my hope.
For the Lord is merciful to the lowly,
    and He is a saviour to those who trust[15] in Him.
Hear, O Lord, my supplication,
    Attend,[16] I pray Thee, to my prayer.
How long, O Lord, wilt Thou forsake me?
    Make haste[17] to redeem Thy servant.
By day[18] and by night I wait unto Thee,
    Wherefore shall I perish before[19] Thine eyes?
Unto Thee, O Lord, I lift up my voice,
    For in Thee alone[20] is my salvation.

NOTES ON LIV

[1] XXIV, 34.   [2] XX, 37.   [3] אֱנוֹשׁ, XI, 17.

[4] 'in his being'—infinitive construct with suffix; see also I, 58.

[5] A passive is often expressed by an impersonal 3rd person active verb. This line may be rephrased to 'they pronounced me happy'. The Piel of אשׁר conveys this sense.

[6] V, 31 (a) and (b).

[7] This phrase had best be expressed as 'The (ones) blessing me', i.e. the Piel participle masculine plural with the suffix.

[8] The imperfect implies continued action.

[9] As in note 7 above, rephrase 'the (ones) praising me', i.e. the Piel participle masculine plural (of הלל or שׁבח) with the suffix.

[10] V, 42.   [11] 'instead of'.   [12] Niphal participle.

[13] 'While yet (בְּעוֹד)'.   [14] Expand to 'my life', II, 6.

[15] 'to the (ones) trusting'—Qal participle masculine plural.

[16] LII, 4.   [17] For the verb see LIII, 6.   [18] LII, 7.

[19] X, 25.   [20] I, 58.

LV

FOR Zion's sake I will not be silent,
  And for Jerusalem's sake I will not rest.
Until her deliverance appeareth[1] as brightness,
  And her glory as a lamp doth shine.[1]
No more shalt thou be called[2] Forsaken,[3]
  Nor thy land be likened to the wilderness.
For, as a bridegroom rejoiceth over his bride,
  So shall thy God rejoice over thee.
No more shall thy corn be given to thine enemies,
  Nor shall strangers drink the wine of thy vineyards,
But they that toil[4] for it shall eat it,
  and they that gather[4] the grapes shall drink its wine.
Go ye through the gates, cast up a highway,[5]
  Gather up[6] the stones, make a way for the people.
Lift up a standard unto all the nations,
  For the Lord hath proclaimed[7] to the ends of the earth:
'Behold, the salvation of Zion cometh,
  Lo, the sound of the feet of one bringing tidings.[8]
Thy children shall be called[9] a holy people, the redeemed[10] of
    the Lord,
  And thy land shall be much[11] sought.
For I shall bring back the glory of Zion,
  And make[12] Jerusalem a praise in all the earth.'
Put aside,[13] then, thy garments of mourning,[14]
  Clothe thyself[15] with royal raiment.[16]
Rejoice and be glad, for thy deliverance shineth,[17]
  And shall illumine[18] thy land all around.[19]

NOTES ON LV

[1] Imperfect, since the future is indicated.
[2] 'shall it be called to thee'.   [3] Niphal participle feminine singular.
[4] Here the perfect is best, since it means 'those who have toiled', 'those who have gathered'.

[5] The verb and noun are cognate: the verb is סָלַל and the noun מְסִלָּה.

[6] סָקַל in Piel means 'cleared away stones'.   [7] XLVII, 14.

[8] בָּשַׂר in Piel: use the participle.

[9] 'To thy children it shall be called'.

[10] Passive participle Qal, masculine plural construct of פָּדָה, WHG 217.

[11] 'exceedingly'.   [12] The verb שָׂם (root שׂים).

[13] XVIII, 30.   [14] LI, 15.   [15] לָבַשׁ in Qal.

[16] 'raiment of kingship', I, 56. Two words are used for clothes: בֶּגֶד and שִׂמְלָה.

[17] Hiphil of יָפַע (originally וּפַע).   [18] XLIV, 35.   [19] XXXIX, 6.

INDEX TO THE NOTES

*The notes indicated below should be read in conjunction with the contexts
to which they refer*

defective verbs, *see under* verbs.

emphasis, effected by (1) the cohortative, III, 44;
  (2) the infinitive absolute (*a*) before the finite verb, II, 50, and (*b*) after the finite verb, with ◘ֱ between them, XXII, 22;
  (3) special exclamatory words, II, 17; IV, 36; XXIX, 45;
  (4) placing first the word to be emphasized, II, 4, 37 (*b*), 41, 55; III, 41; IX, 39; X, 14;
  (5) cognate verb and noun, XIX, 23.

feminine adjective (singular and plural), without associated noun, implies 'thing(s)', *see under* adjectives.

imperative: (1) implying 'thou' or 'ye', II, 9; VIII, 5;
  (2) emphatic form, expressing urgency, III, 23; XI, 18;
  (3) followed by another command (in English), the latter being expressed by the perfect with Waw consecutive, III, 29; IV, 10.
imperfect, with effect of a frequentative future, II, 24; XXVI, 39 (*b*).
inclusive categories, of people or things, XIII, 43; XXIII, 14.
infinitive absolute before and following the finite verb for emphasis, II, 50; XII, 22.
infinitive construct as verbal noun, I, 21; II, 40; III, 2.
interrogative clause, III, 38.
interrogative particle with negative, implying expected positive response or positive assertion, VII, 20.

negative commands or prohibitions, I, 61 (*a*).
negative interrogative implying positive response or assertion, VII, 20.
Niphal, with active meaning in English, I, 27, 29; II, 1.
nouns: (1) formed with preformative Mem, III, 27 (*a*), XLIV, 15;
  (2) plural denoting prepositional ideas, II, 5; X, 25;
  (3) plural, with singular meanings in English, VII, 45;
  (4) repeated, to express 'each', 'every', XVI, 25; XXI, 34.
numerals, V, 13; XX, 18.

oath, formula for taking, III, 24; XIII, 22.
objective relationship, implied by the construct and suffix, XV, 23.
order of (1) subject, verb, and object, I, 11, 19.
  (2) nouns in apposition, one being a proper noun, II, 26; III, 7.
ordinals, IV, 44.

participle: (1) as verbal adjective, III, 10; XIX, 9, 11; XX, 3, 4.
  (2) difference between it (as verbal adjective) and the infinitive construct (as verbal noun), I, 21.
  (3) difference between the participle and perfect of a stative verb, *see under* stative verbs (2).
  (4) with article, representing the English relative with verb, *see under* article.

ENGLISH–HEBREW VOCABULARY

A

Aaron: אַהֲרֹן

abhorred: *Piel of* תעב (*also of* תאב)

Abihail: אֲבִיחַיִל

Abimelech: אֲבִימֶלֶךְ

able, was: יָכֹל (*stative*), *imperf.* יוּכַל, WHG 238 D

abode (*n.*): מָעוֹן, מִשְׁכָּן, מוֹשָׁב, (*vb.*): (i) יָשַׁב, *imperf.* יֵשֵׁב, *with Waw consec.* וַיֵּשֶׁב, *imper.* שֵׁב, *inf. const.* שֶׁבֶת, *with suff.* שִׁבְתִּי; (ii) שָׁכַן

abominated: *see* 'abhorred'

abomination: תּוֹעֵבָה

about (concerning): עַל

above: לְמַעְלָה *followed by* מִן, מִמַּעַל *followed by* לְ

Abraham: אַבְרָהָם

abundance: רֹב

abundantly: לָרֹב

accomplished: (i) עָשָׂה (did, performed), WHG 225 (*b*); (ii) was accomplished מָלֵא (was full)

according to: כְּ (as)—*the insepar-able prep.*

account: on . . . of: עַל־אֹדוֹת (by reason of), בַּעֲבוּר (out of), מִן (for the sake of)

Achan: עָכָן

acknowledged (confessed): *Hithp. of* ידה (וֹדה)—הִתְוַדָּה

across: מֵעֵבֶר לְ (of the side to)

added: יָסַף *in Qal and Hiph.*—

הוֹסִיף. *When followed by another vb. in the inf. const., it is used in an auxiliary sense of* 'continued to (do)', '(did) again'

admonished: *Hiph. of* זהר—הִזְהִיר

adversary: צַר; *with the art.* הַצַּר; צֹרֵר

advice (counsel): עֵצָה

afar: רָחוֹק

affair (matter, thing): דָּבָר

afflicted: *Piel of* ענה—עִנָּה

affliction: *abs. and const.* עֳנִי, *in pause* עֹנִי (*segholate*), *with suff.* עָנְיִי, *&c.*

affrighted, was: *Niph. of* בהל—נִבְהַל

afraid: (i) was afraid: יָרֵא (*stative*), *imperf.* יִירָא, *inf. const.* יִרְאָה, I, 61 (*b*), WHG 211; (ii) made afraid: *Hiph. of* חָרַד (trembled)—הֶחֱרִיד (caused to tremble), *and* (iii) *of* פָּחַד (feared, trembled)—הִפְחִיד

after: אַחַר, אַחֲרֵי, *with suffs. of the pl. n.*, WHG 87

again: עוֹד, שֵׁנִית (a second time). *In association with a vb., the Hiph. (generally) of* יָסַף, *followed by the inf. const. of the vb., may be used with the primary sense of* 'added to . . .', *e.g.* 'he spoke again'—הוֹסִיף לְדַבֵּר (he added to speak)

against: בְּ, עַל; *over against* = op-posite

age: old age זְקֻנִים ,זִקְנָה (*pl. n.*)

aged, was: זָקֵן (*stative*), *imperf.* יִזְקַן

alas: אֲהָהּ

alive: חַי, *fem. sing.* חַיָּה

all: כֹּל, *with maqqeph* כָּל־, *with suff.* כֻּלִּי, *&c.*, I, 5 (*a*), XI, 5 (*a*) *and* (*b*)

allowed: נָתַן (gave). *See under* 'gave' *for the main parts of the vb.*

alone: לְבַד, *usually with suff.* לְבַדִּי (I alone), *&c.*

also: גַּם

altar: מִזְבֵּחַ, *pl.* מִזְבְּחוֹת

ancestors: אָבוֹת *pl. of* אָב (father), X, 39

angel: מַלְאָךְ (messenger)

angry, was: (i) קָצַף *followed by* עַל; (ii) חָרָה ל (it was hot to) *and* אַף (the anger was hot)

anointed: מָשַׁח

another: אַחֵר, *pl.* אֲחֵרִים (other); one another: אִישׁ ... זֶה ... זֶה ... רֵעֵהוּ ,אָחִיו ... אִישׁ *for the masc.,* and אִשָּׁה ... זֹאת ... זֹאת, אֲחוֹתָהּ ,רְעוּתָהּ ... אִשָּׁה *for the fem.,* VI, 42

answered: עָנָה, *imperf.* יַעֲנֶה, *with Waw consec.* וַיַּעַן, *imper.* עֲנֵה, *inf. const.* עֲנוֹת. Cf. WHG 225 (*b*)

anyone: כָּל־אִישׁ

appearance: מַרְאֶה

appeared: *Niph. of* רָאָה (saw)— נִרְאָה (was seen, showed himself), *imperf.* יֵרָאֶה, *with Waw consec.* וַיֵּרָא

approached (drew near): (i) קָרַב *and* קָרֵב (*stative*), *imperf.* יִקְרַב; (ii) *the perf. is* נִגַּשׁ—*Niph. of* נגש;

the *imperf.* יִגַּשׁ, *imper.* גַּשׁ, *and inf. const.* גֶּשֶׁת (*with suff.* גִּשְׁתִּי, *&c.*) *are in* Qal, WHG 141, 142

Aram, Aramea: אֲרָם

ark: אָרוֹן

arm: זְרוֹעַ, *pl.* זְרֹעוֹת

arms (weapons): כֵּלִים—*pl. of* כְּלִי (implement, vessel)

arose: קָם ,קוּם√, *imperf.* יָקוּם, *jussive* יָקֹם, *imperf. with Waw consec.* וַיָּקָם, *imper.* קוּם

arose early (in the morning): *Hiph. of* שכם—הִשְׁכִּים

as: כְּ (*inseparable prep.*) *with n. and adj.,* כַּאֲשֶׁר *when followed by a vb.* (*lit.* 'as that which'), I, 10. *Note: When* 'as' *does not mean* 'like' *but rather* 'for' *it is* ל, I, 56

ascended: עָלָה, *imperf.* יַעֲלֶה, *jussive* יַעַל, *imperf. with Waw consec.* וַיַּעַל, *imper.* עֲלֵה, WHG 225 (*b*)

ashamed, was: בּוֹשׁ (*stative*), *imperf.* יֵבוֹשׁ, WHG 205, 206

Ashera (sacred pole): אֲשֵׁרָה

Ashtoreth (Astarte, goddess of love): עַשְׁתֹּרֶת

aside, turned: סָר ,סוּר√, *imperf.* יָסוּר, *with Waw consec.* וַיָּסַר, *imper.* סוּר

asked: שָׁאַל

ass: חֲמוֹר; she-ass אָתוֹן

assembled (gathered together): (i) *trans.:* קִבֵּץ ,אָסַף (Piel), הִקְהִיל (Hiph.); (ii) *intrans.: usually in the pl.* (*though the sing. is used with a collective n.*)—'were assembled, assembled themselves'

—in Niph. נִקְבְּצוּ וְנֶאֶסְפוּ, and also אסף and קבץ in נִקְהֲלוּ; in Hithp.—הִתְקַבְּצוּ, הִתְאַסְּפוּ.

assembly: קָהָל

astounded, was: Hithpoel of שמם —הִשְׁתּוֹמֵם, XLIII, 17

astray: (i) went astray תָּעָה; (ii) led astray: Hiph. הִתְעָה (caused to go astray)

ate: אָכַל, imperf. יֹאכַל, imper. אֱכֹל, WHG 162

attended: (i) listened: Hiph. of אזן הֶאֱזִין—הַקְשִׁיב, קשב; (ii) paid heed שָׂם לֵב (set one's heart)

availed: Hiph. of יעל (וְעַל)—הוֹעִיל

avenged (oneself): Niph. of נקם—נִקַּם, imperf. יִנָּקֵם

awoke: perfect הֵקִיץ, i.e. Hiph. of קוץ; imperf. יִיקַץ., i.e. Qal of יקץ—a defective vb., IV, 34

axe: גַּרְזֶן

B

Baal: בַּעַל, pl. בְּעָלִים

babe: עוֹלֵל

Babylon: בָּבֶל

bad (evil): רַע, with the art. הָרָע, fem. sing. רָעָה

bade (commanded): Piel of צוה—צִוָּה, imperf. יְצַוֶּה, with Waw consec. וַיְצַו, imper. צַוֵּה and the shortened form צַו

baked: אָפָה, imperf. יֹאפֶה

baker: אֹפֶה—Qal active part.

band (company, troop): אֹרְחָה (a travelling company), גְּדוּד (a troop)

bank (of river): שָׂפָה

banner: נֵס, with suff. נִסִּי, &c.

Barak: בָּרָק

bathed: (intrans.) רָחַץ

battle: מִלְחָמָה, const. מִלְחֶמֶת, with suff. מִלְחַמְתִּי, &c.

battled (fought): Niph. of לחם—נִלְחַם followed by ב

beast: חַיָּה, a wild beast חַיָּה רָעָה (an evil beast)

beautiful: יָפֶה, fem. sing. יָפָה

became: הָיָה (was), usually followed by ל

because: כִּי, יַעַן or, more fully, יַעַן אֲשֶׁר; because of: מִפְּנֵי (from the face of), בַּעֲבוּר (for the sake of)

befell: קָרָה (happened), followed by ל

before: (i) לְעֵינֵי, לִפְנֵי (to the face of, to the eyes of); before me: לְעֵינַי, לְפָנַי (to my face, to my eyes), &c.; (ii) in time—לִפְנֵי with the inf. const. or טֶרֶם, בְּטֶרֶם with the imperf., IX, 23 (a)

begot: Hiph. of ולד—יָלַד (bore a child)—הוֹלִיד (caused to bear a child). Cf. WHG 190

beheld: (i) רָאָה (saw), imperf. יִרְאֶה, jussive יֵרֶא, imperf. with Waw consec. וַיַּרְא; (ii) חָזָה (beheld a vision, prophetically)

behind: (i) אַחַר, אַחֲרֵי, with suffs. of the pl. n., WHG 87; (ii) מֵאָחוֹר (from the rear)

behold: הִנֵּה, with suff. הִנְנִי (behold I), &c.

belonged (to): הָיָה (ל)

below, beneath: תַּחַת, *with suffs. of the pl. n.*, WHG 87; *adverbially* מִתַּחַת

bereaved, was: שָׁכֵל (*stative*), *imperf.* יִשְׁכַּל

beside: אֵצֶל, עַל יַד

besieged: צָר √צור, *imperf.* יָצוּר

best: מִבְחָר, מֵיטָב (choice)

bestowed: גָּמַל

Bethlehem: בֵּית־לֶחֶם

between: בֵּין, *with suff.* בֵּינִי, *&c.*

beyond: (i) across, at the other side of מֵעֵבֶר ל; (ii) without limit —עַד אֵין (till there is not)

bird: (i) צִפּוֹר, *pl.* צִפֳּרִים; (ii) עוֹף, *used also collectively* (birds)

birthplace (kindred): מוֹלֶדֶת

bitter: מַר, *fem. sing.* מָרָה

blackness: צַלְמוּת, LI, 10

blemish: מוּם

blessed: (*vb.*) *Piel of* ברך—בֵּרַךְ, *imperf.* יְבָרֵךְ; (*adj.*) בָּרוּךְ—*Qal passive part.*, מְבֹרָךְ—*Pual part.*

blessing: בְּרָכָה, *const.* בִּרְכַּת

blind: עִוֵּר

blood: דָּם; bloodshed דָּמִים (*pl.*)

bolt: בְּרִיחַ

bondage: עַבְדוּת; house of bondage בֵּית־עֲבָדִים (house of slaves)

book: סֵפֶר (*segholate*), *with suff.* סִפְרִי, *&c.*

booty: בַּז, שָׁלָל

border: גְּבוּל

bore: (i) carried: נָשָׂא, *imperf.* יִשָּׂא, *imper.* שָׂא, *inf. const.* שְׂאֵת *and* נְשֹׂא, WHG 185 (*c*); (ii) bore a

child: יָלְדָה (ילד) √יָלַד, *imperf.* תֵּלֵד (*fem.*)

borrowed: לָוָה, *imperf.* יִלְוֶה

borrower: לֹוֶה—*Qal active part.*

both: (i) *with suff.* שְׁנֵינוּ, *&c.*, (both of us), *&c.*, *from the numeral* שְׁנַיִם (two); (ii) both . . . and גַּם . . . גַּם

bound: (i) (with cords) אָסַר; (ii) bound up wounds חָבַשׁ

bounty: טוּב (goodness)

bowed (oneself down): *Hithpalel of* שָׁחָה (שחו)—'was low, bowed down'—הִשְׁתַּחֲוָה, *imperf.* יִשְׁתַּחֲוֶה, *with Waw consec.* וַיִּשְׁתַּחוּ, II, 61

bowels: מֵעִים (*pl.*)

boy: יֶלֶד (*segholate*), נַעַר

branch: עָנָף

bread: לֶחֶם (*segholate*), *with suff.* לַחְמִי, *&c.*

breath (of life): רוּחַ; נְשָׁמָה, *const.* נִשְׁמַת

breathed: נָפַח, *imperf.* יִפַּח

bride: כַּלָּה

bridegroom: חָתָן

brightness: זֹהַר

brimstone: גָּפְרִית

broad places: רְחוֹבוֹת—*fem. pl.*

broke: שָׁבַר; broke in pieces, *i.e.* shattered: *Piel* שִׁבֵּר; broke down (a wall) נָתַץ, *imperf.* יִתֹּץ; broke off (a yoke) פָּרַק; broke out (of a plague) פָּרַץ, (of the spirit of prophecy) צָלַח, (of joy) פָּצַח

brother: אָח, *const.* אֲחִי, *with suff.* אָחִיךָ, אֲחִי, *&c.*, *pl.* אַחִים, WHG 288

brought (in): *Hiph. of* בּוֹא√ בָּא
(came in)—הֵבִיא (caused to
come in): brought forth, out:
Hiph. of יָצָא√ (וצא—went out)—
הוֹצִיא (caused to go out):
brought up: *Hiph. of* עָלָה (went
up)—הֶעֱלָה (caused to go up);
brought back: *Hiph. of* שָׁב
שׁוּב√ (came back)—הֵשִׁיב (caused
to come back); brought across:
Hiph. of עָבַר (crossed)—הֶעֱבִיר
(caused to cross), XV, 3;
brought near: *Hiph. of* נגש√,
הִקְרִיב, הִגִּישׁ—קָרַב (drew near)
(caused to draw near)

built: בָּנָה, *imperf.* יִבְנֶה, *with Waw*
consec. וַיִּבֶן

burden: מַשָּׂא

burial, burial place: קְבוּרָה

buried: קָבַר

burned: (i) שָׂרַף; (ii) *Hiph. of* בָּעַר
(was alight)—הִבְעִיר (caused to
be alight, set fire to)

but: רַק, אַךְ, וּ (only); *as conj.* ו, I,
45, *after a negative clause* כִּי,
כִּי אִם, XLII, 34

by: (i) instrument בּ (*inseparable
prep.*); (ii) beside; עַל־יַד, אֵצֶל

C

calamity: שֵׁד, שֶׁבֶר

called: קָרָא, *imperf.* יִקְרָא; *followed by* ל (summoned, named)
and by אֶל (addressed, prayed)

came (in): בּוֹא√ בָּא, *imperf.* יָבֹא,
imper. בֹּא, WHG 212 (*d*). *In
association with* 'word' *or* 'spirit'

it is הָיָה (was)—XXI, 24 (*a*);
came back (returned): שׁוּב√ שָׁב,
imperf. יָשׁוּב, *jussive* יָשֹׁב, *imperf.*
with Waw consec. וַיָּשָׁב, *imper.*
שׁוּב; came forth, out (departed)
יָצָא, *imperf.* יֵצֵא, WHG 212 (*c*),
imper. צֵא, *inf. const.* צֵאת; came
near, nigh: (i) קָרַב *and* קָרֵב
(*stative*), *imperf.* יִקְרַב; (ii) *the
perf. is* נִגַּשׁ—*Niph. of* נגש; *the
imperf.* יִגַּשׁ, *imper.* גַּשׁ, *and inf.
const.* גֶּשֶׁת (*with suff.* גִּשְׁתִּי, &*c*.)
are in Qal, WHG 141, 142:
came down (descended) יָרַד,
imperf. יֵרֵד, *with Waw consec.*
וַיֵּרֶד, *imper.* רֵד, *inf. const.* רֶדֶת
(*with suff.* רִדְתִּי, &*c*.), cf. WHG
188; came up (ascended) עָלָה,
imperf. יַעֲלֶה, *with Waw consec.*
וַיַּעַל, *imper.* עֲלֵה, WHG 225 (*b*)

came to pass = was: הָיָה

camel: גָּמָל, *pl.* גְּמַלִּים

camp: מַחֲנֶה, *const.* מַחֲנֵה, *pl.* מַחֲנוֹת

Canaan: כְּנַעַן, XVIII, 6

Canaanite: כְּנַעֲנִי, XVIII, 6

captive: שָׁבוּי—*Qal passive part.*
of שָׁבָה (took captive)

captive, took: (i) שָׁבָה; (ii) *Hiph.*
of גָּלָה (went into exile)—הִגְלָה
(caused to go into exile); (ii)
was taken captive: *Niph. of*
שָׁבָה—נִשְׁבָּה *and Hoph. of* גָּלָה—
הָגְלָה

captivity: גָּלָה, גָּלוּת, שְׁבוּת; שְׁבִי

care, took: *Niph. of* שָׁמַר (kept,
watched)—נִשְׁמַר (kept, watched
himself)

cared for (paid attention to): שָׂם לֵב לְ (set one's heart to)

carried (bore): נָשָׂא, *imperf.* יִשָּׂא, *imper.* שָׂא, *inf. const.* שְׂאֵת *and* נְשׂא, WHG 185 (*c*)

cast (away): *Hiph. of* שלך—הִשְׁלִיךְ; cast down: *Hiph. of* נָפַל (fell)—הִפִּיל (caused to fall); cast off (clothes): פָּשַׁט; cast up (a highway): סָלַל, *the cognate n. being* מְסִלָּה (highway)

cattle: מִקְנֶה, בָּקָר, בְּהֵמָה (*collective*)

cause: רִיב—רָב: pleaded a cause: רָב √רִיב, *imperf.* יָרִיב, *with Waw consec.* וַיָּרֶב, *imper.* רִיב, WHG 197

cave: מְעָרָה

ceased: חָדַל (*stative*), *imperf.* יֶחְדַּל, *imper.* חֲדַל

celebrated (a festival): חַג, *imperf.* יָחֹג

certain, a: אֶחָד (one) *for the masc. and* אַחַת *for the fem.*

chamber: חֶדֶר (*segholate*), *with suff.* חַדְרִי, *&c.*

chariot: מֶרְכָּבָה: chariots with horses רֶכֶב (*collective*)

chastised: *Piel of* יסר—יִסַּר

chief = head

child: (i) יֶלֶד (*segholate*); (ii) בֵּן (son): children בָּנִים

choice: מֵיטָב, מִבְחָר

chose: בָּחַר *followed by* בְּ *with the object*

city: עִיר (*fem.*), *pl.* עָרִים

clean: טָהוֹר

clean, was (*vb.*): טָהֵר (*stative*), *imperf.* יִטְהַר

cleansed: *Piel of* טָהֵר (was clean)—טִהַר, XXXIII, 38

cleaved (split): בָּקַע

cleaved (unto), adhered: דָּבַק *followed by* בְּ (*stative*), *imperf.* יִדְבַּק

closed: סָגַר: closed the ears אָטַם: closed the eyes עָצַם

clothed (*trans.*): *Hiph. of* לָבַשׁ (put on clothes)—הִלְבִּישׁ (caused one to put on clothes); clothed oneself: לָבַשׁ, *imperf.* יִלְבַּשׁ

comfort, consolation: תַּנְחוּמִים (*pl.*)

comforted: *Piel of* נחם—נִחַם

command(ment): מִצְוָה, *pl.* מִצְוֹת—*written defectively*

commanded: *Piel of* צוה—צִוָּה, *imperf.* יְצַוֶּה, *with Waw consec.* וַיְצַו, *imper.* צַוֵּה *or the shortened form* צַו

companion: רֵעַ (*masc.*), רֵעָה (*fem.*)

company: מַחֲלֹקֶת, *pl.* מַחְלְקוֹת (division), אֹרְחָה (travelling company), גְּדוּד (troop)

compassion, had, showed: (i) *Piel of* רחם—רִחַם; (ii) חָנַן, *imperf.* יָחֹן

compassionate: רַחוּם, חַנּוּן (gracious)

completed (*trans.*): *Piel of* כָּלָה (was finished)—כִּלָּה, XXIX, 25, *Note*: was completed: *Pual* כֻּלָּה

concealed (*vb.*): (i) *Hiph. of* סתר, הֶחְבִּיא, הִסְתִּיר—חבא; (ii) concealed oneself, was concealed: *Niph.* נִסְתַּר, נֶחְבָּא *and Hithp.*

נִסְתָּר (adj.); הִתְחַבֵּא, הִסְתַּתֵּר,
Niph. part.

concerning: עַל, עַל דְּבַר

condemned: Hiph. of רשע (was
in the wrong)—הִרְשִׁיעַ (pronounced to be in the wrong),
L, 25

confessed: Hithp. of ידה (ודה)—
הִתְוַדָּה

congregation: עֵדָה

consumed = ate

continually: תָּמִיד

continued (to do) = added (to do)

contrite: Niph. part. of שָׁבַר (broke)
—נִשְׁבָּר (broken)

cord: חֶבֶל (segholate): thick cord
עֲבֹת (rope)

corn: דָּגָן

corpse: פֶּגֶר (segholate), נְבֵלָה

correction: מוּסָר

corrupted: Hiph. of שחת—הִשְׁחִית

couch: מִטָּה, עֶרֶשׂ (segholate)

counsel: עֵצָה; counselled יָעַץ
(ועץ); took counsel: Niph. נוֹעַץ,
imperf. יִוָּעֵץ, WHG 191; coun-
sellor: יֹעֵץ—Qal active part.

counted: מָנָה, סָפַר

countenance = face—פָּנִים

country: אֶרֶץ (segholate), pl.
אֲרָצוֹת

courage, had: אָמַץ (stative), imperf. יֶאֱמַץ

covenant: בְּרִית; made a covenant
—כָּרַת בְּרִית (cut a covenant)

coveted: חָמַד

created: בָּרָא, imperf. יִבְרָא

cried: (i) called out, prayed—קָרָא;
(ii) cried out in pain—צָעַק

crossed: עָבַר; crossed over—עָבַר
אֶת־, crossed through—עָבַר בְּ

crown: עֲטָרָה, כֶּתֶר, נֵזֶר; const. עֲטֶרֶת

crowned (king): the Hiph. of כתר
—הִכְתִּיר is rare. The usual
phrase in Hebrew thinking is
'anointed a person as king'

cry: צְעָקָה, const. צַעֲקַת

cunning: (adj.) עָרוּם; (n.) עָרְמָה

cursed: אָרַר, imperf. יָאֹר; Piel of
of קָלַל—קִלֵּל; (adj.—accursed)
אָרוּר—Qal passive part.

custom: מִשְׁפָּט

cut (off): קָצַץ, כָּרַת

D

daily: יוֹם יוֹם

dainties: מַעֲדַנִּים

Daniel: דָּנִיֵּאל

dark, was: חָשַׁךְ (stative), imperf.
יֶחְשַׁךְ

darkness: חֹשֶׁךְ (segholate)

daughter: בַּת, with suff. בִּתִּי, &c.,
pl. בָּנוֹת

David: דָּוִד

day: יוֹם, dual יוֹמַיִם, pl. יָמִים;
to-day: הַיּוֹם; by day: יוֹמָם

dead: (adj.) מֵת: was dead, died
(vb.), מֵת √מוּת, imperf. יָמוּת
(stative), WHG 206

deaf: חֵרֵשׁ

death: מָוֶת, const. מוֹת, with suff.
מוֹתִי, &c.; put to death: Hiph.
of מֵת √מוּת (died)—הֵמִית (caused
to die); was put to death: Hoph.
הוּמַת

deceit: מִרְמָה

declared: (i) informed: *Hiph. of*
הִגִּיד—נגד; (ii) related: *Piel of*
סִפֵּר—ספר

deep: עָמֹק, *fem.* עֲמֻקָה; *deep sleep*
תַּרְדֵּמָה

defiled: *Piel of* חִלֵּל—חלל

deliverance: יֵשַׁע, *with suff.* יִשְׁעִי,
יְשׁוּעָה

delivered: (i) saved: *Hiph. of* נצל
הִצִּיל—and of ישע (וישע)—
הוֹשִׁיעַ. Cf. WHG 211; (ii)
handed over: נָתַן (gave), מָכַר
(sold)

departed: (i) יָצָא (וצא)—went
forth), *imperf.* יֵצֵא, *imper.* צֵא,
inf. const. צֵאת, WHG 212 (c);
(ii) turned aside: סוּר√ סָר, *imperf.* יָסוּר, *with Waw consec.*
וַיָּסַר

descended: יָרַד (ורד), *imperf.* יֵרֵד,
with Waw consec. וַיֵּרֶד, *imper.*
רֵד, *inf. const.* רֶדֶת, *with suff.*
רִדְתִּי, &c. Cf. WHG 188, 189

descent, slope: מוֹרָד

desert, wilderness: מִדְבָּר, X, 9

desired: (i) coveted חָמַד; (ii) de-
lighted (in)—(ב) חָפֵץ

desisted = ceased: חָדַל, *imperf.*
יֶחְדַּל, *imper.* חֲדַל

desolate: שׁוֹמֵם; was desolate שָׁמֵם,
imperf. יִשַּׁם

desolation: שְׁמָמָה

despised: בָּזָה

despoiled: (i) בָּזַז, *imperf.* יָבֹז;
(ii) שָׁלַל, *imperf.* יָשֹׁל

destroyed: (i) *Hiph. and Piel of*
שׁחת—הִשְׁחִית *and* שִׁחֵת; (ii) *Hiph.*

of הִשְׁמִיד—שמד; (iii) *Hiph. of*
אָבַד (perished)—הֶאֱבִיד (caused
to perish); (iv) of buildings:
נָתַץ

devoured: בָּלַע (swallowed up) *and*
אָכַל (ate)

did: עָשָׂה, *imperf.* יַעֲשֶׂה, *jussive*
יַעַשׂ, *imperf. with Waw consec.*
וַיַּעַשׂ, *imper.* עֲשֵׂה, *inf. const.* עֲשׂוֹת,
WHG 225 (b)

died (= was dead): מוּת√ מֵת, *imperf.* יָמוּת (stative), *with Waw
consec.* וַיָּמָת, WHG 205, 206

diminished: *Hiph. of* מָעַט ('was
small'—*in pl.* 'were few')—
הִמְעִיט; was diminished: מָעַט,
חָסֵר, *imperf.* יֶחְסַר

dismayed, was: *Niph. of* חתת—
נֵחַת, *imperf.* יֵחַת

dispersed: *Hiph. of* פוץ—הֵפִיץ *and*
Piel of פֵּזַּר—פזר; were dis-
persed: *Niph. of* פוץ—נָפֹצוּ *and*
Pual of פֻּזְּרוּ—פזר

distant = far: רָחוֹק; made distant:
Hiph. of רָחַק (was far)—הִרְחִיק
(caused to be far)

distinguished (divided): *Hiph. of*
הִבְדִּיל—בדל

door: דֶּלֶת (*segholate*), *pl.* דְּלָתוֹת

drank: שָׁתָה, *imperf.* יִשְׁתֶּה, *with
Waw consec.* וַיֵּשְׁתְּ; gave to drink:
Hiph. of שקה—הִשְׁקָה, *defective*,
WHG 238 c

dreaded (terrible): *Niph. part. of*
יָרֵא (was afraid, feared)—נוֹרָא,
(being feared).

dream: חֲלוֹם, *pl.* חֲלוֹמוֹת

dreamed, dreamt: חָלַם, *imperf.*
יַחֲלֹם

dreamer: (i) חֹלֵם—*Qal active part.*
(one dreaming); (ii) בַּעַל־
חֲלוֹמוֹת (master of dreams)

drew near: (i) קָרַב and קָרֵב (*sta-tive*), *imperf.* יִקְרַב; (ii) *the perf.
is* נִגַּשׁ—*Niph. of* נגשׁ; *the imperf.*
יִגַּשׁ, *imper.* גַּשׁ, *and inf. const.* גֶּשֶׁת
(*with suff.* גִּשְׁתִּי, *&c.*) *are in Qal*,
WHG 141, 142

drove (out): *Piel* גֵּרֵשׁ, *imperf.*
יְגָרֵשׁ

dug: כָּרָה, חָפַר

dust: עָפָר

dweller (inhabitant): יֹשֵׁב—*Qal ac-tive part. of* יָשַׁב (dwelt)

dwelt: יָשַׁב, *imperf.* יֵשֵׁב, *with Waw
consec.* וַיֵּשֶׁב, *imper.* שֵׁב, *inf. const.*
שֶׁבֶת (*with suff.* שִׁבְתִּי), WHG 188,
189

E

each: כֹּל, *with maqqeph* כָּל־

each other: *see* 'one another' *under*
'another'

ear: אֹזֶן (*segholate*), *with suff.* אָזְנִי,
&c.; dual אָזְנַיִם; gave ear to:
Hiph. of אזן—הֶאֱזִין, *with direct
object*

earth: (i) אֶרֶץ (*segholate*), *with suff.*
אַרְצִי, *&c.*; (ii) אֲדָמָה, *const.* אַדְמַת

earthquake: רַעַשׁ

ease (security): שַׁלְוָה; was at ease
(*vb.*): שָׁלֵו, שַׁאֲנָן

east: מִזְרָח, קֶדֶם

Eden: עֵדֶן

edge: (i) קָצֶה; (ii) שָׂפָה (lip); edge
of the sword (*in the Authorized
English Bible*): פִּי־הַחֶרֶב (mouth
of . . .)

Edom: אֱדוֹם

Egypt: מִצְרַיִם, *the dual referring to
the upper and lower Egypts*;
Egyptian: מִצְרִי, I, 17

eight: שְׁמֹנָה *with masc. ns. and*
שְׁמֹנֶה *with fem. ns.*, WHG 243,
244

eighth: שְׁמִינִי, *fem.* שְׁמִינִית

elder: (i) community leader: זָקֵן,
XLII, 26 (*b*); (ii) (older) גָּדוֹל
(big)

Elhanan: אֶלְחָנָן

Eli: עֵלִי

Eliezer: אֱלִיעֶזֶר

Elijah: אֵלִיָּהוּ

embraced: *Piel of* חבק—חִבֵּק

empty: רֵיק, רֵק

encamped, was encamped: חָנָה,
imperf. יַחֲנֶה, *with Waw consec.*
וַיִּחַן

encompassed (went round): סָבַב,
imperf. יָסֹב

end: קָצֶה, קֵץ

endured (lasted): קָם, עָמַד √קוּם

enemy: אֹיֵב, *with suff.* אֹיְבִי,
&c.

enslaved: *Hiph. of* עָבַד (served,
was a slave)—הֶעֱבִיד (caused to
serve, to be a slave)

entered, (came in): בָּא √בוא, *im-perf.* יָבֹא, *imper.* בֹּא, WHG 212
(*d*)

enticed: *Piel of* פָּתָה—פִּתָּה

entrance: מָבוֹא, פֶּתַח

entreated: עָתַר, *imperf.* יֶעְתַּר

Ephraim: אֶפְרַיִם

epistle, letter: סֵפֶר, מִכְתָּב

escape, place of: מִפְלָט

escaped: *Niph. of* מלט—נִמְלַט

established: (i) *Hiph. of* קָם√קוּם—
הֵקִים; (ii) *Polel of* כון√—כּוֹנֵן.
Cf. WHG 201

eternity: עַד, עוֹלָם

even: גַּם

evening: עֶרֶב

event: מַעֲשֶׂה

ever, for: לָעַד, לְעוֹלָם

everlasting = of eternity, I, 57

every: כֹּל, *with maqqeph* כָּל־;
everyone: כָּל־אִישׁ

evil: (*adj.*): רַע, *with the art.* הָרָע,
fem. רָעָה, *masc. pl.* רָעִים; (*n.*):
(i) רֹע; (ii) רָעָה, *fem. sing. adj.*,
V, 43; did evil: *Hiph. of* רַע√רעע
(was evil)—הֵרַע *and* הָרַע (caused
it to be evil, VII, 26, XVII, 38;
evil-doer = doer of evil

exceedingly: עַד־מְאֹד, מְאֹד

except: רַק (only); אִם . . . לֹא, בִּלְתִּי
(if . . . not)

exile: שְׁבִי, שְׁבוּת, גֹּלָה, גָּלוּת; went
into exile: (i) גָּלָה; (ii) *Niph. of*
שָׁבָה (took captive)—נִשְׁבָּה (was
taken captive); exiled: (i) שָׁבָה;
(ii) *Hiph. of* גָּלָה—הִגְלָה

exulted: עָלַץ

eye: עַיִן (*fem.*), *with suff.* עֵינִי, *dual*
עֵינַיִם.

eyelid: עַפְעַף, *dual* עַפְעַפַּיִם

F

face: פָּנִים

fair (beautiful): יָפֶה, *fem. sing.* יָפָה

faithful: נֶאֱמָן—*Niph. part.*

faithfulness: אֱמוּנָה

false = of falsehood; falsehood:
שֶׁקֶר

family: מִשְׁפָּחָה, *const.* מִשְׁפַּחַת; *also*
בַּיִת (house)

far: רָחוֹק; was far (*vb.*): רָחַק;
kept far: *Hiph. of* רחק—הִרְחִיק
(caused to be far)

fashioned: יָצַר, *imperf. with Waw
consec.* וַיִּיצֶר

fat: (*adj.*) שָׁמֵן, בָּרִיא (of cattle);
(*n.*) חֵלֶב

father: אָב, *const.* אֲבִי, *with suff.*
אָבִי, אָבִיךָ &c., *pl.* אָבוֹת, X, 39,
WHG 288

fatherless (orphan): יָתוֹם

favour (grace): חֵן, *with suff.* חִנִּי,
&c.

fear: פַּחַד, יִרְאָה

feared: יָרֵא (stative), *imperf.* יִירָא,
inf. const. יִרְאָה, I, 61 (*b*). N.B.
'was afraid of' *is* יָרֵא מִפְּנֵי;
'feared' *in a reverential sense is*
יָרֵא אֶת־, VII, 31

feast: מִשְׁתֶּה; Feast = festival

fed: *Hiph. of* אָכַל (ate)—הֶאֱכִיל
(caused to eat)

fell: נָפַל, *imperf.* יִפֹּל

festival: חַג, *pl.* חַגִּים

few: *pl. of* מְעַט (little)—מְעַטִּים

field: שָׂדֶה, *const.* שְׂדֵה, *pl.* שָׂדוֹת

fierce = fierceness of: *const. of*
חָרוֹן (burning)

fifth: חֲמִישִׁי, *fem.* חֲמִישִׁית

filled, was: מָלֵא (*stative*), *imperf.*
יִמְלָא, *inf. const.* מְלֹאת: filled
(*trans.*) *Piel*, מִלֵּא. *This vb. takes
a direct object. It means* 'was
filled with' (*Piel*—'filled with'),
XXII, 13

finished, was: כָּלָה; finished (*trans.*)
Piel, כִּלָּה, XXIX, 25 *Note*

fire: אֵשׁ; set fire to: *Hiph. of* בָּעַר
(was alight)—הִבְעִיר (caused to
be alight)

firmament: רָקִיעַ

first: רִאשׁ‍ן; at first (earlier):
בַּתְּחִלָּה, בָּרִאשׁ‍נָה

first-born: בְּכוֹר

five: חֲמִשָּׁה *with masc. ns. and* חָמֵשׁ
with fem. ns., WHG 242, 244

fled: (i) בָּרַח; (ii) נָס, נוס√, *imperf.*
יָנוּס, *with Waw consec.* וַיָּנָס.
Cf. WHG 197

flesh: בָּשָׂר

flocks: צאן (*collective*)

flood: מַבּוּל

followed = went after

folly: סִכְלוּת, נְבָלָה

food: מַאֲכָל, אָכְלָה, אֹכֶל

for: (*prep.*) לְ; (because) כִּי

force: כֹּחַ, חֶזְקָה (*segholate*), חֹזֶק

forgave: מָחַל, סָלַח

forgot: שָׁכַח

formed = fashioned

forsook: עָזַב; נָטַשׁ, *imperf.* יִטּשׁ

fortress: מִשְׂגָּב, מְצוּדָה

forty: אַרְבָּעִים

fought: *Niph. of* לחם—נִלְחַם *followed by* בְּ

found: מָצָא

founded: יָסַד (וסד); was founded:
Niph. נוֹסַד. Cf. WHG 191

four: אַרְבָּעָה *with masc. ns. and*
אַרְבַּע *with fem. ns.*, WHG
242, 244

fourth: רְבִיעִי, *fem.* רְבִיעִית

from: מִן

full: (*adj.*): מָלֵא; (*vb.*) was full:
מָלֵא (*stative*), *imperf.* יִמְלָא *followed by direct object*—'was full
with', V, 31 (*a*), 32

G

gall (poison): רֹאשׁ, לַעֲנָה

garden: גַּן, *with art.* הַגָּן

garment: (i) בֶּגֶד (*segholate*), *with
suff.* בִּגְדִי; (ii) שִׂמְלָה

gate: שַׁעַר, *pl.* שְׁעָרִים

gathered together: (*trans.*) אָסַף
(*Qal*), קִבֵּץ (*Piel*), הִקְהִיל (*Hiph.*);
(*intrans.*—'were gathered to-
gether', 'gathered themselves
together') *in Niph.* נֶאֶסְפוּ,
נִקְהֲלוּ, נִקְבְּצוּ, *and Hithp.* הִתְאַסְּפוּ,
הִתְקַבְּצוּ

gathering: of people קָהָל (assembly)

gave: נָתַן, *imperf.* יִתֵּן, *imper.* תֵּן,
inf. const. תֵּת, *with suff.* תִּתִּי, &*c.*,
WHG 148

generation: דּוֹר, *pl.* דּוֹרוֹת

gentile (nation): גּוֹי

gift: מִנְחָה, מַתָּנָה

Gilead: גִּלְעָד

girded: חָגַר

girl: יַלְדָּה, נַעֲרָה

glad: (adj.) שָׂמֵחַ; was glad (vb.)
שָׂמַח; made glad, gladdened:
Piel—שִׂמַּח. Cf. XXII, 13, 26

glorious = of glory

glory: כָּבוֹד

go: let go: Piel of שָׁלַח (sent)—שִׁלַּח
(sent away)

God: אֱלֹהִים, often with the art.
הָאֱלֹהִים, 'the God'

gods: אֱלֹהִים

gold: זָהָב

good: (adj.) טוֹב; (n.) טוֹבָה—fem.
sing. adj., V, 44; was good (vb.)
perf. טוֹב, imperf. יִיטַב (√יטב)—
defective, WHG 238 B; did
good: Hiph. of יטב—הֵיטִיב

goods: כֵּלִים, pl. of כְּלִי (vessel)

Goshen: גֹּשֶׁן

grace: חֵן, with suff. חִנִּי, &c.

gracious: חַנּוּן; was gracious to:
חָנַן, imperf. יָחֹן—with direct object

granted = gave

grape: עֵנָב

grass: עֵשֶׂב, דֶּשֶׁא

great: גָּדוֹל; was great: (vb.) גָּדַל
(stative), imperf. יִגְדַּל; made
great: Hiph. הִגְדִּיל (caused to be
great)

green, fresh, luxuriant (of trees):
רַעֲנָן

grew (of plants): צָמַח

grew up: גָּדַל (stative), imperf.
יִגְדַּל

grievous: כָּבֵד (heavy)

ground: אֶרֶץ, אֲדָמָה (earth)

guarded: שָׁמַר

H

Ha‘ai הָעַי

habitation: מִשְׁכָּן, מָעוֹן, מוֹשָׁב

hand: יָד, dual יָדַיִם

handmaid: שִׁפְחָה, אָמָה

happy = Oh, the happinesses of!:
אַשְׁרֵי (const. pl. of אֶשֶׁר); happy
is he = Oh, his happinesses!—
אַשְׁרָיו

hard (adj.): כָּבֵד, קָשֶׁה; was hard
(vb.): כָּבֵד (stative); made hard:
Piel and Hiph.—הִכְבִּיד and כִּבֵּד,
XXII, 26

harm: רָעָה (fem. sing. adj., V, 43),
רַע

harvest: קָצִיר

hastened: מִהַר—Piel

hated: שָׂנֵא, imperf. יִשְׂנָא

haughty was: (i) רָם √רום (was
high); (ii) Hithp. of נָשָׂא (lifted
up)—הִתְנַשֵּׂא (lifted himself up,
exalted himself)

he: הוּא

head: רֹאשׁ, pl. רָאשִׁים

healed: רָפָא and Piel

heap (mound): תֵּל, pl. תִּלִּים

heard: שָׁמַע

hearing (n.): אָזְנֵי (ears of)

hearkened unto: שָׁמַע אֶל

heart: (i) לֵב, with suff. לִבִּי, pl.
לְבָבוֹת; (ii) לֵבָב, pl. לִבּוֹת

heavens: שָׁמַיִם, const. שְׁמֵי

heavy (adj.) כָּבֵד; was heavy (vb.)
כָּבֵד (stative), imperf. יִכְבַּד

Hebrew: עִבְרִי

Hebron: חֶבְרוֹן

heeded: שָׂם לֵב (set one's heart):

took heed: *Niph. of* שָׁמַר (kept)
—נִשְׁמַר (kept himself)

help: עֶזֶר, *with suff.* עֶזְרִי; עֶזְרָה;

helped: עָזַר

herds: מִקְנֶה, בָּקָר (collective)

herdsman: אִישׁ מִקְנֶה (man of herds)

here: פֹּה

heretofore: תְּמוֹל שִׁלְשׁוֹם (yesterday, the day before yesterday)

hero: גִּבּוֹר (mighty man)

hid: (i) *trans.*: *Hiph. of* סתר, חבא—הֶחְבִּיא, הִסְתִּיר; (ii) hid himself: *Niph.* נֶחְבָּא, נִסְתַּר, *and Hithp.* הִסְתַּתֵּר, WHG 120 *Note*, הִתְחַבֵּא;

hidden: נִסְתָּר—*Niph. part.*

high (*adj.*): רָם, גָּבֹהַּ; most high: עֶלְיוֹן; on high: לַמָּרוֹם, בַּמָּרוֹם; was high (*vb.*): (i) רום√, רָם, *imperf.* יָרוּם, *with Waw consec.* וַיָּרָם, WHG 197; (ii) גָּבַהּ, *imperf.* יִגְבַּהּ

highway: מְסִלָּה; cast up, made a highway: *the cognate vb.* סָלַל

hither: הֵנָּה; hither and thither: הֵנָּה וָהֵנָּה

holiness: קֹדֶשׁ (segholate)

holy: קָדוֹשׁ; made holy: קִדֵּשׁ—*Piel. Cf.* XXII, 13, 26

honour: כָּבוֹד

honoured (*vb.*): *Piel* כִּבֵּד; (*adj.*) מְכֻבָּד *Pual part.*

horse: סוּס

host: צָבָא, *pl.* צְבָאוֹת

house, household: בַּיִת, *const.* בֵּית, *with suff.* בֵּיתִי, &*c.*; *pl.* בָּתִּים, II, 21

hundred: מֵאָה, *const.* מְאַת; *dual* מָאתַיִם (two hundred)

hunger: רָעָב

hungry (*adj.*): רָעֵב; was hungry (*vb.*): רָעֵב (stative)

hurt (*n.*): רָעָה (evil—V, 43); פֶּצַע (wound)

husband: אִישׁ

I

I: אָנֹכִי, אֲנִי

idle: (i) vain = of vanity, שָׁוְא; (ii) (lazy) עָצֵל

idol: אֱלִיל

if: אִם, *sometimes* כִּי, XL, 6

illumined: *Hiph. of* אוֹר (was light) —הֵאִיר (caused to be light)

in: בְּ

inclined: (*intrans.*) נָטָה, *imperf.* יִטֶּה, *with Waw consec.* וַיֵּט; (*trans.*)—*Hiph.* הִטָּה (caused to incline), *imperf.* יַטֶּה, *with Waw consec.* וַיֵּט, WHG 224

increased: *Hiph. of* רָבָה (was much)—הִרְבָּה

indeed: אָמְנָם, אָכֵן; *to emphasize a vb. the inf. abs. is used before the finite vb.*

inhabitant: יֹשֵׁב—*Qal active part.*

inhabited = dwelt

inheritance: יְרֻשָּׁה, נַחֲלָה

inherited: (i) נָחַל, *imperf.* יִנְחַל, WHG 144 *Note*; (ii) יָרַשׁ, *imperf.* יִירַשׁ, *imper.* רַשׁ *and* רֵשׁ, *inf. const.* רֶשֶׁת (with suff. רִשְׁתִּי, &*c.*), II, 22

inquired: (i) inquired after: שָׁאַל

followed by לְ; (ii) inquired of
the oracle: שָׁאַל *followed by* ב
instead of: תַּחַת *with suffs. of the*
pl. n., WHG 87
instruction: מוּסָר (correction), XX,
23
instrument: כְּלִי, *pl.* כֵּלִים
interpretation: פִּתְרוֹן
interpreted: פָּתַר
iron: בַּרְזֶל
Isaac: יִצְחָק
Israel: יִשְׂרָאֵל

J

Jacob: יַעֲקֹב
Jeremiah: יִרְמְיָהוּ
Jericho: יְרִיחוֹ
Jerusalem: יְרוּשָׁלַיִם (*read as* יְרוּשָׁלַםִ)
jested: *Piel of* צָחַק (laughed)—צִחֵק
Jonathan: יְהוֹנָתָן
Jordan: יַרְדֵּן
Joseph: יוֹסֵף
Joshua: יְהוֹשֻׁעַ
journey: דֶּרֶךְ (way)
journeyed: נָסַע, *imperf.* יִסַּע
joy: שִׂמְחָה; shout of joy: רִנָּה, רַנֵּה
Judah: יְהוּדָה
judge: שֹׁפֵט—*Qal active part.*
judged: שָׁפַט
judgement: מִשְׁפָּט
just: צַדִּיק
justice: צֶדֶק, מִשְׁפָּט

K

keeper: שֹׁמֵר—*Qal active part.*
kept: שָׁמַר
killed: (i) הָרַג; (ii) *Hiph. of* מֵת

מוּת√ (died)—הֵמִית (caused to
die), *imperf.* יָמִית, *with Waw*
consec. וַיָּמֶת
kinsman = brother
kissed: נָשַׁק, *imperf.* יִשַּׁק, *followed*
by לְ
knew: יָדַע (וְדַע), *imperf.* יֵדַע, *im-*
per. דַּע, *inf. const.* דַּעַת, WHG 210
knowledge: דַּעַת (*inf. const.*)

L

Laban: לָבָן
lad: נַעַר
laid: (i) שִׂים√ שָׂם (placed), *imperf.*
יָשִׂים, *jussive* יָשֵׂם, *imperf. with*
Waw consec. וַיָּשֶׂם, *imper.* שִׂים,
WHG 197; סָמַךְ (laid hands upon)
lament: אֵבֶל, מִסְפֵּד (mourning)
lamented: (i) סָפַד; (ii) *Hithp. of*
הִתְאַבֵּל—אבל
lamp: מְנוֹרָה
land: (i) אֶרֶץ (*segholate—fem.*);
(ii) אֲדָמָה, *const.* אַדְמַת
language: שָׂפָה (lip)
latter (end): אַחֲרִית
laughed: צָחַק
law: מִשְׁפָּט (judgement)
lay down (slept): שָׁכַב (*stative*),
imperf. יִשְׁכַּב, WHG 97 *Note*
leader = head
leaf: עָלֶה
Leah: לֵאָה
learned: לָמַד, *imperf.* יִלְמַד
led: (i) נִהֵל, נָהָה, נָהַל (*Piel*); (ii)
הָלַךְ לִפְנֵי (went before)
left (*vb.*): עָזַב; (direction) שְׂמֹאל

length: אֹרֶךְ (segholate), with suff.
אָרְכִּי

lent: Hiph. of לָוָה (borrowed)—
הִלְוָה (caused to borrow)

lest: פֶּן

letter (epistle): סֵפֶר, מִכְתָּב

lie (lying): כָּזָב

life: (i) duration of existence חַיִּים
(pl.); (ii) the vital element נֶפֶשׁ

lifted up: (i) נָשָׂא, imperf. יִשָּׂא,
imper. שָׂא, inf. const. נְשׂא and
שְׂאֵת, WHG 185 (c); (ii) Hiph.
of רום√ רָם (was high)—הֵרִים
(caused to be high)

light (n.): אוֹר; was light (vb.):
אוֹר, imperf. יָאוֹר; gave light:
Hiph. הֵאִיר (caused to be
light)

lightning: בָּרָק

like (as): כ (inseparable); in
poetry כְּמוֹ

likeness: דְּמוּת

lion: אַרְיֵה, אֲרִי

lip: שָׂפָה, dual שְׂפָתַיִם

little: קָטֹן, קָטָן, fem. קְטַנָּה; was
little (stative vb.) קָטֹן, imperf.
יִקְטַן; little ones (babes) טַף,
with suff. טַפִּי (collective)

lived: חַי√ חיי and חָיָה

living: חַי

lo (behold): הִנֵּה

lofty: רָם—Qal active part., נֹשֵׂא—
Niph. part. of נָשָׂא (lifted up) and
גָּבֹהַּ

long, how . . .? עַד־מָתַי (till when?)

looked: Hiph. of נבט שׁקף—הִבִּיט,
הִשְׁקִיף

loosened: Piel of פָּתַח (opened)—
פִּתַּח

Lord, the = Yahweh—יהוה

lord: בַּעַל, אָדוֹן. The suffs., with the
exception of the first sing., are
attached to the pl. n.

lost, was: אָבַד, imperf. יֹאבַד

Lot: לוֹט

loud (voice, sound): גָּדוֹל (great)

loved: אָהַב, אָהֵב (stative), imperf.
יֶאֱהַב, V, 17

lovingkindness: חֶסֶד (segholate)

low (adj.): שָׁפָל and שָׁפָל, const.
שְׁפַל; was low (vb.): שָׁפֵל (stative), imperf. יִשְׁפַּל; brought low:
Hiph. הִשְׁפִּיל (caused to be low)

M

made: עָשָׂה, imperf. יַעֲשֶׂה, jussive
יַעַשׂ, imperf. with Waw consec.
וַיַּעַשׂ, WHG 225 (b)

magnified: Hiph. of גָּדַל (was
great)—הִגְדִּיל (caused to be
great)

maiden: נַעֲרָה, בְּתוּלָה

maidservant: (i) שִׁפְחָה, pl. שְׁפָחוֹת;
(ii) אָמָה, pl. אֲמָהוֹת

man: אִישׁ, אֱנוֹשׁ, אָדָם, גֶּבֶר; fellow
man: רֵעַ (neighbour); young
man: נַעַר, בָּחוּר, pl. בַּחוּרִים

manner: מִשְׁפָּט

manservant: עֶבֶד (segholate)

many: pl. of רַב (much)—רַבִּים

master: בַּעַל, אָדוֹן. The suffs., with
the exception of the first sing.,
are attached to the pl. n.

matter: דָּבָר

mean (small): קָטֹן

melted, was melted: *Niph. of* נָמֵס—מסס, *imperf.* יִמַּס

merchant: סֹחֵר

merciful: רַחוּם

mercy: רַחֲמִים; had mercy: *Piel of* רִחַם—רחם

merry: שָׂמֵחַ; made merry: טוֹב לִבּוֹ (his heart was good)

met: פָּגַשׁ; to meet (*meaning* 'towards')—לִקְרַאת, *with suff.* לִקְרָאתִי, &c., IX, 33

midday: צָהֳרַיִם

middle (half): חֲצוֹת, חֲצִי

Midian: מִדְיָן; Midianite: מִדְיָנִי, XVIII, 6

midst: (i) תָּוֶךְ, *const.* תּוֹךְ; (ii) קֶרֶב, *with suff.* קִרְבִּי.

mighty: גִּבּוֹר, עָצוּם; was mighty (*vb.*): חָזַק, *imperf.* יֶחֱזַק

minister: *Piel part. of* שרת—מְשָׁרֵת

ministered: *Piel of* שרת—שֵׁרֵת, *imperf.* יְשָׁרֵת

misfortune: רָעָה (evil—V, 43), שֹׁד, שֶׁבֶר

Mizpah: מִצְפָּה

mocked: לֵעַג, לוּץ√ לָץ, *and Piel of* חֵרֵף—חרף (reviled)

money: כֶּסֶף (silver—*segholate*)

monster: תַּנִּין

month: חֹדֶשׁ (*segholate*)

morning: בֹּקֶר; morning star: שַׁחַר

morrow: מָחֳרָת

Moses: מֹשֶׁה

mother: אֵם, *with suff.* אִמִּי, *pl.* אִמּוֹת

mound: תֵּל, *pl.* תִּלִּים

mountain: הַר, *with art.* הָהָר, *pl.* הָרִים

mourned: (i) סָפַד; (ii) *Hithp. of* הִתְאַבֵּל—אבל

mourning (*n.*): אֵבֶל

mouth: פֶּה, *const.* פִּי, *with suff.* פִּיךָ, &c., *pl.* פִּיּוֹת, WHG 288

much: רַב, (*adv.*) הַרְבֵּה—*Hiph. inf. abs. of* רָבָה (was much)

multiplied: *Hiph. of* רָבָה (was much)—הִרְבָּה (caused to be much)

multitude: הָמוֹן

music: זִמְרָה; musical = of music

musician: *Piel part. of* נגן (played an instrument)—מְנַגֵּן

N

Nabal: נָבָל

naked: עָרֹם (עֲרֻמִּים *pl.*) *and* עֵירֹם

name: שֵׁם, *with suff.* שְׁמִי, שִׁמְךָ, &c., *pl.* שֵׁמוֹת

named (*vb.*): קָרָא לְ (called to); קָרָא אֶת־שְׁמוֹ (called its name)

nation: (i) גּוֹי, *pl.* גּוֹיִם; (ii) עַם, *with suff.* עַמִּי, *pl.* עַמִּים; (iii) לְאֹם, *pl.* לְאֻמִּים

nay: לֹא

Nebuchadnezzar, Nebuchadrezzar: נְבוּכַדְרֶאצַּר, נְבוּכַדְנֶאצַּר

neck: עֹרֶף (*segholate*): צַוָּאר *and the pl.* צַוָּארִים

needy: דַּל, אֶבְיוֹן

neighbour: רֵעַ (fellow man)

neither . . . nor: אֵין . . . לֹא, לֹא . . . וְאֵין . . .

nephew = son of a brother *or* sister

net: רֶשֶׁת

new: חָדָשׁ

night: לַיְלָה (*masc.*—VI, 2), *pl.*
לֵילוֹת

Nile, the: הַיְאוֹר

nine: תִּשְׁעָה *with masc. ns. and*
תֵּשַׁע *with fem. ns.*, WHG 243, 244

ninth: תְּשִׁיעִי, *fem.* תְּשִׁיעִית

no, not: לֹא; there is (*or* are) not
אֵין; not to . . . .: לְבִלְתִּי *followed
by the inf. const.*, XXXVIII, 22;
no one: *the neg. with* אִישׁ (man,
person)

noise: שָׁאוֹן, קוֹל (tumult)

north: צָפוֹן; northern = of the
north

nothing: לֹא . . . מְאוּמָה,אַיִן (not . . . a
thing) *usually there would be a
vb. between*; for nothing חִנָּם

now: (*in point of time*) עַתָּה; (*emphatic*) נָא, I, 4

number: מִסְפָּר

numbered: סָפַר, מָנָה

numerous: *pl. of* רַב (much)—רַבִּים

O

O (vocative): *use the art. or suff.*,
I, 62; XXIII, 17

offered up (sacrifice): (i) זָבַח; (ii)
Hiph. of קָרַב (was near)—הִקְרִיב
(caused to be near, brought
near); (iii) *Hiph. of* עָלָה (went
up)—הֶעֱלָה (caused to go up,
brought up), II, 38

offering (sacrifice): זֶבַח, קָרְבָּן,
עוֹלָה; (gift) מִנְחָה

officer (of the army): שַׂר, *with art.*

הַשַּׂר, *pl.* שָׂרִים; (administrative):
שֹׁטֵר

old (*adj.*): זָקֵן; was old (*vb.*): זָקֵן
(stative), *imperf.* יִזְקַן, see II, 35;
. . . years old: בֶּן־ *or* בַּת־ *followed by* שָׁנִים (years)

old age: זִקְנָה, זְקֻנִים (*pl. n.*)

olive, oliveyard: זַיִת, *const.* זֵית, *pl.*
זֵיתִים

on (upon, over): עַל *with suffs. of
the pl. n.*, WHG 87

one: אֶחָד, *fem.* אַחַת; one another:
see under 'another'; no one: *the
neg. with* אִישׁ (man, person)

only: רַק, אַךְ

open (*adj.*): פָּתוּחַ—*Qal passive
part.*

opened: פָּתַח; (of the eyes) פָּקַח;
(of the mouth) פָּצָה

opposite: מוּל, נֶגֶד, II, 11 (*b*)

oppressed: עָשַׁק, לָחַץ

oppression: לַחַץ, עֹשֶׁק

oppressor: (*Qal active part.*) לֹחֵץ,
עֹשֵׁק

or: אוֹ; whether . . . or: הֲ . . . אִם,
III, 40

ordinance: מִשְׁפָּט

orphan: יָתוֹם

other: (i) another אַחֵר, other(s)
אֲחֵרִים (*pl.*); (ii) the other (one)
= the second (one); one another: *see under* 'another'

out of: מִן

over (on, upon): עַל *with suffs. of
the pl. n.*, WHG 87

over against = opposite

overtook: *Hiph. of* נשׂג—הִשִּׂיג

ox: שׁוֹר, *pl.* שְׁוָרִים; פַּר, *with art.* הַפָּר, *pl.* פָּרִים

P

palace: הֵיכָל

parched (thirsty): צָמֵא

passed: עָבַר; passed over (to the other side)—עָבַר אֶת; passed through (from place to place)—עָבַר ב; came to pass = was

Passover: פֶּסַח

pasture: מִרְעֶה

pastured: רָעָה

path: אֹרַח, דֶּרֶךְ

peace: שָׁלוֹם; peaceably = in peace

people, a (nation): (i) עַם, *with art.* הָעָם, *pl.* עַמִּים; (ii) גּוֹי, *pl.* גּוֹיִם; (iii) לְאֹם, *pl.* לְאֻמִּים; group of individuals: אֲנָשִׁים, *pl. of* אִישׁ (man, person)

perfect: שָׁלֵם, תָּמִים

perished (was lost): אָבַד, *imperf.* יֹאבַד

permitted: נָתַן (gave)

person: אִישׁ (man)

Pharaoh: פַּרְעֹה

Philistine: פְּלִשְׁתִּי

pillar: עַמּוּד

pit: בּוֹר, שַׁחַת

pitched (tent): נָטָה (stretched out), *imperf.* יִטֶּה, *jussive* יֵט, *imperf. with Waw consec.* וַיֵּט, WHG 224

pitcher: כַּד, *pl.* כַּדִּים

pitied: רִחַם, חָמַל (*Piel*) *followed by* עַל (had mercy upon)

pity: רַחֲמִים (*pl. n.*); was moved to pity: נִכְמְרוּ רַחֲמָיו (... was warm)

place: מָקוֹם, *pl.* מְקוֹמוֹת; in place of = instead of

placed (set): (i) שָׂם √שׂים, *imperf.* יָשִׂים, *jussive* יָשֵׂם, *imperf. with Waw consec.* וַיָּשֶׂם, *imper.* שִׂים, WHG 197; (ii) שָׁת √שׁית, *imperf.* יָשִׁית, *with Waw consec.* וַיָּשֶׁת. Cf. WHG 197

plague: נֶגַע, מַגֵּפָה

plagued: (i) נָגַף, *imperf.* יִגֹּף; (ii) *Piel of* נגע—נִגַּע

plain: עֵמֶק, בִּקְעָה, מִישׁוֹר (valley)

plant: מַטָּע

planted: נָטַע, *imperf.* יִטַּע

played (instrument): *Piel of* גגן—נִגֵּן *followed by* ב

player: מְנַגֵּן—*Piel part.*

pleaded (a cause): רָב √ריב *imperf.* יָרִיב, *jussive* יָרֵב, *imperf. with Waw consec.* וַיָּרֶב, *imper.* רִיב. Cf. WHG 197, XXIX, 8

pleased: (i) טוֹב בְּעֵינֵי (was good in the eyes of); (ii) מָצָא חֵן בְּעֵינֵי (found favour in the eyes of)

pleasing = good—טוֹב; was pleasing (*vb.*): *perf.* טוֹב, *imperf.* יִיטַב (√יטב)—*defective*, WHG 238 B

ploughed: חָרַשׁ

plucked up: עָקַר

plunder: בַּז, שָׁלָל

plundered: (i) שָׁלַל, *imperf.* יָשֹׁל; (ii) בָּזַז, *imperf.* יָבֹז

poor: אֶבְיוֹן, עָנִי, דַּל

position (*n.*): מַצָּב; took up position: *Niph. or Hithp. of* יצב—הִתְיַצֵּב *or* נִצָּב

possessed: (i) רָכַשׁ; (ii) הָיָה לְ (was unto)

possession: יְרֻשָּׁה, נַחֲלָה, אֲחֻזָּה (inheritance); possessions, goods: רְכוּשׁ; took possession of: (i) יָרַשׁ, II, 22; (ii) נָחַל, *imperf.* יִנְחַל, WHG 144 *Note*

poured (out): (i) שָׁפַךְ; (ii) יָצַק, *imperf.* יִצֹּק, WHG 192 *Note*

power: (i) חַיִל; (ii) יָד (hand)

practised = did

praise: תְּהִלָּה

praised: *Piel of* הלל—הִלֵּל, שׁבח—שִׁבַּח

pray, I pray thee: אָנָּה, נָא, II, 17

prayed: *Hithp. of* פלל—הִתְפַּלֵּל

prayer: תְּפִלָּה

precious: יָקָר

prepared: *Hiph. of* √כון—הֵכִין; prepared oneself: *Niph.* נָכוֹן

presence, in the presence of = before = לְעֵינֵי, לִפְנֵי

prevailed (i) גָּבַר; (ii) קָם בִּפְנֵי (rose in the face of); (iii) יָכֹל לְ (was able for), *imperf.* יוּכַל

prey: עַד, טֶרֶף

priest: כֹּהֵן, *pl.* כֹּהֲנִים; the High Priest = הַכֹּהֵן הַגָּדוֹל

prince: שַׂר, *with the art.* הַשָּׂר, נָשִׂיא

proclaimed: *Hiph. of* שָׁמַע (heard) —הִשְׁמִיעַ (caused to hear); קָרָא (called, cried out)

produce (*n.*): יְבוּל, תְּבוּאָה

profaned: *Piel of* חלל—חִלֵּל

prophecy: נְבוּאָה

prophesied: *Niph. or Hithp. of* נבא—נִבָּא, הִתְנַבֵּא

prophet: נָבִיא

prospered: *Hiph. of* צלח—הִצְלִיחַ

protected: *Hiph. of* גנן—הֵגֵן *followed by* עַל

provisions: צֵידָה (*collective*)

provoked (to anger): *Hiph. of* כָּעַס (was angry)—הִכְעִיס (caused to be angry)

pure: זַךְ, טָהוֹר

pursued: רָדַף; ran after: רָדַף אַחֲרֵי; persecuted: רָדַף אֶת־

put = placed. put off (clothes): (i) פָּשַׁט; (ii) *Hiph. of* סור√—סָר—הֵסִיר (caused to depart, removed)

Q

quaked: רָעַשׁ

queen: מַלְכָּה

quiet (*adj.*) שָׁקֵט—*Qal active part.*; was quiet (*vb.*): שָׁקַט

R

Rachel: רָחֵל

rain: גֶּשֶׁם, מָטָר

rained: (*intrans.*)—the rain came down; (*trans.*)—*Hiph. of* מטר—הִמְטִיר (caused it to rain)

raised: (i) *Hiph. of* קום√ קָם (rose) —הֵקִים (caused to rise); (ii) *Hiph. of* רום√ רָם (was high)— הֵרִים (caused to be high); (iii) נָשָׂא (lifted up), *imperf.* יִשָּׂא, *imper.* שָׂא, WHG 185 (*c*)

ran: רוּץ√ רָץ, *imperf.* יָרוּץ, *with Waw consec.* וַיָּרָץ. Cf. WHG 197

reached: *Hiph. of* נָגַע (touched)— הִגִּיעַ (caused to touch) read: קָרָא *followed by* בּ

reaped: קָצַר

reaping (*n.*), harvest: קָצִיר

rear: אָחוֹר; in the rear: מֵאָחוֹר (from the rear)

reason, by reason of: מִן, עַל אֹדוֹת (out of), בַּעֲבוּר (for the sake of)

rebelled: פָּשַׁע, מָרַד; rebelled against: מָרַד, פָּשַׁע *followed by* בּ

rebuilt = built

recalled (brought to mind): *Hiph. of* זָכַר (remembered)—הִזְכִּיר (caused to remember)

reckoned (counted, numbered): מָנָה, סָפַר

reckoning (counting, number): מִסְפָּר

redeemed: פָּדָה, גָּאַל

redeemer: גֹּאֵל—*Qal active part.*

redemption: פִּדְיוֹן, גְּאֻלָּה

refrained: *Hithp. of* אפק—הִתְאַפֵּק

refused: *Piel of* מאן—מֵאֵן, *imperf.* יְמָאֵן

rejected: מָאַס, *usually followed by* בּ

rejoiced: שָׂמַח; made rejoice: *Piel* שִׂמַּח. Cf. XXII, 13, 26

rejoicing: גִּיל, שִׂמְחָה

related: (i) narrated: *Piel of* סָפַר—סִפֵּר; (ii) informed: *Hiph. of* נגד—הִגִּיד

remained: (i) stayed: יָשַׁב (sat, dwelt); (ii) was left over: *Niph. of* שאר—נִשְׁאַר *and of* יתר (וֹתר)—נוֹתַר, *imperf.* יִוָּתֵר. Cf. WHG 191

remembered: זָכַר

reminded: *Hiph. of* זָכַר (remembered)—הִזְכִּיר (caused to remember)

remnant: שְׁאֵרִית

removed: *Hiph. of* סור√ סָר (departed)—הֵסִיר (caused to depart)

rent: (i) (*vb.*) tore—קָרַע; (ii) (*adj.*) torn—קָרוּעַ—*Qal passive part.*

repented: (i) *Niph. of* נחם—נִחַם; (ii) שׁוּב√ שָׁב (turned back)

report: שְׁמוּעָה (a thing heard)

reproach (shame): חֶרְפָּה

reproached: *Piel of* חרף—חֵרֵף

reproved (corrected): *Piel of* יסר—יִסֵּר

required: (i) דָּרַשׁ; (ii) *Piel of* בקשׁ—בִּקֵּשׁ (sought)

requited: (i) גָּמַל; (ii) שִׁלֵּם—*Piel* (repaid)

rest: מְנוּחָה, מָנוֹחַ

rested: (i) נוּחַ√ נָח, *imperf.* יָנוּחַ, with Waw consec. וַיָּנַח; (ii) שָׁבַת (ceased)

restored: *Hiph. of* שׁוּב√ שָׁב (came back)—הֵשִׁיב (caused to come back)

restrained: עָצַר, חָשַׂךְ

Reuben: רְאוּבֵן

revealed: גָּלָה *and* גִּלָּה—*Qal and Piel*

reviled: *Piel of* גדף, חרף—חֵרֵף, גִּדֵּף

rich: (*adj.*) עָשִׁיר; was rich (*vb.*) עָשַׁר, *imperf.* יֶעְשַׁר

right: (i) good, proper: טוֹב, יָשָׁר; (ii) (direction) יָמִין

righteous: צַדִּיק

righteousness: צְדָקָה, צֶדֶק

ring: טַבַּעַת

river: נָהָר; the river Nile: הַיְאוֹר

robbed: שָׁדַד, גֶּזַל

robber: שֹׁדֵד

robe: מְעִיל

rock: (i) צוּר; (ii) סֶלַע (segholate), with suff. סַלְעִי

rod: מַטֶּה, שֵׁבֶט

rode: רָכַב, imperf. יִרְכַּב

rolled: גָּלַל

room: חֶדֶר (segholate), with suff. חֲדָרִי

root: שֹׁרֶשׁ (segholate), pl. שָׁרָשִׁים

rose: קוּם√ קָם, imperf. יָקוּם, with Waw consec. וַיָּקָם, imper. קוּם, WHG 197; rose up early (in the morning)—Hiph. of שכם—הִשְׁכִּים

round: סָבִיב; round about (adverbially) מִסָּבִיב; went around: סָבַב, imperf. יָסֹב, with Waw consec. וַיָּסָב, WHG 231

royal = of kingship—מַלְכוּת . . .

ruins: (i) שְׁמָמָה (desolation); (ii) שְׁבָרִים (breaches in walls)

rule (dominion): מֶמְשָׁלָה, const. מֶמְשֶׁלֶת, with suff. מֶמְשַׁלְתִּי, &c.

ruled: מָשַׁל; ruled over: מָשַׁל followed by ב

ruler: מֹשֵׁל—Qal active part.

S

Sabbath: שַׁבָּת

sack: שַׂק, אַמְתַּחַת

sacred: קָדוֹשׁ

sacrifice: עוֹלָה, קָרְבָּן, זֶבַח

sacrificed: (i) זָבַח; (ii) Hiph. of קרב

(was near)—הִקְרִיב (brought near); (iii) Hiph. of עָלָה (went up)—הֶעֱלָה (brought up), II, 38

said: אָמַר, imperf. יֹאמַר, with Waw consec. וַיֹּאמַר in pause, but וַיֹּאמֶר when associated with a following word; said unto himself: אָמַר בְּלִבּוֹ (said in his heart)

sake: for the sake of (i) לְמַעַן, with suff. לְמַעֲנִי, &c.; (ii) בַּעֲבוּר, with suff. בַּעֲבוּרִי, &c.

salvation: יֵשַׁע (segholate), with suff. יִשְׁעִי; תְּשׁוּעָה, יְשׁוּעָה

Samuel: שְׁמוּאֵל

sanctified: Piel of קדשׁ—קִדַּשׁ

sanctuary: מִקְדָּשׁ

sang: שִׁיר√ שָׁר, imperf. יָשִׁיר, with Waw consec. וַיָּשַׁר

Sarah: שָׂרָה

sat: יָשַׁב, imperf. יֵשֵׁב, with Waw consec. וַיֵּשֶׁב, imper. שֵׁב, inf. const. שֶׁבֶת, with suff. שִׁבְתִּי, &c., WHG 188, 189

sated, was: שָׂבַע

satiety: שֹׂבַע

Saul: שָׁאוּל

save (only): רַק

saved: Hiph. of נצל and ישע (ושע)
—הוֹשִׁיעַ and הִצִּיל. Cf.WHG 211

saviour: מוֹשִׁיעַ—Hiph. part.

saw: רָאָה, imperf. יִרְאֶה, with Waw consec. וַיַּרְא

saying: לֵאמֹר meaning 'as follows'

scattered: (i) Piel of פזר—פִּזַּר; (ii) Hiph. of פוץ—הֵפִיץ; were scattered: (i) Pual פֻּזְּרוּ; (ii) Niph. נָפֹצוּ

scoffed: (i) √לוּץ לָץ; (ii) Piel of חָרַף—חרף

scoffer: (i) לֵץ; (ii) מְחָרֵף, Piel part.

sea: יָם, pl. יַמִּים

searched: (i) Piel of חפשׂ—חִפֵּשׂ; (ii) דָּרַשׁ—(inquired); (iii) Piel of בקשׁ—בִּקֵּשׁ (sought)

season: (i) עֵת, pl. עִתִּים; (ii) מוֹעֵד (fixed time)

second: שֵׁנִי, fem. שֵׁנִית

secret: סוֹד; secretly, בַּלָּט, חֶרֶשׁ, בַּסֵּתֶר

seed: זֶרַע (segholate), with suff. זַרְעִי, &c.

seized: (i) אָחַז, imperf. יֹאחֵז; (ii) Hiph. of חזק—הֶחֱזִיק

sent: שָׁלַח; sent away (dismissed, let go): Piel—שִׁלַּח

separated (trans.): Hiph. of פרד, הִבְדִּיל, הִפְרִיד—בדל; was separated: Niph. of either root

serpent: נָחָשׁ

set (placed): (i) √שׂים שָׂם, imperf. יָשִׂים, with Waw consec. וַיָּשֶׂם, WHG 197; (ii) √שׁית שָׁת, imperf. יָשִׁית, with Waw consec. וַיָּשֶׁת

set up: Hiph. of (i) √קוּם קָם (rose)—הֵקִים (caused to rise), and of (ii) יצב—הִצִּיב (caused to stand), WHG 192 Note

seven: שִׁבְעָה with masc. ns. and שֶׁבַע with fem. ns., WHG 243, 244

seventh: שְׁבִיעִי, fem. שְׁבִיעִית

seventy: שִׁבְעִים

shame: בֹּשֶׁת, בּוּשָׁה, חֶרְפָּה (segholate); put to shame: Hiph.

of בּוֹשׁ (was ashamed)—הֵבִישׁ (caused to be ashamed)

Shechem: שְׁכֶם

shed (spilled, poured out): (i) שָׁפַךְ; (ii) יָצַק, imperf. יִצֹּק, WHG 192 Note

sheep: צֹאן, used as collective

Sheol: שְׁאוֹל (abode of the dead)

shepherd: רֹעֶה or, more fully, רֹעֵה צֹאן (a tender of sheep)

ship: אֳנִיָּה

shone: Hiph. of יפע (וּפַע)—הוֹפִיעַ (made light)

shoulder: שְׁכֶם

shouted (in triumph): Hiph. of רוע—הֵרִיעַ (made a noise); shouted for joy: Piel רָנַן, imperf. יְרַנֵּן

shout of joy: רִנָּה or רְנָנָה

showed: Hiph. of רָאָה (saw)—הֶרְאָה (caused to see)

sick (adj.): חֹלֶה; was sick (vb.): חָלָה

sickness (disease): חֳלִי, in pause חֹלִי (segholate), with suff. חָלְיִי, &c.

siege: מָצוֹר; laid siege, besieged: √צוּר צָר

sight: (i) appearance: מַרְאֶה; (ii) in the sight of = in the eyes of

sign: אוֹת, pl. אוֹתוֹת

silent, was: חָרַשׁ (stative), imperf. יֶחֱרַשׁ, XLV, 28

silver: כֶּסֶף (segholate), with suff. כַּסְפִּי, &c.

sin: חָטָא, with suff. חֶטְאִי, &c., and חַטָּאת, XXXIX, 24

Sinai: סִינַי

sinned: חָטָא, *imperf.* יֶחֱטָא

sinner: חֹטֵא—*Qal active part., or* חַטָּא *as n.*

sister: אָחוֹת, *pl.* אֲחָיוֹת

situated (referring to a city): יֹשֶׁבֶת (dwelling)—*Qal active part. fem. sing. of* יָשַׁב

slain: (i) חָלָל (pierced); (ii) הָרוּג —*Qal passive part.*

slaughter: הֶרֶג, הֲרֵגָה

slaughtered: שָׁחַט

slave: עֶבֶד (segholate), *with suff.* עַבְדִּי, *&c.*

slavery: עַבְדוּת; brought into slavery: *Hiph. of* עָבַד (served, was a slave)—הֶעֱבִיד (caused to serve, be a slave)

sleep: שֵׁנָה; deep sleep: תַּרְדֵּמָה

slept (was asleep): (i) יָשֵׁן (stative), *imperf.* יִישַׁן; (ii) שָׁכַב (stative), *imperf.* יִשְׁכַּב, WHG 97

slew: (i) הָרַג; (ii) *Hiph. of* מות/מֵת (died)—הֵמִית (caused to die)

slope (incline, descent): מוֹרָד

small: קָטֹן, קָטָן, *fem.* קְטַנָּה; was small (*stative vb.*) קָטֹן, *imperf.* יִקְטַן

smoke: עָשָׁן

smote: *Hiph. of* נכה—הִכָּה, WHG 225

snare: מוֹקֵשׁ, פַּח

soared: (i) עוף√ עָף, טוש√; (ii) טוש√ טָשׂ

sold: מָכַר

Solomon: שְׁלֹמֹה

son: בֵּן, *with suff.* בִּנְךָ, בְּנִי, *&c., pl.* בָּנִים

song: שִׁיר, שִׁירָה

sorrow: יָגוֹן

sought: *Piel of* בקש—בִּקֵּשׁ

soul (life): נֶפֶשׁ (segholate), *with suff.* נַפְשִׁי, *&c., pl.* נְפָשׁוֹת

south: נֶגֶב—strictly a geographical area in the south; דָּרוֹם

sowed: זָרַע

spilled = shed

spirit: רוּחַ, *with suff.* רוּחִי, *pl.* רוּחוֹת

splendour: תִּפְאָרָה, הָדָר, הוֹד, *const.* תִּפְאֶרֶת

split (divided): בָּקַע

spoil: שָׁלָל, בַּז; took as spoil: שָׁלַל *and* בָּזַז

spoke: *Piel of* דבר—דִּבֶּר

spread (out): פָּרַשׂ

spring (of water): מַעְיָן, עַיִן, *const.* עֵין

sprinkled: זָרַק

spy: מְרַגֵּל—*Piel part.*

staff: מַטֶּה

star: כּוֹכָב

statute: חֹק, *with suff.* חֻקִּי, *&c., pl.* חֻקִּים, *and* חֻקָּה, *pl.* חֻקּוֹת, XI, 5 (a)

stayed: (i) remained יָשַׁב; (ii) restrained, held back: עָצַר, חָשַׂךְ

stiff (hard): קָשֶׁה

still (*adj.*), quiet: שֹׁקֵט—*Qal active part.*; was still (*vb.*) שָׁקַט

stole: גָּנַב

stone: אֶבֶן (segholate), *with suff.* אַבְנִי, *&c.*; cleared away stones: *Piel of* סקל—סִקֵּל

stood: (i) עָמַד; (ii) took a stand: *Niph. and Hithp. of* נצב—יצב *and* הִתְיַצֵּב (placed himself) stood on end (of hair, in terror): סָמַר

stopped up: סָתַם

stout (brave, strong): אַמִּיץ

straight: יָשָׁר; was straight: יָשַׁר, imperf. יִישַׁר; made straight: Piel יִשַּׁר, XLIII, 37, also Hiph.

strange: זָר

stranger: (i) a protected one, גֵּר; (ii) a hostile one, זָר

street (usually in the pl.): חוּצוֹת, רְחוֹבוֹת

strengthened: Piel of חָזַק (was strong)—חִזַּק (made strong). Cf. XXII, 13, 26

stretched out: נָטָה, imperf. יִטֶּה, with Waw consec. וַיֵּט, WHG 224; stretched out a hand: שָׁלַח יָד

strife: רִיב, מְרִיבָה

strong: (adj.) חָזָק; was strong (vb.) חָזַק (stative), imperf. יֶחֱזַק; made strong: Piel חִזַּק. Cf. XXII, 13, 26

strove: רָב √ריב, imperf. יָרִיב, with Waw consec. וַיָּרֶב, WHG 197

stubbornness: שְׁרִירוּת

substance (wealth): רְכוּשׁ

suddenly: פִּתְאֹם

sun: שֶׁמֶשׁ (segholate), with suff. שִׁמְשִׁי, &c.

supported: תָּמַךְ

supreme (most high): עֶלְיוֹן

surely: הֲלֹא (is not?), VII, 20

swarm (of bees): עֵדָה

swept away: Piel of בער—בִּעֵר

swooped (down): טָשׂ √טושׂ

sword: חֶרֶב (segholate), with suff. חַרְבִּי, &c., pl. חֲרָבוֹת

swore: Niph. of שׁבע—נִשְׁבַּע

T

table: שֻׁלְחָן, pl. שֻׁלְחָנוֹת

tablet: לוּחַ, pl. לוּחֹת

taught: (i) Piel of לָמַד (learned)— לִמַּד; (ii) Hiph. of יָרָה (ורה)— הוֹרָה

tax: מַס, pl. מִסִּים

temple: הֵיכָל

ten: עֲשָׂרָה with masc. ns. and עֶשֶׂר with fem. ns., WHG 243, 244

tended (sheep): רָעָה, שָׁמַר (kept, watched)

tent: אֹהֶל (segholate), with suff. אָהֳלִי, &c.

tenth: עֲשִׂירִי, fem. עֲשִׂירִית

terrible: Niph. part. of יָרֵא (feared) —נוֹרָא (to be feared)

terror: רְעָדָה, פַּחַד

testimony: עֵדוּת

thanks, gave: Hiph. of ידה (ודה)— הוֹדָה

that: demonstr. הוּא, fem. הִיא; in order that: לְמַעַן; introducing a clause: כִּי; that which: אֵת אֲשֶׁר = the (thing) which, I, 38

then: in point of time אָז; as emphatic word נָא, I, 4

thence: מִשָּׁם (from there)

there: שָׁם

there is, there are: יֵשׁ

therefore (on that account): לָכֵן, עַל־כֵּן; as emphatic word נָא, I, 4

these: אֵלֶּה

they: הֵם, הֵמָּה, *fem.* הֵנָּה, הֵן

thing: דָּבָר

third: שְׁלִישִׁי, *fem.* שְׁלִישִׁית

thirsty: (*adj.*) צָמֵא; was thirsty
(*vb.*) צָמֵא (*stative*), *imperf.* יִצְמָא

this: זֶה, *fem.* זֹאת

thither: שָׁמָּה

thought: (*n.*) מַחֲשָׁבָה; (*vb.*) (i) אָמַר
בְּלִבּוֹ (said in his heart); (ii) חָשַׁב
(planned, devised)

three: שְׁלֹשָׁה *with masc. ns., const.*
שְׁלֹשֶׁת, *with suff.* שְׁלָשְׁתֵּנוּ, &*c.*,
XXIX, 37, *fem.* שָׁלֹשׁ, WHG 242,
244

threw: (i) threw away: *Hiph. of*
שׁלך—הִשְׁלִיךְ; (ii) threw down:
Hiph. of נָפַל (fell)—הִפִּיל (caused
to fall), נָתַץ (demolished)

throne: כִּסֵּא, *with suff.* כִּסְאִי

through: בְּעַד; (by the agency of), בְּיַד

thrust: *Hiph. of* נדח—הִדִּיחַ; was
thrust: *Niph.* נִדַּח

thunder: קוֹלוֹת, רַעַם (sounds)

thus: כֹּה, כָּזֹאת (like this), II, 25

tidings, good: בְּשׂוֹרָה; brought tidings: *Piel* בִּשַּׂר

tithe: מַעֲשֵׂר

to, unto: אֶל, *with suffs. of the pl. n.*,
WHG 87; לְ, I, 2

together: יַחַד, יַחְדָּו, *and* יַחְדָּיו

toiled: עָמָל

told: (i) *Hiph. of* נגד—הִגִּיד (informed); (ii) *Piel of* ספר—סִפֵּר
(narrated)

tomorrow: מָחָר

took: לָקַח, *imperf.* יִקַּח, *imper.* קַח,
inf. const. קַחַת, *with suff.* קַחְתִּי,

&*c.*, WHG 149–50; *in the
sense of* 'captured' לָכַד; took
hold: (i) אָחַז, *imperf.* יֹאחֵז;
(ii) *Hiph. of* חזק—הֶחֱזִיק; took as
spoil: שָׁלַל *and* בָּזַז

top: רֹאשׁ (head)

Torah: תּוֹרָה, X, 35

tore: קָרַע; tore prey: טָרַף

touched: נָגַע, *imperf.* יִגַּע, *imper.* גַּע

towards: (i) to meet: לִקְרַאת, *with
suff.* לִקְרָאתִי, &*c.*, IX, 33; (ii) *in
point of time*, לִפְנוֹת, XXI, 13

tranquillity: שַׁלְוָה

transgressed: עָבַר (crossed over,
trespassed), פָּשַׁע (rebelled)

transgression: פֶּשַׁע (*segholate*), *with
suff.* פִּשְׁעִי, XXXIX, 24

traversed: עָבַר ב (crossed through)

tree: עֵץ

trembled: חָרַד

tribe: שֵׁבֶט (*segholate*), *with suff.*
שִׁבְטִי, &*c.*

trouble: עָמָל (toil)

troubled: עָכַר (disturbed); was
troubled (of spirit): *Niph. of*
פעם (struck, beat)—נִפְעַם (was
agitated)

true = of truth; *in the sense of*
'faithful'—נֶאֱמָן

trusted: בָּטַח, II, 37 (*a*)

truth: אֱמֶת

tumult: שָׁאוֹן

turned: turned over: הָפַךְ; turned
again, returned: שׁוּב√שָׁב; turned
aside: (*intrans.*) סוּר√סָר, (*trans.*)
Hiph. הֵסִיר; turned away: (*intrans.*) פָּנָה, (*trans.*) *Hiph.* הִפְנָה

twain = two: שְׁנַיִם

twelve: שְׁנֵים עָשָׂר *with masc. ns.,*
שְׁתֵּים עֶשְׂרֵי *with fem. ns.*

twice: פַּעֲמַיִם (*dual*)

two: שְׁנַיִם *with masc. ns., const.* שְׁנֵי,
שְׁתַּיִם *with fem. ns., const.* שְׁתֵּי,
WHG 243 (*b*)

U

uncovered (revealed): *Qal* גָּלָה
and Piel גִּלָּה

under: תַּחַת, *with suffs. of the pl. n.,*
WHG 87

understanding: בִּינָה, תְּבוּנָה

understood: √בִּין בָּן, *imperf.* יָבִין,
jussive יָבֵן *imperf. with Waw
consec.* וַיָּבֶן, *imper.* בִּין. Cf.
WHG 197

until: עַד (*with a n.*) *and* עַד־אֲשֶׁר
(*with a vb.*)

unto: אֶל *with suffs. of the pl. n.,*
WHG 87; לְ

upheld (a cause): √רִיב רָב, *imperf.*
יָרִיב, *with Waw consec.* וַיָּרֶב,
imper. רִיב. Cf. WHG 197

upon: עַל *with suffs. of the pl. n.,*
WHG 87

upright: (morally) יָשָׁר; upright
stature: קוֹמְמִיּוּת

uprightness: יֹשֶׁר (*segholate*)

uprooted: עָקַר

upwards: מַעֲלָה

utterly: *inf. abs. with the finite vb.
and, sometimes,* עַד־תֹּם (till the
finishing of √תמם—*inf. const.*)

V

vain = of vanity

valiant = of valour

valley: עֵמֶק, בִּקְעָה

valour: חַיִל

vanity: שָׁוְא, הֶבֶל

vengeance: נְקָמָה; exacted vengeance: *Niph. of* נקם—נָקַם

very: מְאֹד, עַד־מְאֹד

vessel: כְּלִי, *with suff.* כֶּלְיִי, &c.,
pl. כֵּלִים

victory: יְשׁוּעָה, I, 31

vineyard: כֶּרֶם (*segholate*)

violence: חָמָס

visited: פָּקַד

voice: קוֹל, *pl.* קוֹלוֹת

W

wailed: *Hiph. of* יָלַל—הֵילִיל

wait, lay in wait: אָרַב

walked: הָלַךְ, *imperf.* √ילד יֵלֵךְ,
with Waw consec. וַיֵּלֶךְ, *imper.*
לֵךְ, *inf. const.* לֶכֶת, *with suff.*
לֶכְתִּי, &c., *defective,* WHG 237;
walked about: *Hithp.* הִתְהַלֵּךְ

wall: (of a city) חוֹמָה, (of a house)
קִיר, *pl.* קִירוֹת

war: מִלְחָמָה, *const.* מִלְחֶמֶת, *with
suff.* מִלְחַמְתִּי, &c.

warrior = man-of-war

was: הָיָה, *imperf.* יִהְיֶה, *jussive* יְהִי,
imperf. with Waw consec. וַיְהִי,

washed: (i) bathed: רָחַץ; (ii)
washed clothes: *Piel of* כבס—
כִּבֵּס

waste: שְׁמָמָה, חָרְבָּה, חֹרֶב; laid
waste: *Hiph. of* חרב—הֶחֱרִיב

watched: שָׁמַר

watchman: שֹׁמֵר—*Qal active part.*

water: מַיִם, const. מֵי (sometimes
found as מֵימֵי)

watered (irrigated): Hiph. of שקה
—הִשְׁקָה (caused to drink)—defective, WHG 238 c

weak: רָפֶה, חַלָּשׁ

weakened: Piel of רפה—רִפָּה

wealth: הוֹן, עֹשֶׁר, רְכוּשׁ

weapon: כְּלִי, with suff. כֶּלְיִי, pl.
כֵּלִים

weary: יָגֵעַ, עָיֵף

welfare, well-being: שָׁלוֹם

well (spring): בְּאֵר; (adverbially)
הֵיטֵב—Hiph. inf. abs. of יטב
(making good)

went = walked

wept: בָּכָה, imperf. יִבְכֶּה, with
Waw consec. וַיֵּבְךְּ

west: יָם (sea), מַעֲרָב

what?: מֶה, מָה, מַה־, WHG 42 B

whatsoever: כֹּל אֲשֶׁר (all which)

when: כִּי; when?: מָתַי

whence: אֲשֶׁר . . . מִשָּׁם (that . . .
from there); whence?: מֵאַיִן

where: אֲשֶׁר . . . שָׁם (that . . . there);
where?: אַיֵּה, אֵיפֹה

wherefore?: לָמָּה, מַדּוּעַ

whether . . . or: אִם . . . הֲ, III, 40

which (relative): אֲשֶׁר

whither: אֲשֶׁר . . . שָׁמָּה (that . . .
thither); whither?: אָנָה

whithersoever: בְּכֹל אֲשֶׁר (in all
which)

why?: לָמָּה, מַדּוּעַ

wicked: רָשָׁע, XLII, 26 (a)

widow: אַלְמָנָה

wife = woman

wild (animal): רָעָה (חַיָּה)—(evil . . .)

wilderness: מִדְבָּר, X, 9

wind: רוּחַ, pl. רוּחוֹת

wine: יַיִן, const. יֵין, with suff. יֵינִי, &c.

wing: כָּנָף, dual כְּנָפַיִם

winter: חֹרֶף (segholate), with suff.
חָרְפִּי, &c.

wisdom: חָכְמָה

wise: חָכָם, XLII, 26 (a)

with: (i) as instrument בְּ; (ii) together with, עִם, with suff. עִמִּי,
&c., and אֵת, with suff. אִתִּי, &c.

without: מִבְּלִי, בְּלִי

witness: עֵד; gave, bore witness:
Hiph. of עוד√—הֵעִיד

woe: אוֹי

woman: אִשָּׁה, const. אֵשֶׁת, with suff.
אִשְׁתִּי, &c., pl. נָשִׁים

wonder: מוֹפֵת

wonderful, wondrous: Niph. part.
of פלא—נִפְלָא

word: דָּבָר

work: (i) service, עֲבוֹדָה; (ii)
manufacture, מַעֲשֶׂה

worked: עָבַד

world: תֵּבֵל

wormwood (poison): רֹאשׁ, לַעֲנָה

worshipped: (i) עָבַד (served); (ii)
Hithpalel of שחה (שחו), was bowed
down, was low—הִשְׁתַּחֲוָה (made
himself bow down, low), II, 61

would that: מִי יִתֵּן (who will
grant?)

wound: פֶּצַע (segholate), with suff.
הַבּוּרָה, &c., פִּצְעִי

wrath: קֶצֶף, חֵמָה, אַף, with suff.
קִצְפִּי, &c.

wrote: כָּתַב

wroth, was: (i) קָצַף; (ii) חָרָה לְ
(was hot to) and חָרָה אַף (anger
was hot)

Y

Yahweh: יהוה

ye: אַתֶּם, *fem.* אַתֵּנָה

year: שָׁנָה, *dual* שְׁנָתַיִם, *pl.* שָׁנִים, V, 25

yet: עוֹד, *with suffs.* עוֹדְךָ, עוֹדֶנִּי,

&c., not yet (*with vb.*) = before—טֶרֶם *with imperf.*, IX, 23
(b)

yoke: עֹל, *with suff.* עֻלִּי, &c. Cf.
XI, 5 (a)

young: קָטָן, צָעִיר (small)

young man, youth: נַעַר, בָּחוּר,
pl. בַּחוּרִים

Z

Zion: צִיּוֹן

PRINTED IN
GREAT BRITAIN
AT THE
UNIVERSITY PRESS
OXFORD
BY
CHARLES BATEY
PRINTER
TO THE
UNIVERSITY

Thin
11.vi.57

Edinburgh University Library

RETURN BY

05. APR 89

~~22 AUG 89~~

FINES RATE:

1. 10p per volume per day for NORMAL loans (6 wks).
2. 50p per volume per day for RECALLED books.